THE LAFAYETTE ESCADRILLE

THE LAFAYETTE ESCADRILLE

A Photo History of the First American Fighter Squadron

STEVEN A. RUFFIN

CASEMATE
Philadelphia & Oxford

First published in the United States of America and Great Britain in 2016.
Reprinted as a paperback in 2020 by
CASEMATE PUBLISHERS
1950 Lawrence Road, Havertown, PA 19083, USA
and
The Old Music Hall, 106–108 Cowley Road, Oxford OX4 1JE, UK

Copyright 2016 © Steven A. Ruffin

Paperback Edition: ISBN 978-1-61200-852-3
Digital Edition: ISBN 978-1-61200-351-1

A CIP record for this book is available from the British Library

Printed and bound by Megaprint, Turkey

For a complete list of Casemate titles, please contact:

CASEMATE PUBLISHERS (US)
Telephone (610) 853-9131
Fax (610) 853-9146
Email: casemate@casematepublishers.com
www.casematepublishers.com

CASEMATE PUBLISHERS (UK)
Telephone (01865) 241249
Email: casemate-uk@casematepublishers.co.uk
www.casematepublishers.co.uk

To the men of the Lafayette who saw peace only in death: Chapman, Rockwell, Prince, McConnell, Genet, Hoskier, Dressy, de Laage, MacMonagle, Campbell, Pavelka, Lufbery, Maison-Rouge, Doolittle, and Verdier-Fauvety.

CONTENTS

Foreword   ix
Preface   xi
Acknowledgements   xv
Introduction   xvii
Prologue   xxi

1   An All-American Idea Takes Shape   1
2   The Escadrille Américaine Is Born   13
3   First Blood   29
4   Into the Grinder   41
5   Season of Discontent   55
6   The Battle Continues   65
7   The Best and the Bravest   75
8   Misery in the Somme   85
9   Mac Goes West   97
10   The Heartbreak of Ham   109
11   Chaudun and Beyond   121
12   Hard Times at Senard   135
13   From Falcons of France to American Eagles   149
14   Aftermath   161

Epilogue   175
Appendices   179
Selected Bibliography   183
Archival Sources   186
Museums   187
Index   188

FOREWORD

On April 20, 1916, seven young American airmen converged on a large grass flying field near Luxeuil, France. Arriving from various locations and a diversity of backgrounds, they were all there for the same reason: to fly for France as combat pilots. The First World War was raging all around them and since their own homeland still steadfastly maintained its neutrality, they had plunged themselves into the conflagration without any compelling reason to do so.

These seven Americans were not, strictly speaking, mercenaries. They did not volunteer their services to another country for compensation. Rather, they were there—at least, in part—because of an ideal in which they believed: the cause of freedom. France and Belgium had been invaded by a brutal enemy, intent on subjugating their citizens. As a consequence, this group of pilots—along with dozens of other American citizens who were fighting in France's army—had deemed it their duty and a matter of honor to do as a young French nobleman had more than a century earlier. In 1777, the 20-year-old Marquis de Lafayette had traveled to America to fight with the American patriots in their struggle for independence in the Revolutionary War. It was finally time to return that favor.

The unit these founding seven pilots formed—and in which a total of 38 Americans would eventually serve—earned a place in history as the first American fighter squadron. Best remembered as the "Lafayette Escadrille," it served the French Aéronautique Militaire with honor until February 18, 1918, when it became the 103rd Aero Squadron of the US Air Service. As such, this famed group of men, who might be considered the founding fathers of American combat aviation, formed the embryo of what would become the greatest air power ever known, the United States Air Force.

This unique photo history traces the footsteps of the 38 pilots who flew for the Lafayette Escadrille, from their first patrol to the day they became a part of the US Air Service. In so doing, it tells the story of this fabled unit in a way that words alone never could.

T. MICHAEL MOSELEY
General (Ret.) United States Air Force
18th Chief of Staff

PREFACE

As any World War I aviation enthusiast can tell you, there are dozens of excellent histories, biographies, and autobiographies dealing with the Lafayette Escadrille. There are so many, in fact, that this World War I all-American volunteer unit is, without doubt, one of the best-known fighter squadrons ever to take to the skies.

Given the preponderance of works dealing with this iconic squadron, readers may (understandably) wonder why yet another history is needed. What more could be said that has not already been written? The answer is simple: this unique photographic history of the Lafayette Escadrille—set to appear during its centennial—not only "tells," it *shows* the story of this elite unit. My intent was to create a written and visual history that both World War I aviation aficionados and those with a more passing interest could appreciate. If a photograph is worth a thousand words, this book of photographs is worth a million.

To accomplish my goal, I spent an entire year gathering hundreds of black and white photographs and other documents relating to the Lafayette Escadrille from various university and museum archives in the United States and France. Fortunately, there is no shortage of images, as innumerable snapshots were made of the famed squadron—not only by the pilots themselves, but also by the constant flow of journalists and other visitors to the squadron. The resulting prints were widely reproduced and distributed among squadron members, who then passed them on to family and friends. Many copies of these old photographs still exist in collections all over the world. Although smudges, scratches, creases, and fading are standard fare for 100-year-old, multi-generation photographs, most of the images I chose for this work are of excellent quality—especially the ones I was fortunate enough to scan from original negatives. The result may well be the best photographic collection—both in terms of number and quality—available in any existing publication portraying the men, machines, and mascots of the Lafayette Escadrille.

These black and white photographs, which were the norm for that era, are fascinating and revealing to look at. They serve the singular function of recording real events involving these men and their airplanes in real time. However, another element—that of color—is also necessary for today's readers to fully appreciate this historical experience. In order to demonstrate that World War I-era colors were, in fact, as vivid as they are now, I also included in this work numerous photographs of existing museum relics relating to the squadron. Only by seeing century-old objects—aircraft, uniforms, insignia, etc.—the way they really appeared can readers gain a truly accurate perspective.

To add yet another dimension to this work, I traveled extensively through both the United States and France to photograph existing markers and memorials honoring the men of the Lafayette Escadrille. I was pleasantly surprised at the number of these I was able to find and at how well maintained they generally were. As a bonus, I also went to great—some might say inordinate—lengths to seek out locations in France where the squadron operated, where important events occurred, and where the pilots spent their leisure time. Wherever possible, I matched the color photos I took with black and white contemporary images of the same scene, thus creating a provocative "then and now" comparison. This work is further enhanced by aircraft profiles and artistic scenes, which are not only in brilliant full color, but are also historically accurate—again giving readers a realistic glimpse of how aircraft and events appeared during the Great War years.

One final point has to do with the potentially confusing terminology regarding the Lafayette Escadrille. Readers should understand that the squadron had several names during its existence. Its first official designation was "Escadrille N.124," the "N" denoting that it was equipped with the Nieuport fighter. When the squadron eventually replaced its Nieuports with the new Spad VII fighter, N.124 became "SPA.124."

Likewise, the squadron's unofficial name also evolved. It was originally called "Escadrille Américaine," but diplomatic expediency later forced a name change, first to "Escadrille des Volontaires," and finally, to "Escadrille de Lafayette"—the Lafayette Escadrille. As a matter of accuracy, I used the squadron name in effect at the time of the events being described. However, readers should rest assured that N.124, SPA.124, Escadrille Américaine, Escadrille des Volontaires, and Lafayette Escadrille all refer to the same unit.

Readers should also be aware that this book focuses exclusively on the squadron known as the Lafayette Escadrille, and not the larger World War I aviation entity known as the "Lafayette Flying Corps." The two are not the same, and to this day, there is widespread confusion between them. The Lafayette Flying Corps is a broad designation referring to all the 269 Americans who volunteered to fly for France during World War I. Of these, 38 served in the Lafayette Escadrille—the only squadron composed almost solely of Americans—while the remaining volunteers served with various other

French squadrons. Hence, while all the pilots of the Lafayette Escadrille were members of the Lafayette Flying Corps, only 38 men from the Lafayette Flying Corps served in the Lafayette Escadrille.

Readers will judge for themselves whether or not this book achieved its intended purpose, but I sincerely believe they will find it to be the most complete visual history of this famous Franco-American fighter squadron ever published.

Steven A. Ruffin
April 2016

ACKNOWLEDGEMENTS

A work containing as many parts and pieces as this cannot possibly happen without the help of many talented and dedicated individuals. My list of those to whom I am indebted is virtually endless but I feel compelled to acknowledge some of those whose efforts on my behalf were especially crucial: the editorial staff at Casemate helped make this work as good as it could possibly be; the Lafayette Escadrille Memorial Working Group provided crucial support, without which, this work would not have been possible; Jerry Hester, of the US World War I Centennial Commission, was a constant source of help and encouragement; Alan Toelle and Tomasz Gronczewski teamed to produce the beautiful and historically accurate aircraft profiles that appear within—and a special thanks to Alan for his help acquiring and interpreting some of the rare photos; aviation artist Russell Smith created the artistic scenes that add color and realism; Frédéric Castier of Historical Consulting Tourism & Patrimony and Benoît Odelot, director of the Office National des Anciens Combattants et Victimes de Guerre, took time out of their busy schedules to take me to important sites and introduce me to local French historians; Patrice Platelle and Didier Trebuchet, city leaders of Grugies, France, disclosed to me historical secrets I would not otherwise have discovered—and treated me to a feast worthy of a king; Mme. Danielle Lanco, mayor of Flavy-le-Martel, France, escorted me to the beautifully maintained James McConnell memorial; Jacques Calcine helped me discover some secrets of the aerodrome at Ham; Mathilde Schneider, curator at the Musée franco-américain, Chateau de Blérancourt, graciously granted me an entire day and full reign of the museum's extraordinary Lafayette Escadrille archives collection; Mr. Willis Haviland Lamm generously allowed me to use photographs from his magnificent Willis B. Haviland Collection; Alain Vezin, author of *Escadron de chasse La Fayette, Du Nieuport au Mirage 2000N*, kindly provided me with the photograph of France's still-operational Lafayette Escadrille. Others who provided crucial support include: Alexander Blumrosen, Président de la Fondation du Mémorial de l'Escadrille La Fayette; Gen. Yvon Goux, Président des Anciens du "La Fayette" et Vice-président de la Fondation du Mémorial;

Gen. T. Michael Moseley, US Air Force (Ret.); Lt. Gen. David A. Deptula, US Air Force (Ret.); Maj. Gen. Rick Devereaux, US Air Force (Ret.); Maj. Gen. Walter D. Givhan, US Air Force (Ret.); Col. Terry L. Johnson, US Army (Ret.); Col. Charles E. Metrolis, US Air Force, Defense Air Attaché from the US Embassy in Paris; Lt. Col. Stephen Miller, US Air Force (Ret.); Dana Garrow; Monique B. Seefried; Peter Kilduff; Greg VanWyngarden; Dieter Gröschel; Chuck Thomas; Charles Woolley; Dr. Joseph C. Porter and Eric Blevins of the North Carolina Museum of History; Dr. Mary Elizabeth Ruwell and Dr. Charles D. Dusch Jr., US Air Force Academy McDermott Library Special Collections; the staff at the University of Virginia Albert and Shirley Small Special Collections Library; Dr. Forrest L. Marion and William M. Russell, Air Force Historical Research Agency; the staff at the Archives Division of the Smithsonian National Air & Space Museum; Diane B. Jacob, Archives and Records Management, Special Collections, Preston Library, Virginia Military Institute; and Brett Stolle of the National Museum of the US Air Force Archives. A note of special gratitude is due to Prof. Thomas E. Camden and his colleagues at Washington and Lee University Leyburn Library Special Collections. Their help and cooperation during the two full weeks I spent researching their fabulous Paul Ayres Rockwell collection was a major factor in making this work possible. And finally, my wife, Janet, who did everything possible to support me throughout the process, my daughter, Katie, who provided critical technical support, and my son, Daniel, who meticulously reviewed the manuscript. Thanks to each and every one of you.

INTRODUCTION

At sunrise on the morning of May 12, 1916, a group of five French Nieuport fighter planes took off en masse from a large open grass flying field. The aerodrome was located on the outskirts of Luxeuil-les-Bains, an ancient resort town situated in the Vosges Mountains, near the eastern border of France. Those on the ground watched as the formation disappeared into the morning mist, and they were still watching an hour or so later when the pilots of the small, open-cockpit biplanes bounced safely back onto the grass field and taxied in. When the flight leader penciled his observations into the squadron operational log, it read simply "RAS" (Rien à Signaler): nothing to report.

World War I had been raging for 21 months and the war's newest weapon, the airplane, had already become an important instrument of military strategy. Consequently, this patrol was, by all appearances, completely routine; however, in truth, it was anything *but* routine. History had just been made. The five French single-seat fighters belonged to a newly formed squadron, designated N.124. Though a typical French squadron in most ways, it had one unique quality: it was composed entirely—with the exception of its two French commanders—of American volunteers. These seven young men had, for reasons of their own, decided to ignore their own country's rigid neutrality stance—one that the United States would maintain for nearly another full year before officially entering the war—in order to come to the aid of France.

The squadron was widely referred to as the Escadrille Américaine—a name that upset leaders in the German government. Understandably, they vehemently opposed the idea of a unit composed of citizens from a neutral nation waging war against them. Because of the protests they lodged, Escadrille Américaine would undergo two politically driven name changes—first, to "Escadrille des Volontaires," and finally, to "Escadrille de Lafayette"—the Lafayette Escadrille. As the unit winged its way to the various other hotspots along the Western Front, it blazed a path of glory and sacrifice across the skies of France. The American volunteers created a legacy and achieved a level of fame that extended far beyond their wildest dreams—their names became household words throughout the United States and France. A hundred years later, this fabled band of brothers we now remember as the Lafayette Escadrille remains one of history's best-known combat units.

A total of 38 American pilots served with the Lafayette Escadrille from its creation on April 20, 1916, until February 18, 1918, when it became the 103rd Aero Squadron of the US Air Service. Of these so-called "Valiant 38," several would—before the November 11, 1918, Armistice finally brought hostilities to a halt—receive serious wounds in combat, three would become prisoners of war, and eleven would lose their lives.

The men who made up the Lafayette Escadrille were a highly diverse socioeconomic mix of early-20th century American culture. They ranged from wealthy scions of prominent families to uneducated vagabonds of modest means and beginnings to those who were somewhere in between. Most were—as popularly portrayed—well-heeled, educated, and idealistic East Coast Ivy Leaguers. Thirty had attended college, mostly at elite educational institutions, and several had earned degrees. They were lawyers, architects, engineers, and businessmen; but they were also sailors, men of leisure, dayworkers, and ne'er-do-well drifters. Rich and poor, educated and otherwise, they made their way to France to volunteer, first as ambulance drivers or soldiers in the French Foreign Legion, and eventually as pilots.

Some of these men came because of family ties with France or an abiding belief in the cause. Others were motivated by curiosity and a desire to be where the action was. A few of these volunteers were wanderers who simply found themselves in the wrong place at the right time. In the end, however, most sought the prospect of adventure and a chance to make a name for themselves. Regardless of pedigree and motivation, these 38 men—idealists, thrill-seeking adventurers, and itinerants, alike—lived, flew, fought, and died together as one cohesive unit.

This is not to say that these 38 American volunteer pilots all liked one another or that they always got along together. They often did not. Regardless of their basic motivations, most of them were also driven, at least to some extent, by an ambitious desire for fame and glory. This sometimes brought the more tightly strung of these testosterone-laden alpha males into opposition with one another. As with almost any group, there were personality conflicts and opposing cliques—and not surprisingly, their widely disparate social statuses often put them at further odds with one another. These clashes, along with the petty jealousies and bruised egos, come through loud and clear in letters these men wrote at the time.

Similarly, the assumption should not be made that all of the American pilots in the Lafayette Escadrille were equally courageous and effective in combat. They were not. As a unit, this squadron was more or less average, at least in terms of the measure generally used to judge a fighter squadron: destroying enemy aircraft. Establishing official confirmation for aerial victories in World War I was, at best, an inexact science, and official documents and previously published accounts are often in conflict; however, research conducted by respected World War I aviation historians Dennis Connell and Frank W. Bailey indicates that the 38 Americans who flew for the Lafayette Escadrille officially downed a total of only 33 enemy aircraft over its 22-month period of existence. Sixteen of these belonged to one pilot, the escadrille's shining star and highly regarded ace, Raoul Lufbery. No other member downed more than four enemy aircraft while flying with the squadron (although some later scored additional victories with other squadrons and even became aces), and a whopping 25 of them—well over half of the squadron's roster—scored no victories at all.

None of this should be construed as a criticism of the men of the Lafayette Escadrille. On the contrary, all of the above was more or less typical of an "average" World War I flying squadron. It was not unusual for squadron members to sometimes feud with one another. Nor was it unusual for a fighter pilot to down no enemy airplanes: in fact, *most* pilots in the First World War failed to score a single confirmed victory. Shooting down enemy aircraft was a far more dangerous, gut-wrenchingly terrifying, and technically difficult thing to do than most people today can adequately appreciate. As squadron member James McConnell—who failed to score a single victory during his 10 months of active service—put it, "but God in Boston it's a hard job." It took equal measures of skill, courage, and luck to find an enemy airplane, maneuver into a favorable position, and then shoot accurately enough to bring it down—all while the highly skilled opposing enemy airman was doing his best to accomplish precisely the same thing. Most average pilots were simply lacking in at least one of these three essential factors, so only a handful of World War I fighter pilots—like Lufbery—achieved any degree of success.

Still, there was much more to successfully flying in World War I than simply shooting down enemy airplanes. The majority of the men who flew for the Lafayette Escadrille rose to the occasion, conquered their fears, and dutifully flew their daily patrols. In so doing, they earned the respect of their peers as combat airmen—even in the absence of any recorded kills. Those remaining few squadron members who, on the other hand, established practically no record at all and flew only a few missions were silently condemned by their fellow airmen as slackers, incompetents, or something worse.

All things considered, the Lafayette Escadrille, with its many metaphorical ups and downs, was a successful and effective—if not outstanding—fighter squadron. Its historical significance comes, instead, from the American volunteer pilots that manned it and the ideals they represented.

Just as the men of the Lafayette Escadrille differed from one another during the war years, not all fared equally well after leaving the squadron. A quarter of the 38 men who served with the squadron either wrote or were the subject of books about their experiences. One became an internationally acclaimed author, and a few went on to successful military or business careers. However, the majority lived their post-Lafayette lives in relative obscurity. Two died in military aircraft accidents and another in a freak non-flying accident, soon after leaving the squadron. One later died of probable suicide and two were convicted of crimes that earned them prison time. Only a relative few succeeded in living to a ripe old age. Whether their collective problems were due to the extreme physical and mental stresses they suffered during the war—or to the hard-driving, heavy-drinking, chain-smoking lifestyle so typical of such men of that era—is anyone's guess. However, the average lifespan of the 27 American pilots who survived the war was only about 60 years, and barely half of them lived past that age.

Such are the plain facts that define the men of the Lafayette Escadrille. They were a heterogeneous group of young adventurers—some of them more courageous, dedicated, and skilled than others—who found themselves together in the same place at a unique and deadly crossroads in history. Worthy or not, they all played a role: each belonged to history's first predominantly American fighter squadron and was therefore subject to the rewards that came with it, along with the hardships. Their renown has faded but little from the days when they streaked across the skies above war-torn France, flying open-cockpit biplanes bearing the image of an American Indian warrior. They and the squadron to which they belonged will forever live in history.

BLOOD IN THE SOIL

"… that rare privilege of dying well."

It was a sunny October day when I stood in an Alsatian cornfield, looking down on a tiny piece of earth that had once been hallowed by American blood. It had been a long journey getting to this place: a tiring overnight flight to Paris; a gauntlet of passport and customs checkpoints; and then, the complicated maze of roads and heavy morning traffic surrounding Paris, through which I had to navigate in my little gazole-powered rental car. Eventually, I broke free and began speeding my way southeastward, across the picturesque countryside of rural France.

A couple of hours later, as I wound my way through the beautiful Vosges Mountains of Eastern France, I rolled into the commune of Roderen. The quaint little village sits in the Haut-Rhin department of Alsace, near where France, Germany, and Switzerland converge. As I passed through the town and into the countryside, the narrow paved road gradually deteriorated to a dirt cow path, where I was finally obliged to park the car. From there, I continued on foot—loaded down with camera equipment and a folder full of documentation—into the wilderness, such as it exists in modern France.

I proceeded across the fields and pastures, carefully stepping through electrical livestock fences, over cow paddies, and well clear of a sinister-looking mob of milk cows. Finally, after consulting the documents I carried with me—a nearly century-old, hand-drawn map copied from a dusty archival collection, a Google Earth aerial view printout, and a handful of World War I-era photo reprints—I knew I had arrived at my destination. Even without the maps and photos, I could *feel* it. Here, 98 years ago, on the ground in front of me, a courageous 24-year-old American fighter pilot had crashed to his death. His life ended at this lonely spot after he had traveled all the way from his home in North Carolina, to fight for the cause of France in the Great War. His name was Kiffin Yates Rockwell.

An image of the long-since-removed wreckage of his Nieuport 17 open-cockpit biplane, which dived vertically into the earth on September 23, 1916, was recorded in an old photograph I carried with me. The impact had been so great that no part of the crumpled airplane protruded more than a few inches above the ground. The engine had embedded several feet into the earth and the pilot's lifeless remains—still present when the photograph was taken—lay crushed beside the wreckage. The state of his broken body was immaterial, however, as his spirit had exited it long before it hit the ground: high in the sky above this place, a German airman had sent a machine gun slug through young Rockwell's chest, killing him instantly.

On the day I was there, the unmarked crash site was hidden in a field of corn. Pushing my way through a half-dozen rows to the point of impact, I made a curious discovery. There, where I had determined that Rockwell and his plane had plunged into the earth, was a mysteriously odd clearing in the midst of a forest of ten-foot-high cornstalks. Why did nothing grow there, of all places? There were no other similar clearings in sight. Was it simply a quirk of nature, or did a patriotic farmer—aware of the tragic event that had occurred there—avoid planting seeds into such hallowed ground? Or was the tiny area devoid of growth for another reason? Could it be that the mixture of gasoline, oil, and blood that trickled from the crash into the ground that day poisoned the earth such that nothing would ever grow there again? It is a mystery that still intrigues me.

★ ★ ★

Thus began my pilgrimage across France, treading in the footsteps of the men who flew, fought, and died while serving with the legendary Franco-American volunteer aviation squadron known as the Lafayette Escadrille. There were more long-hidden secrets for me to discover in the days to come.

> *Yet sought they neither recompense nor praise,*
> *Nor to be mentioned in another breath*
> *Than their blue-coated comrades, whose great days*
> *It was their pride to share—aye, share even to the death!*
> *Nay, rather, France, to you they rendered thanks*
> *(Seeing that they came for honor, not for gain),*
> *Who opening to them your glorious ranks*
> *Gave them that grand occasion to excel—*
> *That chance to live the life most free from stain*
> *And that rare privilege of dying well.* ★

★ Verse three of *Ode in Memory of the American Volunteers Fallen for France*, from *Poems* by Alan Seeger (Charles Scribner's Sons, 1916). Seeger was another of those American volunteers who, like Kiffin Rockwell, had the "rare privilege of dying well." He was killed on July 4, 1916, fighting on the Western Front with the French Foreign Legion. He was the uncle of the late American folk singer, Pete Seeger.

CHAPTER I

AN ALL-AMERICAN IDEA
TAKES SHAPE

"I do not feel that I am fighting for France alone, but for the cause of all humanity,
the greatest of all causes… I pay my debt for Lafayette and Rochambeau."

On August 7, 1914, two brothers from North Carolina boarded the SS *St. Paul* in New York, bound for Europe. Neither of the two, aged 21 and 25, had ever before left the shores of North America nor was either of them a professional soldier. Yet, they were on their way to France to fight in a war that was just beginning, and one in which they had no obligation to fight. Within three weeks they were wearing the uniform of the 2nd Regiment of the Légion étrangère française, as soldiers in the French Foreign Legion.

They were not alone. Dozens of other Americans—some already living or visiting in France and others making their way across the Atlantic in various ways—had the same idea. Rich and poor, young and old, educated and illiterate, they congregated in Paris, and on August 25, 1914, the highly diverse group of enthusiastic American volunteers marched as a unit through its streets and boulevards. Waving an American flag past throngs of cheering Parisians and completely caught up in the moment, they were on their way to fight another country's war. For all of them, it was a life-changing decision—and for nearly half, including one of the young brothers from North Carolina, a life-ending one.

A World War Begins

History's first "world war"—remembered now as simply the Great War or World War I—began in August 1914. It was triggered by the June 28, 1914, assassination of Archduke Franz Ferdinand and his wife, Sophie, in the Bosnian city of Sarajevo. This murder of the heir to the Austro-Hungarian Empire by 19-year-old Serbian nationalist Gavrilo Princip precipitated a series of political ultimatums, declarations, and behind-the-scenes maneuvering throughout the highly politically charged continent. By the end of the first week in August, most of Europe was at war.

The complex political situation that led to this global conflict is well beyond the scope of this book. Suffice it to say, however, that the First World War was a cataclysmal event involving the mobilization of at least 70 million men and women and causing the deaths of some 18 million people. This conflagration, unlike anything ever seen before, radically altered the political and social makeup of the entire world, set the stage for yet another world war, and reconfigured the future of all humanity.

The First World War started as a strictly European conflict, involving the Central Powers of Germany and the Austro-Hungarian Empire, pitted against the Triple Entente: France, Britain, and the Russian Empire. In time, however, numerous other countries from Europe and elsewhere around the world were drawn into it. It began as a war of mobility but soon became an entrenched stalemate. The primary combat zone, known as the "Western Front," became a mostly static line of trenches that extended southeastward from the North Sea across Belgium and France, all the way to the border of neutral Switzerland.

Another country, besides Switzerland, dedicated to maintaining its neutrality, as the great nations of Europe began systematically destroying one other, was the United States of America. President Woodrow Wilson was intent on keeping it that way. A few days after hostilities began, he expressed a "solemn word of warning" to the American people. In an August 19, 1914, address to Congress, he cautioned that "the United States must be neutral in fact as well as in name during these days that are to try men's souls." He further implored Americans to remain "impartial in thought as well as action" and to "put a curb upon our sentiments as well as upon every transaction that might be construed as a preference of one party to the struggle before another."

A Call to Arms

Wilson's policy of neutrality was not universally accepted. A few Americans decided, for reasons of their own, to ignore their president's warning and take sides in the war. A case in point was one of the young North Carolinian brothers, Paul A. Rockwell, who was working as a newspaper reporter in Atlanta, Georgia. On August 3, 1914—two days before the war's first major battle, the German assault on Liège, he wrote a letter to the French Consul in New Orleans, stating:

> I desire to offer my services to the French government in case of actual warfare between France and Germany.... I am twenty-five years old, of French descent, and have had military training at the Virginia Military Institute. I am very anxious to see military service, and had rather fight under the French flag than any other, as I greatly admire your nation.

In truth, Rockwell's French heritage was distant, at best, and he never attended VMI; nonetheless, he and his younger brother, Kiffin, who had written a similar letter—and who actually *had* briefly attended VMI, did not bother to wait for a reply. Within four days, they were on their way to Europe and, by the end of the month, marching with the French Foreign Legion—earning the exorbitant equivalent of one penny per day.

North Carolinians Kiffin Rockwell (sitting) and his brother Paul were among the first to volunteer to fight for France in 1914. Both were wounded while serving with the Foreign Legion. Paul was invalided out, while Kiffin escaped the ground war by transferring into aviation. Here, they are pictured during Kiffin's convalescence leave in Paris, July 1915. (Washington and Lee University Archives)

One of the two would never return to North Carolina but instead remain eternally buried in the French soil he had been so eager to defend.

The Rockwell brothers were just two of hundreds of Americans who had similar ideas. It was not just that they wanted to fight for a cause in which they believed: they wanted to be where the action was, to be a part of history in the making. These were men who lived large and who would stop at nothing in their quest for adventure. Most had grown up listening to their grandfathers and other veterans of the US Civil War tell of the glorious battles in which they had participated, and of how they had fought with honor and gallantry. Now, these members of this younger generation wanted their own war, so they could experience these things for themselves.

Not all of these men were partial to France. They flocked to all the warring countries, volunteering to serve the nation of their heritage or with which their family had some ties—be it France, England, or even Germany. Others chose to join the cause they felt was most just. Since France, a traditional American ally going all the way back to the Revolutionary War, was about to take the brunt of the Teutonic onslaught, many fair-minded young Americans enthusiastically took up her cause. Kiffin Rockwell explained his own decision to volunteer to serve France by stating simply, "I pay my debt for Lafayette and Rochambeau," in reference to the two French nobleman who had come to the aid of the United States during its darkest days of the Revolutionary War. Ted Parsons, another of these young Americans who would eventually become a member of the Lafayette Escadrille, was somewhat less high-minded in his assessment of these men's motivations. He wrote in his classic and highly entertaining 1937 book *The Great Adventure* that "some sought adventure, others revenge, while a pitiful few actually sacrificed themselves in the spirit of purest idealism." Another volunteer, an ex-boxer named Eugene Bullard, enlisted in the Legion for reasons that were not nearly as clear, stating that, "it must have been more curiosity than intelligence." Bullard eventually wangled his way into the French Air Service and, though he never served with the Lafayette Escadrille, went on to become history's first African-American combat pilot.

Americans Serving in France

There were serious legal implications for Americans who volunteered to fight in the army of a foreign nation. The most important of these was the potential loss of citizenship. A group of these men, already in Paris, sought out US Ambassador Myron T. Herrick to get his opinion on this matter. Herrick dutifully explained the illegality of neutral Americans serving in the French Army, but then he slammed his fist down on the table and said, "That is the law boys; but if I was young and in your shoes, by God I know mighty well what I'd do!" With a "hurrah!" the young Americans ran out of his office and signed up for the Foreign Legion. At least in this branch, they were not required to swear an oath of allegiance to France, thus decreasing their likelihood of having their citizenship revoked. This highly diverse mercenary branch of the French army, made

Kiffin Rockwell (center) with Dennis Dowd and Charles Trinkard, serving with the 2ème Régiment étranger in the Aisne trenches near Craonnelle, France, December 1914. All three eventually transferred from the Foreign Legion to the Aéronautique Militaire (French Air Service), and all three died flying for France. (Washington and Lee University Archives)

up almost exclusively of foreign nationals, was famed for its fierceness in battle and its esprit de corps, but it was also infamous as a refuge for criminals, troublemakers, and other outcasts. Now, it would add to its ranks a much different classification of fighter: the curious and idealistic young American.

These men could not have had even the slightest notion of the horrendous situation into which they were entering. Most claimed previous military experience to increase the likelihood that the Legion would accept them—one even proudly stating that he had served in the Salvation Army—but in fact, most were not veterans. Even had they been, they could not have fully appreciated that modern warfare, as it had evolved by 1914, bore little resemblance to that of the Civil War, or any other war ever waged. It was far less personal and more deadly, and it was almost completely devoid of glory or honor. Scores of them would pay for their idealism and quest for adventure with their lives. Kiffin Rockwell was one of these. After several months of fighting with the Legion, a serious wound provided him a way out of the mud and allowed him to enter into aviation. He was destined to become the second member of the newly formed all-American squadron to die in combat. After he had arrived in France, he related in a letter to his mother a sentiment shared by many of fellow volunteers: "If I die, I want you to know that I have died as every man ought to die, fighting for what is right. I do not feel that I am fighting for France alone, but for the cause of all humanity, the greatest of all causes."

A somewhat safer avenue for young Americans to see the war firsthand—in terms of both legality and of maintaining life and limb—was to volunteer as an ambulance driver. The war was generating unprecedented numbers of casualties, which in turn, created a great need for ambulances to transport them. Independent civilian ambulance companies, such as the American Field Service and the Norton-Harjes Ambulance Corps, soon formed to help fulfill this need. These companies naturally required

Future Lafayette Escadrille founding member James Rogers McConnell, of Carthage, North Carolina, stands next to his ambulance. Like many other American aviators in World War I, he began his wartime service as an ambulance driver. He served with section S.S.U.2 of the American Field Service for ten months and saw considerable frontline action before transferring to the French Air Service. (US Air Force)

competent drivers—semi-skilled manpower that any nation at war could ill afford. Consequently, hundreds of Americans, young and old—including the likes of Ernest Hemingway, Archibald Macleish, and nearly half of the men who would eventually fill the roster of the Lafayette Escadrille—volunteered to serve as drivers in nearly all of the countries in which the war zone extended. Thus many young Americans—particularly those who could afford to pay their own way to Europe and support themselves while there—gained a front row seat to the war, sitting behind the wheel of a Ford, Fiat, or Peugeot field ambulance.

Warfare Takes to the Skies

Thus, between the young Americans fighting with the Legion and those manning the ambulances, there was a ready pool of talent available to flow into yet another branch of the French military complex: the Aéronautique Militaire, or French Air Service.

Early in the war, there was little demand for new pilots, simply because military aviation at that time barely existed. There were as yet very few airplanes operating at the front, and since military aviation activities had not yet evolved into aerial combat, the attrition rate for the few pilots that were flying missions was relatively low. It did not take long, however, for both of these factors to change dramatically.

The usefulness of aviation became apparent soon after the outbreak of hostilities. The flimsy, unreliable toy that most military leaders of the day considered the airplane to be, proved its value beyond all expectations. In the wake of horse-mounted scouts falling before withering machine gun fire like weeds to a sickle, military pilots quickly established themselves on both sides of the lines as the new eyes of the army. In the first weeks of the war, Allied pilots flying reconnaissance aircraft discovered key movements and weaknesses in the German forces that helped prevent a major Allied defeat—and possibly an early loss of the war. Because of this, along with the newly recognized value of reconnaissance aircraft for artillery spotting, the number of frontline reconnaissance aircraft rapidly increased from a mere handful to dozens of squadrons.

The earliest military aircraft were unarmed, a situation that the realities of warfare quickly changed. Army commanders from both sides took serious exception to being spied upon from above. This prompted them to ask designers to develop fast, maneuverable, and well-armed "scouts"—or "avions de chasse," as the French called them—to attack enemy reconnaissance aircraft and defend their own observation planes from enemy attackers. Thus, was born the concept of the fighter plane. From then on, opposing pilots in nimble machine gun-carrying aircraft would begin meeting, almost daily, all along the front in aerial combat. The skies above the Western Front had now become an aerial battlefield as deadly as the one raging below.

As a result of the new lethal nature of military aviation, the air services of all the warring armies soon became plagued by the constant drain of pilots lost in combat. Before the war ended, France alone would train a total of nearly 17,000 pilots, and the

American expatriates serving in the Foreign Legion and ambulance service formed a tempting pool from which to draw new recruits. They were, by and large, young and healthy, educated—and most importantly—willing and readily available.

Many of these idealistic young men were ripe for the picking. After months of fighting in the trenches or transporting horribly maimed men in their ambulances, they had become disillusioned with war as they experienced it. Even the idealistic Kiffin Rockwell had reached his limit. He still believed in the cause but was ready to support it in a different way. As he wrote to his brother, Paul, who had already reverted back to civilian life:

> If you can get me into a French regiment, get busy, for I want to get out of the Legion. This regiment is no good; the officers are no good. It is just luck I am not dead, owing to their damned ignorance and neglect…. There is no romance or anything to the infantry. It is not a question of bravery, it is a question of being a good day laborer.

American volunteers in the 3rd Marching Regiment, Foreign Legion, while on leave in Paris, July 4, 1915. Standing at center is Victor Chapman, who would later become the first Escadrille Américaine pilot to die in combat. To his immediate left is Eugene Bullard, who survived the war after becoming history's first African-American combat pilot. Sitting in the front row, center, is Edmond Genet, also destined to die while flying with the Lafayette Escadrille. To Genet's left is yet another future member of the famed all-American squadron, William Dugan. (Washington and Lee University Archives)

What they had experienced firsthand was dehumanization at its worst: mechanized murder. Absent in this current war of attrition were the heroic charges and the gallantry that their grandfathers had experienced. Any opportunity for individual bravery and glory was eliminated by swaths of deadly machine gun fire or atomized in indiscriminate artillery barrages. After months of filth, vermin, death, and back-breaking physical exertion, many of these men were actively seeking an honorable way out. The prospect of transferring to aviation provided that, and more. Here, finally, was the opportunity to fight a "clean" war, complete with the individual heroism and the glory they had traveled to France to experience.

An American Squadron

The desire by certain young Americans to fly for France began from the first days of the war. Many of these men—a few of whom were already accomplished pilots—traveled to France for the sole purpose of joining the air service. Some joined the Foreign Legion or the ambulance service only as a way to get into aviation. Although the first of these who succeeded were assigned to French combat squadrons after completing flight training, a plan was in the works to create a single squadron composed almost entirely of Americans.

Within weeks after the war started in August 1914, two young men from wealthy American families independently expressed an interest in forming an all-American unit. William Thaw and Norman Prince, without even knowing one another, came to France already as trained pilots. Both served first as pilots in French squadrons, and both were destined to become founding members of the all-American unit that came to be known as the Lafayette Escadrille. They were not the only ones. By mid-1915, there were several future members of the still nonexistent American squadron who were flying for the French. For all of them, it had been a very hard sell just to get accepted into the French Air Service, let alone convincing the French government to sanction the formation of an all-American squadron. For that to occur, some high-level political support would be necessary.

Up until this point, the French had been less than enthusiastic about a squadron composed of Americans. There simply had been little demand for American aviators, since there were far more French aviation volunteers than were needed. And besides, the French wartime government was exceedingly paranoid about foreigners being in any position where they might wreak havoc. There were spies everywhere—even where there were no spies. Finally, there was a general feeling among top-level French officials that creating an all-American flying squadron might violate a provision of the 1907 Hague Convention, which prohibited recruiting combatants from a neutral country. This, they feared, could negatively affect France's standing in the eyes of the still very neutral American public. The United States was a powerful potential ally they did not want to upset.

By mid-1915, however, all of this had changed. The war, which had not gone particularly well for the French, now promised to be a long one. Already, the casualty rate was astronomically high, and so France was no longer in any position to refuse help. Also, by this time, a handful of American citizens had set an important precedent by managing to enter French aviation via the Foreign Legion. These American pilots—which included several future Lafayette Escadrille members—had more than proven their loyalty and had accounted for themselves well in aerial combat.

Finally, the neutrality issue that had previously concerned the French so much had also more or less resolved itself—with the aid of some behind-the-scenes political maneuvering. Edmund L. Gros, a well-connected San Francisco physician, who had for many years lived and practiced medicine in Paris, was also interested in getting young Americans into French aviation. After learning of Thaw's and Prince's desire to form an all-American flying unit, he teamed with a powerful French ally, an undersecretary of the French Ministry of Foreign Affairs named Jarousse de Sillac, to form an organization that became known as the Franco-American Flying Corps Committee. Under this banner, they lobbied the chief of French military aeronautics to form an all-American squadron in the French Air Service. Consequently, on August 21, 1915, an order was issued to bring all the Americans currently flying for France into a single squadron.

Gros and de Sillac were also lobbying another individual whose help they needed. Their Franco-American Flying Corps Committee required money for operating expenses, so they went to where the money was. Wealthy American industrialist William K. Vanderbilt, who at the time lived in France and was enthusiastic about Americans flying for France, agreed to fund the effort. Because of his influence, other investors eventually also volunteered their financial support. These funds would be used not only for committee administrative and travel expenses but also to supplement the pay of the American aviators who would earn the equivalent of only about 20 cents a day from the French army. The committee would pay each American aviator a generous monthly expense allowance of 100 francs (about $20), which was later doubled to 200 francs. In addition it would award a hefty bonus of 1,000 francs ($200) for each enemy aircraft shot down and from 250 to 1,500 francs ($50-$300) for each medal or citation awarded.

The French authorities laid out these rules: American aviators would have to enter the French Aéronautique Militaire through the Foreign Legion, train in French flying schools and be governed by French regulations. Furthermore, the squadron itself, though manned by American pilots, would be commanded by French officers. The most important provision paved the way for nearly unlimited numbers of future volunteers: it guaranteed that anyone who failed to qualify as an aviator would be under no further obligation to serve in the French army. Thus, the path was finally clear for the formation of an American flying unit in France. It would take several more months for it to

Dr. Edmund L. Gros began World War I as a prominent American physician practicing at the American Ambulance Hospital, located on the outskirts of Paris at Neuilly-sur-Seine. He was instrumental in establishing the American Ambulance Corps, later called the American Field Service, and in helping to pave the way—politically and financially— for the establishment of the all-American unit that became known as the Lafayette Escadrille. (US Air Force)

become reality, but on April 20, 1916, Escadrille N.124—commonly known as the Escadrille Américaine—became officially operational.

★ ★ ★

Thus began what was to be the adventure of a lifetime for the 38 American pilots who would, over the next 22 months, legitimately claim membership in the famed squadron that ultimately became known as the Lafayette Escadrille. For several of these men, that adventure would also prove be their last—for it would also be a deadly one.

CHAPTER 2

THE ESCADRILLE AMÉRICAINE IS BORN

"I only ask that you fly well, that you fight hard, and that you act as a man."

The newly designated Escadrille N.124—the "N" signifying that it was equipped with Nieuport fighters—first formed at a large sprawling flying field on the outskirts of Luxeuil-les-Bains. Located on the far eastern side of France in the foothills of the Vosges mountains, Luxeuil was—and is—a beautiful resort town founded by the Romans, and known for its thermal baths. In April 1916, Luxeuil was comfortably situated more than 30 miles behind the frontlines in the relatively stable Vosges sector, making it an ideal location for the new squadron to cut its teeth. Here, starting in the latter half of April 1916, its initial group of pilots, mechanics, and other support personnel, along with the airplanes, vehicles, tools, spare parts, and other equipment necessary to operate a combat squadron, began to assemble. Here too, the newly assigned American airmen would fly their first missions and begin learning the serious business of aerial combat.

The Capitaine and his Lieutenant

The Lafayette Escadrille would, from its inception until it became a part of the US Air Service in February 1918, be under the command of two French officers: a captain and his lieutenant. This was one condition on which the French Air Service insisted, and it was probably a wise one. The intricacies of commanding a squadron in a French-speaking air service required a level of experience, judgment, and linguistic finesse that no American pilot possessed.

Capitaine Georges Thénault was the highly capable French officer assigned to command Escadrille N.124. Born on October 2, 1887, the 28-year-old career army officer was one of the most experienced aviators in the French Air Service. He applied for the position at the urging of William Thaw, who had previously served under him as a pilot in Escadrille C.42. Thaw, who was to become one of the founding American members of the squadron, heartily endorsed Thénault, whom he admired

Capitaine Georges Thénault (left) confers with Lieutenant Alfred de Laage de Meux. Thénault was the first and only commander of the squadron that became known as the Lafayette Escadrille. After attending the French military academy at St. Cyr, he served in the elite mountain infantry unit, the Chasseurs Alpins, before transferring to aviation. De Laage was Thénault's hand-picked second-in-command. An aggressive leader in the air and a good comrade on the ground, he was universally admired and respected. The two French officers made an effective team in leading their squadron of neophyte American pilots into battle. (Willis B. Haviland Collection)

and respected as a commander. Thénault would prove to be the squadron's only CO during its 22 months of existence, and despite some occasional grumbling on the part of the Americans, he would also prove to be the right man for the job. A natural leader, he was respected for the way he maintained the fine balance between strict military discipline and a cordial atmosphere.

Lieutenant Alfred de Laage de Meux was Thénault's pick as his second-in-command. Born on September 24, 1891, he came from an old French aristocratic military family. He entered hostilities as a cavalryman in the 14th Regiment of the Dragoons, but transferred to aviation after being wounded on August 31, 1914. He served first as a gunner, but in his spare time, somehow taught himself to fly. He received his pilot's wings on March 22, 1915, thus becoming one of the few aviators of the war to receive his "brevet militaire"—the French military pilot rating—without ever attending a flying school. Lieutenant de Laage was to become the most respected man in the squadron, beloved by all who knew him. A natural flyer and leader, his aggressive combat style, offset by his compassion and congenial personality, set the standard that the pilots serving under him strived to meet. As he told each new pilot reporting to the squadron:

> I only ask that you fly well, that you fight hard, and that you act as a man. I demand that you obey, explicitly and without hesitation, any orders I give when I am leading combat patrols…. Accept your share of the responsibility for upholding the good name of the squadron, and we shall get along quite well.

Lt. de Laage was a terror in the sky, yet he wept openly when he lost one of his men. Nearly all of the pilots under his command spoke of him in similarly glowing terms: "the finest man I ever knew," "a wonderful French gentleman," and "no finer soldier ever lived."

The "Founding Seven"

The first seven American members of Escadrille N.124 started arriving at Luxeuil on April 20, 1916. They had come to this time and place in their respective careers in various ways. Some had entered the Aéronautique Militaire after first serving as frontline soldiers in the Foreign Legion, while others had entered from the ambulance service. Two had come to France already trained as pilots and five of them had aviation experience in French combat squadrons before being assigned to N.124. Regardless of background, all had worked their way through the French flying schools like any other prospective pilot.

SOUS-LIEUTENANT WILLIAM "BILL" THAW was the only American member of the escadrille to report as a commissioned French officer, and was thus the ranking American pilot throughout its existence. The heavy-set, bushy mustachioed Thaw was also one the best-liked Americans in the squadron, as demonstrated by the many laudatory comments

The only American in the newly formed Escadrille Américaine holding a French officer's commission was Sous-lieutenant William Thaw, pictured here. An experienced pilot and natural leader, he joined with Lieutenant de Laage to form a buffer between the sometimes unruly American pilots and the more business-like Capitaine Thénault. (Library of Congress)

fellow squadron members made about him during and after the war. Edwin Parsons probably spoke for many others when he wrote, "I can never speak or write about Bill without a certain feeling of awe, amounting almost to reverence."

He was born in Pittsburgh, Pennsylvania on August 10, 1893, to wealthy parents, Benjamin and Elma Thaw. He attended Yale from 1911 to 1913, before leaving to pursue a career in the new business of aviation. After learning to fly in 1913 at the Curtiss School of Aviation, in Hammondsport, New York, he purchased a Curtiss Model E Hydro flying boat and operated it out of Newport, Rhode Island. Here, he gave rides and made a number of highly publicized flights, most notably, one in which he flew under the four East River bridges and around the Statue of Liberty. He eventually made his way to Europe with his flying boat, in search of fame and fortune, and was in France giving rides when the war began. In spite of his considerable flying experience, his services as a pilot were not immediately needed, so he donated his airplane to the French government and joined dozens of other Americans by enlisting in the French Foreign Legion. While a soldier with the 2ème Régiment étranger, he envisioned the possibility of an all-American flying squadron but first had to get himself back into aviation. With great persistence, he eventually gained admission into the French Air Service, first as a gunner and then as a pilot with Escadrille C.42. Here, he earned numerous citations and a commission as a sous-lieutenant, or junior lieutenant, flying Caudrons—making him the first American in World War I commissioned an officer in the French army. When he arrived at Luxeuil in April 1916, the 22-year-old seasoned and decorated veteran of aerial warfare was well qualified to become a leader in the new escadrille of American volunteers.

SERGENT NORMAN PRINCE was the other founding member of N.124, besides Thaw, to have been a pilot prior to coming to France. Also like Thaw, he came from an established and wealthy family. He was born on August 31, 1887, in Prides Crossing, Massachusetts, to Frederick and Abigail Prince. A 1908 graduate of Harvard College and 1911 graduate of Harvard Law School, he was, in August 1911, practicing law in Chicago at Winston, Payne, Strawn and Shaw when he first became interested in aviation. He signed up for flight training—using a pseudonym, since his strong-willed father refused to give his blessing—and in 1912 received Aero Club of America License No. 55.

Prince had spent a considerable part of his childhood in Pau, France, where his family had an estate, so soon after the war broke out, he rallied to her colors. In January 1915, he sailed to France, where he volunteered for the air service and began lobbying the French to establish a squadron of all-American volunteers. After completing the legal technicality of joining the Foreign Legion, he entered directly into French aviation—the first American to do so without first serving as a soldier in the trenches or as an ambulance driver. After receiving his brevet on May 1, 1915, the refined Harvard lawyer served with Escadrille V.B.108, and later V.B.113, before training on the Nieuport and reporting to N.124 at Luxeuil in April 1916.

Escadrille Américaine founding members Elliot Cowdin (left) and Norman Prince had much in common: both were Harvard grads and scions of elite Eastern families, and both had served previously in French flying squadrons. It was Prince and William Thaw, however, who were instrumental in the creation of the new all-American squadron. (Smithsonian National Air and Space Museum)

SERGENT ELLIOT CHRISTOPHER COWDIN was another Harvard man, having graduated in 1907. He was born on March 3, 1886 on Long Island, New York, to John and Gertrude Cowdin. His father was a successful businessman and sportsman, so Elliot grew up in a comfortable and financially secure atmosphere.

Soon after the outbreak of war in Europe, he volunteered for the American Ambulance Field Service. He served there until February 1915, when he gained entry into the French Air Service. After completing flight training on May 1, he joined Norman Prince at Escadrille V.B.108, where he flew until August 1915. He then trained on Nieuport fighters and subsequently served in three different squadrons over the next eight months as a pursuit pilot, before finally ending up at Luxeuil with the Escadrille Américaine. Cowdin had served with some distinction with the French squadrons: he was awarded the Croix de Guerre with two palms and was the first American in the war to receive the French military medal, the Médaille militaire.

SERGENT WESTON BIRCH "BERT" HALL was in many ways the most interesting founding member of the Escadrille Américaine. He was born on November 7, 1885, to George and Georgia Hall on a farm outside of Higginsville, Missouri. Hall's father, while still only a boy, had served in the Civil War with Confederate Colonel Joe Shelby.

A wanderer for most of his life, Bert found himself in Paris driving a taxicab when the war began. Within days, he was marching with William Thaw, the Rockwell brothers, and the other American volunteers through the streets of Paris to l'Hôtel des Invalides to sign up for the French Foreign Legion. His motivation for doing this is anyone's guess. In fact, it is difficult to know just about anything with certainty about this man of many contradictions. In all likelihood, however, it was a sprinkling of idealism laced with a heavy dose of self-promotion that led him to volunteer. After several months of ground fighting, he too managed a transfer to aviation. After receiving his brevet, he served with Escadrille MS.38 for several months before returning to Avord for pursuit training and eventually, assignment to N.124 at Luxeuil.

CAPORAL VICTOR EMMANUEL CHAPMAN was born on April 17, 1890 in New York City. The son of John and Minna Chapman, he was another of the original seven members of N.124 to come from a distinguished East Coast family. Victor was a direct descendant of John Jay, the second governor of New York and first Chief Justice of the US Supreme Court, the grandson of the president of the New York Stock Exchange, and the son of a prominent American writer. Thus, like many of the other founding members, he had little reason to volunteer to fight for France, other than his sincere belief in the cause.

After graduating from Harvard in 1913, he traveled to France to attend the École des Beaux-Arts school of architecture in Paris. When the hostilities commenced, he immediately enlisted in the Foreign Legion, in which he fought for the next several months. On August 8, 1915 he transferred to the French Air Service as an aerial gunner in Escadrille V.B.108—the same squadron in which Prince and Cowdin were serving

One of the most controversial members of the Escadrille Américaine was Westin Birch "Bert" Hall. Born on a Missouri farm, the son of a Confederate soldier, his humble beginnings and worldly experiences ensured him outcast status among some of his elitist squadron mates. However, during his time with the squadron, he proved his courage and ability. (Library of Congress)

Capitaine Thénault poses here with four of the first seven Americans to report to Escadrille N.124 at Luxeuil-les-Bains in late April 1916. James McConnell, Kiffin Rockwell, Thénault, Norman Prince, and Victor Chapman stand in front of the first airplane assigned to the escadrille, Nieuport 10 N.450. Chapman, a 26-year-old Harvard graduate from New York, decided to transfer from the ground war to aviation because he felt he had "neither helped the French nor injured the Germans." Thénault later called this the "tragic photograph"—within a matter of months after it was taken, all four men standing beside him would be dead. (Washington and Lee University Archives)

as pilots. With Prince's help and encouragement, Chapman soon entered into pilot training, where he met up with two other future members of Escadrille N.124, Kiffin Rockwell and Bert Hall. In April 1916, all three were at Luxeuil, reporting to Capitaine Thénault and the new American volunteer squadron.

CAPORAL KIFFIN YATES ROCKWELL was born in Newport, Tennessee, to Reverend James and Loula Rockwell on September 20, 1892. Like Bert Hall, he did not attend Harvard or Yale, nor did he come from an elite Eastern family. Also like Hall, he was a son of the South: both of his grandfathers had fought with the Confederate Army during the Civil War. He spent his childhood on his maternal grandfather's farm in South Carolina before moving with his family at the age of 14 to Ashville, North Carolina. After briefly attending Virginia Military Institute, he received an appointment to the US Naval Academy but turned it down to join his older brother, Paul, at Washington and Lee University. He attended there for two years.

When the war began in August 1914, Kiffin was living in Atlanta with Paul. They soon boarded a ship to Europe to volunteer for what Kiffin called "the cause of all humanity," and by the end of the month, they were wearing the uniform of the French Foreign Legion. Kiffin served in the trenches until May 1915, when he received a bullet wound to the right thigh. By this time, thoroughly disillusioned with both the ground war and the Legion, he volunteered for the air service. The thin, gangling, 6' 2" 23-year-old proved to be a natural pilot as he progressed through the various phases of flight training. After reporting to Escadrille N.124 at Luxeuil, he achieved great success before his luck came crashing to an end.

Thanks to his brother Paul, Kiffin is one of the best-documented members of the squadron. Paul became the squadron's self-appointed historian and spent the rest of his long life memorializing his brother in every way possible. His book *War Letters of Kiffin Yates Rockwell* provides modern-day historians a particularly interesting behind-the-scenes perspective of life in the squadron.

CAPORAL JAMES ROGERS MCCONNELL was born in Chicago, Illinois, on March 14, 1887, to Judge Samuel and Sarah McConnell. He attended high school in New Jersey and Pennsylvania, and when his father moved his family to Carthage, North Carolina, James enrolled in the University of Virginia. He graduated from there in 1910.

He lived for a while in New York City, attempting with future fellow N.124 member Charles Chouteau Johnson to establish a business. When that ended, he moved to Carthage to accept a position with the Randolph and Cumberland Railway. In January 1915, he decided to sail to France to see the war. For the next few months, he drove for the American Ambulance Field Service, and in the process, earned the Croix de Guerre for distinctive service and courage under fire. Eventually, he decided that "it was plainly up to me to do more than drive an ambulance. The more I saw the splendour of the fight the French were fighting, the more I felt like an embusqué—what the British call a 'shirker.'" Consequently, he entered into aviation, and upon completion of training, was assigned to the new Escadrille Américaine currently forming at Luxeuil in April 1916. Though serving faithfully, the intelligent and urbane McConnell's biggest contribution was literary in nature. Thanks to several weeks of convalescence following an injury received in a crash landing, he wrote his classic book *Flying for France*.

Making the Grade

All seven of these young Americans had, before arriving at Luxeuil, worked their way through the highly effective French aviation training pipeline. It was a long and demanding regimen, lasting several months and consisting of several types and levels of flying schools located throughout France.

The first step after acceptance was to pass a physical examination that, in the midst of a desperate world war, seemed little more than a joke. As *Lafayette Escadrille Pilot*

James Rogers McConnell, posing here in front of a Nieuport fighter at Cachy, served as an ambulance driver before volunteering for aviation. Born in Chicago, he graduated from the University of Virginia and was living in Carthage, North Carolina, when he left for France. (Washington and Lee University Archives)

Biographies author Dennis Gordon put it, it was one that "anyone but a blind amputee could pass." Future squadron member, Ted Parsons, agreed with that assessment:

> Standing me off at ten feet in front of a chart whose letters looked as large as the Corticelli sign in Times Square, he [the examiner] commanded me to read. "The second line," he'd say, "the third letter. I see there a B. What do you see?" Sure enough, it was a B, and I'd say so. "*Bon*," he'd explode enthusiastically. Then we'd do some more .... He was right every time. He never tried to cross me by calling the wrong letter. He wasn't taking any chances I'd be wrong, and his "*Bons*" grew bigger and better with every answer.

Once declared physically fit, the "élève pilote," or student pilot, drew his flight gear and reported to the first school. In most cases, flight training began at one of the large flying schools located at Pau, Avord, or Buc. Here, future members of N.124 had their first experience with an airplane. Some received dual instruction on a trainer, such as the Maurice Farman, while others trained on the Blériot. Those who trained on the latter did not immediately leave the ground in it. They first strapped themselves into a machine with wings so short that it could not take off. In this so-called "Penguin," they learned to control an airplane on the ground and to manage the engine, as they raced back and forth across the huge flying field, wheels firmly planted on the grass. From there, they graduated to a "rouleur" with slightly more wing area and power—just enough to hop off the ground. From this, they progressed to bigger and more powerful trainers and longer, higher flights, complete with turns and other increasingly complex maneuvers. At the completion of training, students took a series of flight tests, after which, they received their brevet and were promoted to the enlisted rank of caporal.

Typically, a prospective "aviateur de chasse," or pursuit pilot, would then move on to the next phase of training in higher performance airplanes. When finished with this so-called "école de perfectionnement," he would travel to Cazaux, in Western France, for a course in aerial gunnery. Here, he learned how to shoot at a moving target while throwing himself around the sky in an airplane traveling 100 miles per hour—a skill so challenging that few pilots ever really mastered it.

The next stop in the journey towards becoming a fighter pilot was the school of aerobatics. Here, new pilots perfected the advanced flying skills they would need in order to maneuver against highly accomplished German pilots. Surviving the dogfights in which they would soon be embroiled would require learning every trick known—and sometimes, even that would prove insufficient.

Once pilots had completed training, they were assigned to a pilot pool, officially called the "Groupe des Divisions d'Entraînement" or GDE. Most of the American pilots went through the GDE at Plessis-Belleville, a small town a few miles northeast of Paris. At this sprawling and utterly flat flying field, they were left mostly on their own, with the freedom to fly as much and as often as they wanted, while they waited for an assignment to a frontline squadron. By this time, they had successfully completed a rigorous course of instruction and gained great confidence in their aerial fighting skills. They could fly and they could shoot, so they were ready—at least, as far as they were concerned—for anything the Germans could put up against them. Almost without exception, they were eager to get to the front so they could start knocking down enemy planes and collecting medals.

What these well-prepared, but inevitably overconfident, young pilots could not possibly know was that they were, in reality, still very green-behind-the-ears novices. In spite of their intense training, at which they may have excelled, they still had to learn the hardest lesson of all: how to stay alive in a very dangerous sky. Until they had gained many hours of hazardous combat experience and learned the way the brutal and constantly evolving game of aerial warfare was really played, their chances for survival were not good—especially, if unlucky enough to encounter an experienced enemy airman or to be forced to fight against numerical odds. Such was aerial combat as it existed in World War I, and such was the game of chance that the American pilots reporting to N.124 at Luxeuil in April 1916 faced. Four of the seven would eventually come out losers.

'A Machine of Aces and an Ace of Machines'

The first six new planes assigned to the pilots reporting to the N.124 were the highly touted Nieuport 11 and Nieuport 16 pursuit planes—three of each. The light and highly maneuverable 11, nicknamed the "Bébé," or baby, for its diminutive size, was the first successful French chasse plane of the war. By the spring of 1916, the Aéronautique Militaire was already in the process of upgrading to the Nieuport 17, but the untested Americans were not complaining. They were happy to have the 11 and higher-powered 16, which were still at that time, fighters worthy of aces—and equal to anything Germany had with which to oppose them. The little single-seat sesquiplanes—biplanes with smaller lower wings than upper ones—weighed just over 1,000 pounds fully loaded and were powered by Le Rhône air-cooled rotary engines that developed 80 or 110 horsepower. These engines rotated with the propeller, thus creating a powerful torque with which the pilots had to contend; however, they also created enough power to allow them to scoot across the lines at 100 miles per hour and climb to altitudes above 15,000 feet. To fly a Nieuport was the highest honor any French pilot could have in 1916. It was, as it was known, "a machine of aces and an ace of machines."

Though small, these early Nieuport fighters had a deadly stinger. They were armed with a single .303-caliber Lewis machine gun, fastened to the top of the upper wing so that it could fire forward, just above the arc of the propeller. Because of this innovation, coupled with its superior flying performance, the Nieuport 11 was the first French design capable of countering the infamous German Fokker monoplane fighter. The Germans had been using its "Eindecker," designed and built by the young Dutchman, Anthony Fokker, with such devastating success over the past year that Allied pilots had come to consider themselves "Fokker Fodder."

This machine gun arrangement was an innovation that evened the score for Allied pilots. They had for some time been up against German aircraft equipped with an interrupter gear that allowed their pilots to fire a belt-fed machine gun straight ahead through the propeller. Now, Allied pilots could also "point and shoot" by firing a Lewis machine gun over the top of the propeller arc. However, the early Lewis ammunition drums, like the one seen here, held just 47 rounds and delivered a brief five-second burst—provided it didn't jam. Pilots had to change drums and clear jams in a 100-mile-per-hour gale, while flying the airplane and evading the enemy with the control stick held between their knees. (Source Unknown)

The secret of the Eindecker's success was not its flight performance, but rather its armament. It was equipped with a revolutionary interrupter mechanism that allowed its belt-fed 7.9-mm machine gun, mounted in front of the pilot, to fire forward through the spinning wooden propeller without hitting and splintering it into a million pieces. German airmen had dramatically capitalized on this feature, which allowed them to aim the machine gun simply by pointing the nose of their airplane at the target. Many Allied aircraft had fallen victim to Fokkers, particularly those flown by the early German aces, Max Immelmann and Oswald Boelcke. The Nieuport pilots now had the upper hand, thanks to their own forward-firing gun and the sparkling performance of their Bébé. The nimble, fast Nieuport was superior to the Eindecker in almost every respect, but the primitive-looking German monoplane was still a deadly adversary.

★ ★ ★

An excellent air-to-air view of a Fokker Eindecker E.III in flight—in this case, a replica with famed late stunt pilot Frank Tallman at the controls, circa early 1960s. Though the plane's flying characteristics were mediocre at best, it featured a machine gun synchronized to shoot through the propeller. For that reason alone, the E-series Fokker became the favorite mount for the earliest German aces—and a dangerous adversary for the pilots of Escadrille N.124. (American Aviation Historical Society)

The unique new Escadrille Américaine now had officers, trained pilots, support personnel, and first-rate fighter planes on hand. It was finally time for the world to see, for the first time in history, what an American fighter squadron could do.

CHAPTER 3

FIRST BLOOD

"The heavens are their battlefield; they are the Cavalry of the clouds."

Life at Luxeuil for the men of the new Escadrille Américaine was far better than any of them could ever have expected in the midst of a world war. They were quartered in a

The American pilots reporting to Escadrille N.124 at Luxeuil-les-Bains in April 1916 lived the good life. They were quartered in a villa near the thermal baths and for their meals walked a short distance down Rue Carnot to the Hôtel du Lion Vert restaurant, where they dined in elegance. Until their fighting aircraft arrived, they amused themselves with the local ladies or, as pictured here, playing billiards at Madame Voge's. From left: James McConnell, Victor Chapman, Madame Voge, and Kiffin Rockwell. (Washington and Lee University Archives)

large, comfortable villa located in a resort town dozens of miles behind the frontlines, they ate their meals in a fine hotel restaurant, and they were chauffeured around in an open touring car like famous celebrities.

The Good Life

All aviators in the world's first air war—and especially single-seat fighter pilots—were members of an elite club. These pioneers were among the very few with both the courage and the skill to take to the skies to do battle in warfare's newest weapon. For that reason, they captured the public's imagination. When compared to the grinding, muddy, vermin-infested killing grounds of the trenches, war in the air seemed clean, heroic—even romantic. The one-on-one aerial dogfights, observed for miles around by those on the ground, seemed part of an exciting game. It is, therefore, not surprising that these pilots, twisting and turning all over the sky, were more like sports heroes than fighting men.

They were far more than sports heroes, however. These specially trained men who waged combat in a world arena for all to see were fighting not only for their country, but for their very lives. They flew and fought mostly alone, and when they died, they typically died alone. They were in many ways comparable to the gladiators of ancient Rome or the knights of the Middle Ages. The manner in which British Prime Minister David Lloyd George described these "knights of the air" in an October 29, 1917, speech to the House of Commons expresses how the public typically viewed fighting airmen of that era:

> The heavens are their battlefield; they are the Cavalry of the clouds. High above the squalor and the mud ... they fight out the eternal issues of right and wrong.... Every flight is a romance; every report is an epic. They are the knighthood of this war, without fear and without reproach. They recall the old legends of chivalry, not merely the daring of their exploits, but by the nobility of their spirit, and, amongst the multitude of heroes, let us think of the chivalry of the air.

All combat aviators of this period enjoyed an exalted status, but the Americans who volunteered to fly for France were on an even loftier pedestal. The amount of worldwide publicity the new Escadrille Américaine had already received was staggering. The French were only too happy to put these heroic Americans on public display. It was good for morale and it made for excellent propaganda. Likewise, an increasingly pro-Allied American public was proud to read about its young countrymen who had volunteered to fly and fight for a cause in which they believed. The press coverage converted these men into worldwide celebrities. Their pictures appeared in newspapers, magazines, and newsreels, and everywhere they went, they were hounded by reporters for interviews and photos. The new Escadrille Américaine and the names of each American in it soon became known the world over.

Some of the American pilots not only welcomed this attention, they also contributed to it. One of those who did not was Kiffin Rockwell, who wrote to his brother Paul in a May 6, 1916, letter:

The original members of Escadrille Américaine who reported to Luxeuil in April 1916. From left: Victor Chapman, Elliot Cowdin, Bert Hall, William Thaw, Capitaine Thénault, Lieutenant de Laage, Norman Prince, Kiffin Rockwell, and James McConnell. The captain's German shepherd Fram, along with two other squadron members from the animal world, pose in the foreground. (Washington and Lee University Archives)

> In regard to photographs, every single fellow seems to be trying to beat the others in sending news to the newspapers, so there is going to be a damned sight too much publicity as it is, and every time the least thing happens, four or five will be sending telegrams to the papers. So I had rather not bother with any of it as all this junk they pull off makes me sick.

Accompanying the American pilots' new degree of notoriety was a new lifestyle. For all of them, it was dramatically different from anything they had experienced in the Legion, the ambulance service, or even in flight training. As James McConnell described it in *Flying for France*:

> Rooms were assigned to us in a villa adjoining the famous hot baths of Luxeuil, where Cæsar's cohorts were wont to besport themselves. We messed with our officers … at the best hotel in town. An automobile was always on hand to carry us to the field. I began to wonder whether I was a summer resorter instead of a soldier.

Kiffin Rockwell was equally impressed with the fine reception they received at Luxeuil. After his months in the trenches and the Spartan lifestyle of a student aviator, it must have seemed as though he had arrived in paradise. As he wrote to his mother on April 20, 1916:

I am at last in escadrille but a good distance from the front and, so far, it is like being on a pleasant trip to a resort…. We all eat together at a hotel where wonderfully good meals are served. We occupy a villa that has been requisitioned for us, with orderlies to wait on us. We go down each day about one hundred yards from here to bathe in a bath-house that is over two hundred years old…. If it were not for looking in the glass and seeing myself in uniform I should not be able to believe that I am at war, or that there is such a thing as war.

The quaint Vosges town belonged to the young Americans as they swaggered around the streets of Luxeuil, as did the hearts of many women there, young and old. Deprived of their men by the raging war, the lonely ladies of Luxeuil were completely enamored with the dashing and famous "aviateurs américains." They were veritable gods, and as suggested by letters the men wrote during this period, their opportunities for amour were abundant and their conquests numerous. James McConnell wrote in an April 30, 1916, letter to Paul Rockwell, "Why it's an effort to avoid being raped. I've obliged a couple but have settled down to occupy myself with a very interesting looking young lady of Italian birth…. They're not used to soldiers here and so things flow our way."

Political Opposition

Not everyone, however, approved of the newly formed Franco-American flying unit. Many Americans who strongly favored maintaining strict neutrality decried the establishment of the American squadron as a step closer to US entry into the war. Other detractors felt that these trained pilots should return to the United States and help develop their own country's woefully deficient air service. Most of all, pro-German Americans joined the German government in strongly opposing Americans taking up arms against Germany. Charging that it was a flagrant violation of existing neutrality laws, they bitterly protested to the American government.

The flames of German resentment for the American fliers had been fanned even hotter back in December 1915. William Thaw, Norman Prince, and Elliot Cowdin, all of whom were, at the time, flying with French squadrons and would soon become founding members of the new all-American squadron, returned to the United States for Christmas leave. They arrived on December 23 to great public fanfare and extensive press coverage. The articles in US newspapers regarding the US fliers and their efforts in support of the French were nearly all favorable. These glowing reports about their exploits greatly pleased the French government, but the Germans understandably had an entirely different take on the matter. The issue was brought to a head by a chance encounter and a less-than-friendly exchange of views in a New York barbershop between the German Ambassador to the United States, Herr Johann Heinrich von Bernstorff, and William Thaw. As a result, the three aviators decided to hightail it back to France before US authorities decided to intern them as belligerents in a neutral country. For now, however, the complaints about the Americans flying for France had no tangible effect.

Not everyone approved of citizens from neutral America flying for France. Back in December 1915, Norman Prince, Elliot Cowdin, and William Thaw (pictured here, from left to right)—all of whom had been flying in French squadrons—returned to the United States for Christmas leave. It was a newsworthy event on both sides of the Atlantic, but not all the press was good. An open letter from the editor of the pro-German weekly newspaper, The Fatherland, *appeared in the Christmas edition of the* New York Times, *urging the arrest of the three fliers for neutrality violation. Fearing detainment, they cut short their leave and returned to France. (Library of Congress)*

First Mission

When the first Americans arrived at Luxeuil, the new squadron was already well on its way to becoming operational. As James McConnell described it, in his typically colorful way:

> Everything was brand new, from the fifteen Fiat trucks to the office, magazine, and rest tents. And the men attached to the escadrille! At first sight they seemed to outnumber the Nicaraguan army—mechanicians, chauffeurs, armourers, motorcyclists, telephonists, wireless operators, Red Cross stretcher bearers, clerks! Afterward I learned they totalled seventy-odd, and that all of them were glad to be connected with the American Escadrille.

More work was necessary, however, before the new squadron was ready for wartime missions. Most of the airplanes arrived from the factory in pieces, packed in crates and canvas-covered trailers, so they had to be assembled, and machine guns installed and adjusted. As part of the preparation process, each pilot also instructed his "mécanicien" to paint a personal insignia on his assigned airplane. Though partly ego-driven, it was

Bert Hall posing with his Nieuport 16 N.1208 "BERT." He later flew with his name reversed on one side to read "TREB," so that, as he put it, "Pilots can now tell who I am, no matter how they pass me." Most of the Escadrille N.124 pilots displayed some type of personal insignia so they could be recognized in the air. (Charles Woolley)

also a matter of practicality: it allowed the pilots to recognize each another in the air. Most chose as their personal trademark their initials or a nickname: Rockwell was "R," Hall was "H," and McConnell was "MAC." In the ensuing months, personal insignia would evolve into many different forms, but the practice continued throughout the life of the squadron.

Capitaine Thénault also used this time to familiarize his pilots with the surrounding Vosges countryside and to develop some semblance of the teamwork they would need to accomplish their mission—and remain alive. Specifically, that mission was to fly protection for the French Groupe de Bombardement 4, with which they shared the aerodrome at Luxeuil. This group, led by the famed Capitaine Felix Happe, was planning a series of strategic bombing missions into Germany.

All of the many preparations needed to make the new squadron an effective operational unit took time, but by May 13, 1916, it was ready. At sunrise, five Nieuports took off from the aerodrome at Luxeuil. Leading the "V" formation was Kiffin Rockwell, with James McConnell and Victor Chapman just behind and to either side. The veterans,

All nine pilots of Escadrille N.124 in flight gear at Luxeuil, May 14, 1916. From left: Victor Chapman, Elliot Cowdin, Bert Hall, William Thaw, Lieutenant de Laage, Norman Prince, James McConnell, Kiffin Rockwell, and Capitaine Thénault. In the background, mechanic Michel Plaa-Porte stands in front of the Nieuport. This photo was among the many taken at Luxeuil on May 14, 1916, by a professional film crew. (Library of Congress)

Capitaine Thénault and Sous-lieutenant William Thaw brought up the rear. They patrolled the lines at an altitude of 13,000 feet, with the Swiss Alpine mountain peaks to the south "glistening like icebergs in the morning sun," as James McConnell described it. After an hour or so, they returned to Luxeuil, very cold but with nothing to report other than scattered antiaircraft fire. It was an uneventful mission, but Escadrille N.124 had its first patrol under its belt and was now officially open for business.

To mark the occasion, a film crew and United Press reporter that Cowdin and Prince had brought back with them from Paris recorded for posterity scenes of the men and machines of the famed American escadrille. This interesting and revealing footage still exists today. As Victor Chapman described it in a May 14, 1916, letter:

> Well, we pulled it off this morning despite the rain and low clouds. I never was so be-photo'd or ever hope to be again. In large groups and small ones; singly, talking, and silent; in the air, and on the ground, by "movies" and in poses…. Then one at a time we bumped out [in our planes] and rushed by [the cameraman out in the middle of the flying field]. I must say that he had nerve for we décolle'd [took off] just before him, and, after a turn of the field, we each dived just over him, then came round and landed…. Kiffin and Berty Hall were much peeved to think that some—person was going to make heaps of money out of us, and we'd risked our necks for nothing. (None of us liked to maneuver so close together with the plafond [cloud ceiling] at 300 metres). "Think of the honor," said I. "Oh, no, give me the cash and keep it," said Bert.

Kiffin Rockwell also mentioned this film session in a letter to his mother when he wrote, "About a week ago, we all gave flights before a moving picture concern.

The original members of Escadrille Américaine posing at Luxeuil on May 14, 1916, with the bomber pilots of Groupe de Bombardement 4, with which they shared the aerodrome. The tall, bearded Capitaine Felix Happe, who commanded the bomb group, stands to the right of center between Elliot Cowdin and Capitaine Thénault. The Americans left Luxeuil before flying any missions with Happe but would rejoin him a few months later. (US Air Force)

The pictures are going to be shown in America. If you see them advertised be sure and go, and look for a machine with an "R" on the side and that will be Kiffin."

A Toast to Death

The escadrille soon experienced another significant event at Luxeuil. It occurred only days after their initial mission when, on May 18, Kiffin Rockwell became the first pilot in N.124 to down an enemy airplane. It was a truly phenomenal accomplishment, given Rockwell's total lack of experience—he and his squadron had only been in action for five days and it was his first aerial combat. Perhaps most phenomenally, he accomplished this feat with only four shots fired from his Lewis machine gun.

He was flying alone when he spotted a German two-seat reconnaissance airplane below him. He dove on it, holding his fire, as the enemy observer opened fire on him with his swivel-mounted machine gun. Rockwell felt his own plane being hit, but he waited until he was within 30 feet of the enemy plane—absolute point-blank range. By this time, he only had time to squeeze off four quick shots from his Lewis machine gun before swerving violently to avoid a collision. His aim was either very good or very

Capitaine Thénault briefing his pilots at Luxeuil, May 14, 1916. From left: Kiffin Rockwell, Thénault, Norman Prince, Lieutenant de Laage, Elliot Cowdin, Bert Hall, James McConnell, and Victor Chapman. William Thaw is hidden behind Thénault. (Library of Congress)

An aerial view of the aerodrome at Behonne, as photographed by a German reconnaissance plane in May 1915. The arrow points to the north. The hangars are visible near the center of the photograph and the village of Behonne at the upper left. This is similar to what the pilots of Escadrille N.124 saw on May 20, 1916, as they approached from the southeast on their flight from Luxeuil to Behonne. (Dieter Gröschel)

lucky, because in that half-second burst, he hit both pilot and observer and sent the aircraft down smoking. He watched it crash in German lines, as did French observers on the ground. The escadrille received almost immediate official confirmation for his kill and when Rockwell landed, he received a rousing reception from his fellow pilots— and a recommendation from the Capitaine for the Médaille militaire and promotion to sergent.

The Escadrille Américaine had drawn first blood and Kiffin Rockwell, whose feat was reported in newspapers throughout France and the United States, became an instant international hero. It was an auspicious start for N.124 and one that deserved a special celebration. With that spirit in mind, Kiffin uncorked a rare old bottle of bourbon whisky that his brother, Paul, had given him. He downed a slug and then passed it on to Victor Chapman. Victor, however, had a keener appreciation for the momentous occasion. He made a suggestion that spawned one of the squadron's most famous traditions. Hereafter, he proposed, only when a pilot downed an enemy airplane would he be allowed to take a drink from the "Bottle of Death," as it came to be known. Little by little, over the ensuing months, the bottle was emptied; unfortunately, however, some of those who had the honor of drinking from it would soon join their victims in death. Kiffin Rockwell was one of these.

★ ★ ★

The following day, the squadron received orders to relocate, even though they had not yet flown a single mission with Capitaine Happe and his bombers. The men of N.124 hurriedly packed up their equipment and supplies, and on May 20, the pilots climbed into their Nieuports, and winged their way 90 miles to the northwest. Their destination was an aerodrome adjacent to the tiny village of Behonne, France. This rolling, rocky farm field, known as Ferme Ste. Catherine, was located on a plateau above the larger city of Bar-le-Duc.

Only 30 miles northeast of there, the "real" war was being waged. In progress was a massive, historic battle in which German Army Chief of Staff General Erich von Falkenhayn intended to "bleed France to death" by inflicting so many casualties that she would be forced to capitulate. The brutal conflagration of attrition that became known as "the meat grinder" epitomizes—as much as any battle ever fought—the horror of total war. The newly blooded Escadrille Américaine was about to enter into the Battle of Verdun.

CHAPTER 4

INTO THE GRINDER

"We had hold of the bear's tail and no one to help us let go."

The men of Escadrille N.124 quickly settled into their new environment at Behonne and readied themselves for what promised to be a much more dangerous war than what they had briefly experienced at Luxeuil. Only a few miles away, hundreds of thousands of men were pulverizing each other into oblivion. The terrible battle at Verdun, which began on February 21, 1916, was total warfare at its very worst, and the war in the air reflected this desperate struggle. Enemy airmen had pulled out all stops to prevent French observation aircraft from operating over the lines. This prompted a desperate French Général Philippe Pétain to tell his air commander, Commandant Charles de Tricornot de Rose, "I am blind, Rose. Clear the sky!"

In response, de Rose brought together several escadrilles de chasse, dedicated exclusively to the destruction of enemy aircraft. The Escadrille Américaine had arrived at Behonne to join this group, now recognized as France's first fighter group. The squadron's next few months here would bring more air battles, and with them, more successes—but they would come at a cost.

The Way it Was

It is difficult today to envision what combat flying was really like in the First World War. Nearly a century's worth of fanciful articles, books, movies, comic strips, and other forms of popular culture have distorted and trivialized it beyond any sense of reality.

One common misconception, repeated ad nauseam over the past century, is that World War I airplanes were flimsy kites held together by baling wire and glue. Nothing could be further from the truth. Thanks to unlimited wartime funding and rapidly evolving technology, warplanes had, by 1916, progressed far beyond that. Coming on the heels of the Industrial Revolution, these machines were the culmination of

Kiffin Rockwell models a fur ensemble that his friend, Mrs. Alice Weeks, gave him to ward off the cold. According to many accounts by men who flew open cockpit aircraft in World War I, there was no greater hardship than winter flying in bitterly cold Northern France. At the high altitudes they routinely operated—often exceeding 15,000 feet— temperatures plunged well below zero, and with a 100-mile-per-hour icy slipstream in the face, it was all but unbearable. (Washington and Lee University Archives)

the best engineering technology and scientifically applied art in existence at the time. A close look at any of the few remaining examples of aircraft from this era that are displayed in museums around the world reveals how incredibly beautiful and complex they really were. And though the varnished fabric, wood, and steel wire bracing, from which they were built, tends to give them an almost delicate, kite-like appearance, they were surprisingly sturdy. They were, in fact, deadly weapons possessing dazzling flight performance that steadily increased throughout the war years.

This is not to say that warplanes of 1914–1918 were necessarily safe or easy to fly. They were usually neither. They were built for one reason, and one reason alone: to accomplish military objectives. Thus, very little effort was expended to make them comfortable or aerodynamically stable; and because these airplanes were a new technology, produced in the midst of a frenzied wartime development program, and because they were usually maintained in an austere field environment, they often did not perform as designed. Wings *did* sometimes separate from fuselages in dives, gasoline tanks too often caught fire, and engines routinely quit in midflight. This was flying in the Great War as it really existed, and pilots learned to accept the dangerous level of risk that came with the world-class performance they enjoyed.

Also contrary to popular perception, flying in World War I was not fun. Certainly, it was an exciting adventure that had its good moments and its share of perks, but few of those who actually experienced it considered it anything short of unpleasant. The physical assault on these airmen flying in open-cockpit airplanes in all kinds of weather was unprecedented. The hardships they had to endure were as numerous as they were severe: crushing positive and negative g-forces typical of high-speed flight; the painful effects of rapid changes in air pressure that occurred during steep dives, which included sinus blockages, toothaches, and burst eardrums; the debilitating effects of prolonged high-altitude oxygen starvation; intense cold, made worse by violent wind forces; blinding sun glare; prolonged exposure to sickening engine fumes, noise, and vibration; and dizzying disturbances of the equilibrium that commonly resulted in vertigo and motion sickness. All these exacted a heavy toll on the bodies of these pioneer combat pilots.

Equally oppressive was the psychological shock of flying in mortal combat. It was an exceedingly deadly and utterly terrifying undertaking—one that US "Ace of Aces" Eddie Rickenbacker described as "legalized murder." It was brutal, exacting, instantaneous in nature, and unforgiving in the extreme. It required great skill and courage—and the stakes were the highest possible: life and death. To fight for one's life high in the sky on a daily basis against a highly competent and well-equipped enemy was a challenge to these pilots' very sanity. They knew that sudden death lurked at every turn and could occur anytime they were in the air. They were also well aware that when they fell—whether from structural or engine failure or from enemy bullets—they fell without a parachute. These life-saving devices were not routinely used in World War I, except by observation balloon crews and a few pilots late in the war.

These early combat airmen also knew all too well that when they fell to their inevitable death, they were likely to fall in flames with gallons of spewing gasoline exploding all around them. Fanned by a 100-mile-per-hour slipstream, the resulting inferno would roast them to a charcoal crisp long before they augered into the ground, several thousand feet below. They knew this because they had seen it happen to others too many times before.

It is therefore easy to understand why many pilots who flew in World War I lived in a state of constant fear, compounded by nightmare-induced sleep deprivation. For the men of Escadrille Américaine, this terror was only alleviated by occasional sprees in Paris and regular doses of liquid courage. Many, in fact, could not fly without first fortifying themselves with several stiff drinks. One of the squadron's more eloquently candid pilots, who would join its ranks in January 1917, was Edwin C. "Ted" Parsons. He wryly observed, in one of his classic understatements, that "bullets buzzing past your head have a most depressing effect."

His solution to this problem, as well as the mind-numbing cold, was alcohol—which to him was a form of therapy and an essential coping mechanism, rather than a substance of abuse. As he expressed it, "I can speak authoritatively only for myself, but I was not a whit different than 99% of all other pilots, at least those who had been in it for some time. During the last year and a half of the war, I rarely went up without a couple under my belt." He also admitted to putting a couple more under his belt after he was in the air. He carried a half-pint metal flask filled with brandy in the breast pocket of his tunic. He considered it, "an absolute necessity" that "with judicial nipping, would just about hold out for a two-hour patrol."

The physical and emotional assault that these early combat airmen suffered eventually affected their health. Parsons postulated that every time a man faced danger, it left an invisible scar. "He begins flinching before he knows it. And in the end, the strain cuts into his nerves." These extreme physical and emotional hardships that eventually exceeded the upper limits of human endurance led to a condition equivalent to what the men in the trenches were calling "shell shock," or what modern-day psychologists call "posttraumatic stress disorder" (PTSD). Those lucky enough to avoid being killed outright lasted only a matter of weeks before either physical or mental breakdown forced their removal from combat. Had the young Americans who so enthusiastically volunteered to fly for France in 1916 and 1917 known all of this ahead of time, they might have reconsidered throwing their hats into the ring. Parsons candidly expressed what he and probably many of his fellow squadron members felt at the time:

> None of us had any real idea of what we were getting into. We had hold of the bear's tail and no one to help us let go. With few exceptions, I believe most of us would have welcomed an opportunity to bow out gracefully. In fact, some, after they'd awakened to what they'd let themselves in for, stole away on silent feet before they'd heard any guns fired in anger, perhaps not so gracefully or honorably, but most wisely. While there was some slight criticism at the time, it may well be they

> were the smart ones after all…. Viewed down the mellowing vista of years, the Great Adventure had
> its romantic side, but at the time it was just plain unvarnished hell on wings…. We were merely very
> wild, but very frightened, youngsters, fighting with unfamiliar weapons in a new element, leaping
> to fame and being made heroes overnight by newspaper publicity…. Our sole claim to real heroism
> was in being half scared to death and doing our best in spite of it!

This realistic assessment of flying in the Great War only emphasizes the courage and dedication of the men who volunteered to fly with the Escadrille Américaine— particularly those who stayed with it and fulfilled their duties honorably. It also helps explain why those who "stole away on silent feet" did so—not because they were cowards, but because not everyone is physically or emotionally equipped to deal with such extreme stresses.

Into the Battle

Life at the Verdun front for the men of N.124 was in some ways similar to what they had experienced at Luxeuil. They were once again quartered in a comfortable nearby villa but now had their own mess, complete with a chef. However, it was all too obvious that this sector was a far cry from the relatively quiet one they had just left at Luxeuil. McConnell later wrote:

> Our really serious work had begun, however, and we knew it. Even as far behind the actual fighting
> as Bar-le-Duc one could sense one's proximity to a vast military operation. The endless convoys of
> motor trucks, the fast-flowing stream of troops, and the distressing number of ambulances brought
> realization of the near presence of a gigantic battle.

The ground war also looked much different from above than anything the pilots had seen before. McConnell called it "murdered Nature." He described in a June 13, 1916, letter his impression of the landscape near Verdun, as viewed from the air:

> There is a broad brown band north of Verdun which marks the territory where the fighting has
> taken place. It does not seem of this earth. At each side are shell holes but in the brown band there
> are none to be seen. They are so numerous that they blend into each other. What trees there were
> have all gone, and if villages were there, there is no sign of them left. Even the broad white roads
> have vanished as if erased from a blackboard.

Another difference the men noticed was the increased enemy air activity. This meant better hunting opportunities but also a greater degree of danger. It did not take long for the squadron to make its presence known. On May 22—only two days after arriving at Behonne—Bert Hall earned his first sip from the "Bottle of Death," and along with it, the Médaille militaire and Croix de Guerre with palm. After spotting an enemy machine flying at 13,000 feet altitude, he attacked with good effect and saw it crash just inside the German lines.

The intensity level remained high for N.124, and additional momentous events were in the making. Early on the morning of May 24, Bill Thaw destroyed a German Fokker, for his first confirmed victory. Rather than boast about it, however, he downplayed the feat by telling his fellow pilots, "No credit to me. I just murdered him. He never saw me."

In a wild aerial melee that followed later that day, the squadron shed its first blood—three times over. Thénault, de Laage, Thaw, Rockwell, and Chapman were patrolling when they encountered a formation of 12 German airplanes. The dangerously impetuous Victor Chapman did not wait for an attack signal but simply dived on the large formation, forcing everyone else to follow suit. During the attack, Rockwell's Nieuport took a bullet to the windscreen, which sent glass and metal fragments into his face. Stunned and blinded by the blood, he made his way back to the aerodrome and landed safely. Fortunately, the wound was only serious enough to keep him out of action briefly. After a few days of rest and recuperation in Paris, he was back in business.

While Rockwell was fighting for his life, Victor Chapman was having a similarly unpleasant experience. Bullets whizzed all around him, into his airplane, and through his clothing, one of which grazed his arm. In the same attack, Thaw targeted three enemy planes, and as with Chapman and Rockwell, he came out on the short end. He soon found himself in the midst of a shooting gallery, with himself as the target. The onslaught of enemy bullets bored his airplane full of holes, one of them smashing into his left elbow, creating a serious and painful wound. He barely managed to get down safely behind French lines before fainting from the pain and loss of blood. He would eventually return to flying status but his arm would never be the same again.

New Blood

During this period of fighting at Verdun, new pilots continued to arrive. They slowly filled the ranks of the new escadrille, which had yet to reach full strength. The first one of these to report showed up the same day that Rockwell, Chapman, and Thaw had their painful encounters with straight-shooting enemy airmen. He could not have arrived at a better time, and as future events proved, there could have been no better man to join the squadron.

8. SERGENT GERVAIS RAOUL VICTOR LUFBERY had a unique and highly interesting background. None of his fellow pilots could have predicted that the short, muscular man who reported at Behonne on May 24, 1916, and who spoke—when he bothered to speak at all—with a strange mixed-language accent, would become legendary as the squadron's ranking ace.

He was born on March 14, 1885, in Chamalieres, France, to an American-born father and French mother, Edward and Ann Lufbery. Raoul's mother died when he was a small child, and his father remarried and moved to Connecticut, leaving Raoul

Raoul Lufbery stands next to Nieuport 17 N.1485, wearing the standard-issue flight suit that was specifically designed to protect pilots from the intense cold. Lufbery reported to N.124 at Behonne on May 24, 1916. He was not impressive in appearance or speech, and he initially had so much trouble mastering the fast, maneuverable Nieuport fighter that his instructors nearly washed him out. Understandably, no one could have imagined that he would develop into one of the war's deadliest aces. (Washington and Lee University Archives)

in France with his maternal grandparents. After reaching manhood, he left France to travel the world, spending time in North Africa, Greece, Turkey, the Balkans, and Germany, before eventually ending up in the United States, where he worked his way from Connecticut to San Francisco. In 1908, he enlisted in the US Army, where he became an expert marksman—a skill that would later serve him well. He was discharged in 1911, while stationed in the Philippines. Still feeling the need to wander, he headed further eastward. In Calcutta, he met a man who would become not only his employer, but also a friend who would determine his destiny in life. Marc Pourpe, a French exhibition pilot, took Raoul along as his mechanic on a flying tour across Southeast Asia.

When war broke out, Pourpe enlisted in the air service, while Raoul joined the Foreign Legion in order to remain Pourpe's mechanic. Pourpe was killed in a flying accident in December 1914, which prompted Lufbery—who vowed to avenge his friend's death—to apply for pilot training. He first served with Escadrille V.B.106, flying slow, cumbersome Voisins, before being accepted into training as a chasse pilot. Surprisingly, the future ace and virtuoso of aerial combat had difficulty mastering the fast and highly maneuverable Nieuport fighter. However, he finally qualified and received orders to Escadrille N.124, at Behonne.

9. CAPORAL HORACE CLYDE BALSLEY was born on July 27, 1893, to Reverend Enos and Elizabeth Balsley and was living in San Antonio, Texas, when the war in Europe erupted. In January 1915, intending, as he later wrote to his mother, "to see the war, to see it well," Balsley answered a newspaper ad for "white and colored men to take care of horses and mules from here to Europe." He soon found himself aboard the S.S. *Dunedin*, sailing from New Orleans to Great Britain. After arriving, he needed a job, so he crossed the English Channel and signed on with the American Ambulance Field Service in Paris. He remained here until his transfer to aviation in September 1915. On May 27, 1916, he reported to the Escadrille Américaine at Behonne.

10. CAPORAL CHARLES CHOUTEAU "CHUTE" JOHNSON was born in St. Louis, Missouri, on September 18, 1889. His parents, US Army Captain David and Anne Johnson, were prominent members of St. Louis society. Like fellow Escadrille Américaine pilot James McConnell, Johnson attended the University of Virginia, graduating in 1909. The two were close friends, having partnered in business and shared an apartment in New York City. Soon after the war began, Johnson sailed for France and joined the American Ambulance Field Service, before transferring to aviation on September 2, 1915. He reported to Escadrille N.124 with Clyde Balsley on May 27, 1916.

11. CAPORAL LAURENCE DANA RUMSEY JR. was born on September 2, 1886, in Buffalo, New York, to wealthy parents, Laurence and Jennie Rumsey. After graduating from

Laurence D. Rumsey Jr. poses with his Nieuport 11 N.1290 "RUM" at Behonne on June 16, 1916. After reporting to the squadron on June 4, his tenure there would be relatively short and disappointingly undistinguished. He and Norman Prince had been classmates in Harvard's Class of '08. (Washington and Lee University Archives)

Harvard in 1908, he played professional polo until the war in Europe began, at which time he volunteered for the American Ambulance Field Service. Here, he served from January to July 1915. The following September, he entered into French aviation and was assigned to N.124 on June 4, 1916.

12. CAPORAL DUDLEY "DUD" LAWRENCE HILL reported to N.124 at Behonne on June 9, 1916. Born in Peekskill, New York, to Edward and Jessee Hill, he—like most of his squadron mates—grew up in an affluent family. He graduated from Peekskill Military Academy in June 1914, and spent a short time at Cornell and New York University, before sailing for France to join the American Ambulance Field Service. That he was later accepted into aviation—he was blind in one eye and had once ruptured an eardrum—illustrates the lack of medical scrutiny these men typically received. Hill's acceptance was, however, due more to deception than examiner apathy: he passed the eye exam by memorizing the chart. His handicap was eventually discovered, but only after he had demonstrated superior skills as a pilot.

13. SERGENT PIERRE DIDIER MASSON, like so many of the other men of N.124, already had a fascinating life before joining the squadron. He was born in France on February 23, 1886, to Jules and Sarah Masson. In 1909, he went to work for French aviator Louis Paulhan and soon learned to fly, making him one of history's earliest aviators. The next year, he accompanied Paulhan to the United States to participate in an air exhibition in Los Angeles, and remained in the United States, flying exhibitions and making a name for himself. His greatest pre-war claim to fame, however, was as one of history's first combat pilots. Beginning in May 1913, he flew in the Mexican Revolution as a paid mercenary for General Álvaro Obregón. Flying a Martin biplane, he made a series of attacks on the Federalist gunboat *General Guerrero* with makeshift pipe bombs. When World War I began, Masson returned to France and joined the Aéronautique Militaire. After breezing through flight training, he served with Escadrilles C.18 and N.68 before joining N.124 at Behonne on June 19, 1916.

14. CAPORAL PAUL "SKIPPER" PAVELKA was the last pilot to join N.124 at Behonne. Born on October 26, 1890, to Hungarian immigrants Paul and Anna Pavelka, he did not come from a family of wealth. He did, however, come with a wealth of experience. At the age of 16, he left his father's Connecticut farm and struck out on his own, supporting himself with a series of odd jobs in the United States and Canada that took him all the way to the West Coast and then to Central and South America. Along the way, he was once mistakenly shot by a guard, while stowed away on a freight car, and nearly died of exposure walking across the Andes Mountains. After signing on with a Pacific freighter, he made his way around the world, and later served a stint in the US Navy. It was these latter experiences that earned him his nickname. In 1914,

Dudley Hill reported to N.124 on June 9, 1916. He managed to transfer from the ambulance service into aviation despite being blind in one eye—a defect even the desperate French Air Service had trouble ignoring. He outwitted the medics by memorizing the eye chart and went on to become one of the squadron's longest-serving pilots. (Washington and Lee University Archives)

Paul "Skipper" Pavelka poses beside Nieuport 21 N.1615 at Behonne, where he arrived on August 11, 1916. He had recently transferred from the trenches, fighting with the Foreign Legion. Note the ammunition drum for the wing-mounted Lewis machine gun and the castor oil on the fuselage and wing blown back from the Le Rhône air-cooled rotary engine. Pilots sometimes breathed and swallowed enough of this natural laxative while flying to suffer its unpleasant effects later. (Washington and Lee University Archives)

he traveled to France and joined the Foreign Legion, where he befriended Kiffin Rockwell. After several months of hard fighting, Pavelka transferred to aviation. He arrived at Behonne on August 11, 1916.

★ ★ ★

Meanwhile, the air fighting over Verdun continued in its deadly intensity, and for Escadrille Américaine, the bleeding was not yet finished.

CHAPTER 5

SEASON OF DISCONTENT

"I think that in a few weeks I will be pretty sick with the outfit."

On the early afternoon of June 1, 1916, a formation of German bombers flying at high altitude slowly approached the flying field at Behonne and adjacent residential areas of Bar-le-Duc. Bomb payloads were severely limited in 1916, and the art of bomb aiming virtually nonexistent; nevertheless, their projectiles hit both the aerodrome and town, indiscriminately killing dozens of innocent civilians and maiming more than a hundred more. The men of the squadron responded to this outrage by taking off and giving chase to the enemy but could not gain altitude rapidly enough to achieve any positive results. The enemy gunners in the high-flying bombers, on the other hand, had better luck: they scored decisive hits to Thénault, Prince, and McConnell's Nieuports, forcing them to land. McConnell's landing turned into a crash when he tried to glide into a neighboring field where, as he put it afterward, "the only way to land was the direction I didn't take." Thus ended the career of his Nieuport, "MAC."

The Grumbling Begins

These frantic days of almost constant aerial combat, made worse by the bombing attacks, were grating on the men's nerves. As a result, frictions were developing—not only between the men, but also between them and their Capitaine. Kiffin Rockwell complained to his brother Paul about Thénault in a letter he wrote on June 5, 1916:

> My citation hasn't yet gone through, so can't send you a copy yet. Don't think there is much doubt of the Médaille, but don't expect two citations. There is no reason why I shouldn't have them, except that we are very unlucky in having a captain who is a nice fellow and brave, but doesn't know how to look after his men, and doesn't try to. I have been fighting with him ever since being back, mainly about the fact that I have no machine, he having given my old one to Prince and not managing right about getting me a new one. I think that in a few weeks I will be pretty sick with the outfit.

A bit of drama in front of one of the Bessonneau hangars at Behonne aerodrome, early June 1916. Kiffin Rockwell appears to be having serious words with Capitaine Thénault, as Raoul Lufbery looks on at the far right and Clyde Balsley approaches from the left. Rockwell was, at this time, irritated that he had not yet received the medals he thought he deserved, and that he not been assigned a new airplane since returning from convalescent leave. He complained to his brother Paul that Thénault "doesn't look after his men." Paul responded by trying to exert political pressure to have Thénault replaced. (Washington and Lee University Archives)

There was also discord within the ranks. It had started back at Luxeuil, when James McConnell wrote Paul Rockwell on April 25, 1916, that, "Prince cannot stand the horrors of our warlike existence and is beating it back to Paris to stay until our machines arrive. Kiffin and I are disgusted." Then, on June 8, he wrote, "There seems to be a split up in this outfit. Thaw & Co. v. Cowdin, Prince et al. I don't give a damn and won't join either club." In a later letter dated June 15, 1916, he explained further:

> I don't mean I'm neutral in opinion as to the camps here but I can't see any good in putting my voice in. Here's the way I've got the outfit sized up. Kiffin, Bill, Chapman *et cie* [& Co.] are the most serious, Lufbery included. They are all one could ask for. Prince and Cowdin are in it for the sport, especially the latter and while they do their work, will never ring any gongs. Hall is minus a few cogs but runs along in the average. Johnson & Rumsey, frankly dislike the game and I believe Balsley needs a new pair of drawers whenever he goes out. Hill is a nice sort and I believe will try hard.

One thing about which both "camps" seemed to agree was their disdain for Bert Hall. With his crude, conniving ways and lack of formal education, he was the odd man out with this crowd. Bert was, in just about every way, diametrically opposite from most of the other educated and cultured members of the newly formed squadron. He came from a rural background west of the Mississippi River, his family had no wealth or social standing, and the only college Bert had ever attended was the time-honored school of hard knocks. For his entire life, he had been forced to work for a living—as a farm hand, a chauffeur, a deck hand, and even a "human cannonball" in a circus. Accordingly, his manners and language were rough, and he reputedly lied, cheated at cards, and wrote bad checks. Though sometimes characterized as a "lovable rogue," many of those who knew him best did not find him lovable at all. Consequently, he was branded a boor and made an outcast in this new escadrille of gentlemen. The only men in the squadron sympathetic to Bert were his fellow former Legionnaires—Rockwell and Thaw, in particular. Even with his notable success in aerial combat, it was a situation that would grow worse in the weeks to come.

This cliquish behavior and petty squabbling, though typical of any group of ambitious and diverse young men operating under such pressures, remained a constant throughout the life of the squadron. To these men's credit, they managed to keep most of it among themselves, so that very little of this discord ever escaped the confines of the squadron, except in private correspondence.

Not only did the men have issues with each other, some also begrudged the American newcomers who were arriving in France by the dozens to join the French Air Service. James McConnell particularly seemed to resent these new volunteers that the Aéronautique Militaire now welcomed with open arms. He wrote on June 15, 1916, that, "The general run of see-the-war boys from Amerika [sic] are going to hurt us like hell by coming in. It makes me sore for they are taking the place of good Frenchmen. In other words hurting the cause." He later added that when these "parade loving chaps" learned of the dangers involved, they would "say their country calls them and hie back to the land that likes only picnic wars."

A Bag of Oranges

The air activity around Verdun remained intense and very dangerous. On June 17, Victor Chapman once again impetuously broke formation and went hunting on his own. In a letter dated that same day to his brother, Kiffin Rockwell explained what happened:

> Chapman has been a little too courageous…. He was attacking all the time, without paying much attention. He did the same thing this morning, and wouldn't come home when the rest of us did. The result was that he attacked one German, when a Fokker … got full on Chapman's back, shot his machine to pieces and wounded Chapman in the head. It is just a scratch but a miracle that he wasn't killed. Part of the commands [control cables] on Chapman's machine were broken, but Chapman landed by holding them together with his hand.

Victor Chapman, with head bandaged, posing beside his damaged Nieuport 11 fighter N.1148 after his narrow escape of June 17, 1916. The marksmanship of his German opponent is clearly evident. The bullet entered the fuselage behind him, zipped past his head, taking some scalp with it, and exited through his windscreen. The extreme risks Chapman was taking made it apparent to his comrades that his days were numbered. (Washington and Lee University Archives)

Leutnant Oswald Boelcke was the enemy pilot most likely responsible for grazing Victor Chapman's skull and shooting his airplane full of holes during the June 17, 1916, encounter. Boelcke, who at the time had 18 victories, went on to even greater success, becoming one of Germany's top fighter pilots and aerial tacticians. He was killed on October 28, 1916, after colliding in midair with a fellow squadron member. At his death, he was credited with 40 downed Allied aircraft. (Library of Congress)

The talented pilot of the Fokker that nearly killed Chapman was, according to some historians, the famed German ace, Oswald Boelcke. If so, the impetuous American was indeed lucky to have survived. After Chapman's plane was repaired and his wound dressed, the aggressive New Yorker insisted on going back up immediately to renew the fight. Only Thénault's promise to give him a new 110-horsepower Nieuport kept him safely on the ground.

Two days later, it was new kid Balsley's turn to pay the piper. The young Texan, who Capitaine Thénault later described as having "all the shyness and gentleness of a girl," did not initially impress some of his new squadron mates—as evidenced by McConnell's rather unkind comment about Balsley "needing a new pair of drawers whenever he goes out." Although Balsley would only spend three weeks with the squadron, McConnell and others would soon change their opinions about him.

On June 18, Thénault, Prince, Rockwell, and Balsley were out on an early morning patrol, when they became embroiled in a dogfight with a formation of five German aircraft. Balsley dived on a two-seater, but after firing one solitary round, his Lewis machine gun jammed. When he pulled his Bébé out of the fight to clear it, he found himself centered in a deadly crossfire. One of the enemy bullets found its mark on Balsley, slamming into his leg, splintering his femur, and sending bone and bullet fragments throughout his lower internal organs. The devastating hit, which he later compared to being "kicked in the thigh by a mule," sent him into what could easily have been a death spin. Fortunately, his survival instinct gave him the strength and presence of mind to straighten his fighter and pull up just before he hit the ground. As he was losing consciousness from the intense pain and loss of blood, he managed a hard crash landing just behind the frontline trenches. He somehow crawled free of the wreckage before four French soldiers dragged him "like a sack of grain" to the nearest dressing station, and from there to the evacuation hospital at Vadelaincourt. He had barely survived his first and last fight, but his great ordeal had just begun.

Balsley hovered between life and death for the next few weeks, as he underwent one surgery after another to remove fragments and debris that had been driven deep into his intestines and other organs. The courageous manner in which he handled this horrendous experience gained him the respect of his fellow fliers—including McConnell, who made a point of writing to Paul Rockwell, "Take back everything I said about the poor boy. He's been very brave and decent during his suffering." Similarly, Kiffin Rockwell related in a June 19 letter:

> Well, yesterday was a rather bad day for us. You know we didn't think much of Balsley. It was because he is young and inexperienced, but when he got here to the Escadrille I began to like him fairly well and better every day, as I saw he had plenty of good will to work and was not afraid.

Balsley was in constant pain and had a maddening thirst, since the nature of his internal wounds precluded him from drinking any liquids. When the kind-hearted Victor Chapman—a man who had, as a soldier in the Foreign Legion, offered a battlefield surgeon 100,000 francs to save his friend's life and had bought a cow for a sick comrade who needed milk—visited Balsley in the hospital two days later, he asked what could be done about his friend's thirst. The attending doctor consented to allow Balsley to suck on an orange—if one could be found in the midst of a war zone. Chapman assured Balsley that he'd have those oranges if he had to fly to Paris to get them.

On the afternoon of June 23, Victor Chapman took off from the aerodrome at Behonne, head still bandaged from his wound of six days earlier. He carried with him a package of newspapers, chocolate, a letter Balsley had just received in the mail, and some oranges he had somehow managed to acquire. Chapman's plan was to join up with Thénault, Lufbery, and Prince, who had already taken off for a patrol over the lines, and afterward, as he told his mechanic, Louis Bley, "take the oranges and chocolate to poor Balsley at the hospital, for I think there is little hope of saving him." Bley put the package in the airplane and shook hands with Chapman, who said, "*Au revoir*, I shall not be long."

Exactly what happened to Chapman on this last mission will never be known, but a French Maurice Farman crew operating in the vicinity later reported a lone Nieuport desperately battling four enemy fighters northeast of Douaumont. They saw the Nieuport go down out of control and break into pieces in the air. It could only have been Chapman.

Victor Chapman's loss was a crushing blow to the squadron. The squadron's first fatality brought the grim reality of war painfully close to home—and as one of the most popular and courageous members of the squadron, his absence greatly affected his fellow pilots. However, given the reckless abandon with which Chapman flew, it was only a matter of time. Those around him knew it, as did he himself. As he told his "Uncle Willy"—William Astor Chanler—only three days before his death, "Of course I shall never come out of this alive." McConnell wrote of Chapman:

> Considering the number of fights he had been in and the courage with which he attacked it was a miracle he had not been hit before. He always fought against odds and far within the enemy's country. He flew more than any of us, never missing an opportunity to go up, and never coming down until his gasoline was giving out. His machine was a sieve of patched-up bullet holes. His nerve was almost superhuman and his devotion to the cause for which he fought sublime.

Kiffin Rockwell was especially devastated by Victor's loss, as he wrote to his brother on the day of Chapman's death:

> Well, I feel very blue to-night. Victor was killed this afternoon.… There is no question but that Victor had more courage than all the rest of us put together. We were all afraid that he would be killed, and I rooming with him had begged him every night to be more prudent. He would fight every Boche [German] he saw, no matter where or what odds.… I am afraid it is going to rain to-morrow, but if not, Prince and I are going to fly about ten hours, and will do our best to kill one or two Germans for him.

Capitaine Thénault wrote simply, "Glory to Chapman, that true hero! Men like him are the pride of a nation, their names should ever be spoken with respect."

A Welcome Departure and Official Recognition

On June 25, the squadron experienced yet another—though far less painful—loss. Elliot Cowdin departed, officially, because of "ill health." Much has been made of Cowdin's departure over the years, but there is evidence that he was, in fact, not in good health and that his nerves were shot. Because of this and other related factors, he and Thénault mutually agreed that he should leave the squadron. In fairness, he had seen his share of combat with the previous French squadrons. It could be that the 30-year-old Cowdin—elderly, in fighter pilot years—had simply reached his limit, as nearly all combat pilots eventually did.

Meanwhile, promotions and honors finally began to flow in the direction of the much-publicized American squadron. At a ceremony on June 28, Hall, Rockwell, Balsley (who survived but would never rejoin the squadron), Johnson, and McConnell were all promoted to the next grade. Chapman was posthumously promoted and awarded the Croix de Guerre, while Hall and Rockwell finally received their Médaille militaire. William Thaw, the only commissioned officer among the Americans, made a special trip from Paris to Behonne, his arm still in a sling, to be named a Chevalier de la Légion d'honneur—making him the first American in World War I to receive this high honor.

Paul Rockwell posing beside a Breguet-Michelin BM.2 bomber that happened to be parked at Behonne aerodrome, early summer 1916. Having been invalided out of the Foreign Legion, Paul now worked in Paris as a correspondent for the Chicago Daily News. *He had traveled to Behonne to visit his brother Kiffin, and to report on the famed new American squadron. While there, his camera was used to take numerous photographs of the men and aircraft, the original negatives of which still exist. The light leak defect that appears here and on several other of his images serve to establish the time and location they were taken.* (Washington and Lee University Archives)

Kiffin Rockwell climbing into the cockpit of Bert Hall's Nieuport 16 N.1208 at Behonne, early summer 1916. Pilots did not always fly the airplane to which they were assigned, but rather, whichever one happened to be available and airworthy at the time. Here, Rockwell is about to perform a demonstration flight for his visiting brother, Paul. Upon landing, he careened into one of the bombers parked on the airfield, doing considerable damage and infuriating Capitaine Thénault. (Washington and Lee University Archives)

Chouteau Johnson, Bert Hall, and Kiffin Rockwell pass the time playing cards in front of one of the hangars at Behonne. It is a safe bet that Bert was winning, as he usually did. Their makeshift card table is the lower wing of a Nieuport fighter. A bored-looking young mechanic looks on, as does an unidentified French pilot sitting at the far right. (Washington and Lee University Archives)

The men of the Escadrille Américaine gathered in front of their Nieuport fighters. Paul Rockwell took this snapshot just before he departed Behonne on July 10, 1916. From left to right: Lieutenant de Laage, Chouteau Johnson, Laurence Rumsey, James McConnell, William Thaw, Raoul Lufbery, Kiffin Rockwell, Didier Masson, Norman Prince, and Bert Hall. Missing from the picture are Dudley Hill and Capitaine Thénault. Hall stands noticeably apart from the others, symbolizing the differences he had with his squadron mates. (Washington and Lee University Archives)

★ ★ ★

June 1916 at Behonne had been a stressful and tragic month for the Escadrille Américaine. However, there would be much more flying, fighting, and discord in the weeks to come, as the battle over Verdun continued.

CHAPTER 6

THE BATTLE CONTINUES

"… the hardest struggle we had to face."

On July 9, 1916, a young blond-haired French pilot showed up at the aerodrome at Behonne, displaying a noticeable limp, scarred face, and a gleaming row of gold teeth to match the row of medals on his chest. His name was Charles Nungesser, and he was one of France's top fighter aces. He had come to fly with the Escadrille Américaine.

The famed Sous-lieutenant Nungesser voluntarily latched on to the Escadrille Américaine and flew as a free agent under its auspices for the next few weeks. Already a highly decorated ten-victory ace, he was recovering from injuries suffered in a June 22 landing accident while serving with Escadrille N.65. The hard-driving warrior spent his time with N.124 as a sort of working vacation. Whether he was there because he liked the hospitality and companionship of the Americans or because he was invited there to help mentor them, he used the opportunity to continue his personal war in the air.

Born in Paris on March 15, 1892, he was a natural for the American squadron. Besides being of similar age and temperament to most of the men in N.124, he had—also like many of the Americans—lived a uniquely fascinating life prior to the war. Among other prewar pursuits, he had been a mechanic and racecar driver, before learning to fly. In 1914, he was living in Brazil on his uncle's sugar plantation, when he learned of the imminent outbreak of hostilities. He hurried back to France and enlisted in the French cavalry, in which he served with great distinction.

Nungesser soon joined many other former cavalrymen in transferring to aviation, and before long, had worked his way into Escadrille N.65. It was here that he began racking up kills and where he introduced his infamous macabre personal logo that he displayed on the fuselage of all his airplanes: a skull and crossbones, candles, and a coffin enclosed in a big black heart.

French ace Charles Nungesser at Behonne, stands next to Nieuport 17 N.1490, bearing his personal logo. He arrived there on July 9 and temporarily attached himself to Escadrille N.124, while convalescing from injuries received in a crash. Already with 10 confirmed victories, he finished the war as France's 3rd-ranking ace with 43 confirmed kills. He was destined to disappear in 1927 while attempting to fly nonstop from Paris to New York. (Washington and Lee University Archives)

Nungesser was well known as a hard-partying ladies' man, rumored to have consorted with the infamous Dutch exotic dancer and spy known as Mata Hari. This, along with his outstanding combat record, placed him in good stead with the men of N.124. They also admired the flamboyant gold-toothed Nungesser for his grit and resilience. Though already a physical wreck from his numerous wounds and crash injuries, he continued to fly—sometimes having to be lifted into and out of the cockpit—and blast enemy aircraft out of the sky. He would end the war with 43 confirmed kills to his credit, making him France's third-ranking ace and among the war's top 20 aces from all nations.

While at N.124, he flew almost exclusively lone-wolf patrols—18, to be exact—during which, he recorded his 11th victory, by downing a German two-seater on July 21. Otherwise, his contributions to the squadron—other than providing nonstop photo ops—are unknown. Presumably, the highly successful ace spent at least some time sharing his expertise with the relatively green American pilots—knowledge they sorely needed.

Norman Prince and Didier Masson (foreground) wait as Charles Nungesser (center) talks with two other officers, July 1916, Rue Vieille Côte de Behonne, Bar-le-duc. (Washington and Lee University Archives)

More Grumblings and More Victories

Escadrille N.124 achieved further successes against the enemy during the remainder of its stay at Behonne, luckily without any additional deaths or serious injuries. However, the rigors of the heavy fighting helped bring squadron morale to new lows. This occurred partly because of the physical and emotional stresses involved with day-to-day combat flying, but also because of the inherent personality and cultural differences between the men in the squadron. A third contributor to the sagging morale may have been the squadron leadership. Kiffin Rockwell, in particular, continued to find fault with Thénault's management style.

On July 27, Rockwell assisted Lieutenant de Laage in achieving the gallant French officer's first official victory with N.124. Rockwell, who was becoming increasingly bitter about life in the squadron, vented in a letter to his brother that same day:

> Am pretty disgusted; have been working my poor head off lately, and don't even get thank-you for it. I may ask any day to change escadrilles. Everyone here is scrapping and discontented, and I am about the worst of any.... This morning Lieut. de Laage and I brought one down in their lines. I attacked him first and he went over on his nose. As he came up, the Lieut. opened up on him and he fell. The Lieut. deserves all the credit one gives him, but I certainly ran the most risk this morning, and if I didn't hit him myself, which I may have, I made it possible for the Lieut. to hit him. Yet do you think I got any credit for it? Not at all! Fifteen minutes later I made another

German land just within his own lines, having attacked two, and was seen by Prince, but nothing is said about it. The trouble is that I fight all the time, instead of trying to curry favor in useful quarters. I had a hell of a scrap with the captain about the popote [squadron mess] right after you left, and refused to have anything more to do with it. I think the best thing I can do is to go to another escadrille, but I hate to lose what work I have done here, and to tell you the truth, I want the Légion d'Honneur and a Sous-Lieut.'s grade. I don't give a damned how conceited it may appear, but I think I have well earned the two.

A few days later, he added:

I want to be changed to a French escadrille unless certain conditions change here, and several others will follow my example. I think I have the most hours of flight and the most fights for the month of July on the Verdun front of any Nieuport pilot …. I don't think, however, that a full report of my work has gone out of this office, and a number of times my report on a fight has been changed.

Paul, who was always quick to come to his younger brother's defense, replied in a letter that he had spoken to a "Monsieur L" who was going to recommend to the French Minister of War that Thénault be replaced. He cautioned Kiffin to keep quiet about it and that "an investigation will surely be made, and I believe a new man will take his place." Thénault was never replaced, but these letters show the degree of dissatisfaction that existed at the time.

Kiffin Rockwell at Behonne, summer 1916, in Nieuport 11 N.1148, adjusting its Lewis machine gun. Mechanic Michel Plaa-Porte stands at the propeller, while the unidentified man at the far left loads cartridges into the ammunition drum. Note the patch on the fuselage below Rockwell. This was the aircraft in which Victor Chapman had been wounded on June 17. Rockwell was forced to use this well-worn machine because his was out of commission. The lack of airworthy fighters was a chronic problem and a constant source of irritation for the pilots. (Washington and Lee University Archives)

Bert Hall, for all his failings, was doing good work, having bagged his second confirmed victory on July 23. As he later described it in his book *One Man's War*, the German "turned over on his back, then slipped over on his nose and spun like a bastard for more than 10,000 feet." Regarding this victory, Hall's friend Kiffin Rockwell complained on Bert's behalf to brother Paul that, "X did his best to prove that it wasn't brought down, and so far Bert hasn't even been proposed for a citation." The "X" in this case refers to Rockwell's arch-enemy, Norman Prince. Hall would get yet another confirmed kill—his third—on August 28, by forcing an enemy aircraft to land northeast of Douaumont. However, by this time, his days in the squadron were numbered. He was just a little bit too good at poker, and his personal behavior fell well short of his more cultured squadron mates' standards.

Self-Inflicted Pain

Crashes during this period seemed to be a nearly daily affair, as evidenced by the many photographs of smashed up planes and numerous accounts describing them. James McConnell mentioned in a July 25 letter that, "out of eleven machines in escadrille only four are in commission at present moment from various causes." One of the more notable accidents occurred that same day, as Raoul Lufbery was flying low and fast over

Capitaine Georges Thénault posing with his new Nieuport 17 N.1372, already sporting his personal butterfly insignia. One of the squadron's first of this type, it was equipped with a synchronized, belt-fed Vickers machine gun mounted in front of the pilot. Thénault's performance as a commander was not always appreciated by his men. (Willis B. Haviland Collection)

the field. Suddenly, he yanked his Nieuport into a steep climbing turn to avoid a Farman that was landing from the opposite direction. Instead of climbing, however, Luf snagged a wing on the ground and cartwheeled across the field at a rate of 100 miles per hour. His Nieuport disintegrated "into bits of wood, iron, and cloth," as he later wrote to a friend. Somehow, he crawled from the wreckage and walked away from it. A couple of days later, it was McConnell's turn. As he colorfully described it later:

> I had another beautiful smash-up. Prince and I had stayed too long over the lines…. On my return, when I was over another aviation field, my motor broke. I made for the field. In the darkness I couldn't judge my distance well, and went too far. At the edge of the field there were trees, and beyond, a deep cut where a road ran. I was skimming ground at a hundred miles an hour and heading for the trees. I saw soldiers running to be in at the finish and I thought to myself that James's hash was cooked, but I went between two trees and ended up head on against the opposite bank of the road. My motor took the shock and my belt held me. As my tail went up it was cut in two by some very low 'phone wires. I wasn't even bruised. Took dinner with the officers there who gave me a car to go home in afterward.

McConnell may not have been bruised, but his back was severely wrenched. He remained in pain for the next month before Capitaine Thénault finally ordered him to the hospital, where he would remain for another two months. Even then, he would never again be pain-free from this injury. Thankfully, the down time he received was not wasted, as he spent it penning *Flying for France*.

Also during this period, Sergent Lufbery, a pilot Capitaine Thénault called "simple, modest, silent, and hard-working," finally started to make his presence known. Since reporting to the squadron more than two months ago, he had well over a dozen combats without a decisive victory.

On July 30, his long run of bad luck ended when he shot down a two-seater over the Fôret d'Etain. Apparently figuring out, at long last, how the game of aerial combat was played, he proceeded on a ten-day romp, downing three more enemy airplanes on July 31, August 4 (shared with a French Escadrille N.57 pilot), and August 8. Any doubts about him before that ceased to exist. Nothing could stop him now. Even at this early stage in his meteoric career, his squadron mates recognized and appreciated his exceptional qualities. Kiffin wrote on July 31, regarding Luf's first victory:

> Lufbery is a quiet boy who does good work and when he says he has done something we all believe him. This morning Lufbery brought down a German machine ten kilometers in the German lines. We all know he did because he wouldn't lie about it, yet not a soul saw it. Thénault immediately went in an automobile to the Commandant of the Armée, and proposed Lufbery for the Médaille. All of us will be damned glad to see him get it, as he deserves it.

By August 16, Luf had been awarded the Médaille militaire and Croix de Guerre with palm and was well on his way to greatness. He was now, as Capitaine Thénault wrote, "scoring successes faster than they could recompense him."

As of August 11, the squadron's newest man, Paul Pavelka was on the scene and soon flying regular missions. As a new member of the squadron, he had to accept whatever

Chouteau Johnson seated in the cockpit of Nieuport 16 N.1131 at Behonne. It is notably equipped with Le Prieur rockets, which were used for "sausage hunting"—shooting down heavily defended, hydrogen-filled observation balloons. Johnson's personal logo at the time was the "snake-eyes" motif seen here. Paul Pavelka later inherited this machine, which he called "hoodooed," and with good reason: Bill Thaw had been wounded in it, after which it had suffered a series of mishaps, the last being an in-flight fire with Pavelka at the controls. He barely escaped with his life. (Washington and Lee University Archives)

hand-me-down flying machine was available, which for him was Nieuport 16 N.1131. Pavelka was not thrilled with it, as he wrote on August 14, "I have Victor Chapman's mechanic and a hoodooed machine with 110 HP motor. It is the one Lieutenant Thaw was wounded in, and all the others have had accidents in it. Norman Prince turned it over so now it has new wings."

Pavelka's luck with N.1131 was no better than that of Thaw or Prince. During an August 15 mission over the lines, it caught fire, forcing him to violently side-slip the plane all the way to the ground, so as to fan the flames away from him. He hit hard and barely had time to jump out and run before it exploded—and before German artillery unleashed their fury onto it. It is unlikely that Pavelka or anyone else shed any tears at the loss of this ill-fated airplane.

On August 25, Norman Prince forced down an enemy airplane behind German lines. McConnell, who like Rockwell, was no great fan of Prince, wrote in a letter that same day:

> He was out in morning and claims to have brought down a Boche. He acted like a wild man on landing, turned summersault and yelled. Boche was so far in lines no one saw him. Don't know if it will be official or not but anyway Norman beat it immediately on permission [leave].

Paul Pavelka in Nieuport 16 N.1208, which he inherited from Bert Hall as a replacement for the doomed N.1131. Pavelka painted it in a personal color scheme that noted World War I aircraft markings expert Alan Toelle likened to a white-faced cow—perhaps symbolic of Pavelka's days as a cow puncher in the old west. His personal insignia consisted of a "P" and "V" superimposed on one another to look like a branding iron imprint on the cowhide background. The world traveler and former Legionnaire proved to be a capable and well-liked member of the squadron. (National Archives)

Kiffin Rockwell was even more critical of Prince's claim, as he wrote in a September 1 letter to his brother:

> No one thinks X—— got a German, in fact, everyone is sure he didn't; yet the Captain proposed him for a citation, wanted to propose him for the Médaille, but everyone said if he did they would quit. I am going to have to call him out when he gets back, as he talked awfully big about us behind my back when I was away. We have all agreed to try to run him out of the Escadrille.

On September 9, both Prince and Rockwell, in separate actions, downed an enemy plane. Later that day, Kiffin wrote to Paul, who as a *Chicago Daily News* correspondent continually badgered Kiffin for information concerning the squadron:

> This morning I attacked a Boche at three thousand meters high, killed the observateur the first shot. After that, followed the machine down to eighteen hundred meters, riddling it with bullets. At that height I was attacked at very close range by two other German machines. I succeeded in getting back home.

Life in the Escadrille Américaine had been rocky during its stay at Behonne. Internal strife, daily combat, and painful losses had negatively affected the men, but they were now becoming seasoned veterans. Capitaine Thénault characterized the squadron's role in the Battle of Verdun as, "the hardest struggle we had to face."

> We had had 146 combats, 13 enemy planes, confirmed as having been brought down, one pilot killed and three wounded. It was a fine record .... and later the survivors were wont to recall this

William Thaw, gingerly positions his injured left arm as he poses at Behonne on August 24, 1916. He had only recently rejoined the squadron after his serious elbow wound of May 24. Here, he is standing beside his new Nieuport 17 N.1582, marked by his "T" insignia. The squadron had just begun transitioning to the new model. (National Archives)

A US Army neutral observer at Behonne on August 24, 1916, inspecting Raoul Lufbery's new Nieuport 21 fighter N.1615, in which he had just returned from a patrol. Though similar to the Nieuport 17, it had a smaller 80-horsepower engine and carried only the single machine gun atop the upper wing. Note Lufbery's personal logo on the fuselage. (National Archives)

terrible period when they had hardly time to sleep or eat, when they used to sleep fully dressed in their flying suits beneath their planes so as to be ready to start at the first glimpse of dawn. These were the heroic days of the Escadrille, its glorious prime. Prince, Lufbery, Rockwell and Chapman, were you not worthy rivals of the greatest Heroes of any age or country?

★ ★ ★

On September 12, 1916, the men of Escadrille N.124 learned they were needed elsewhere and ordered to pack up for another move. More battles and more successes were in the making, but first, they would enjoy a short break and welcome an important new member to the squadron.

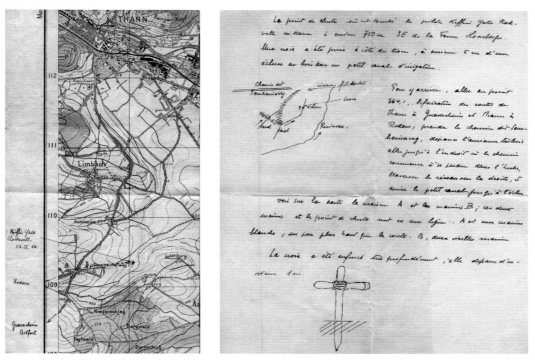

Above: A map and diagrammed letter, dated December 25, 1918, that an Alsatian officer sent to Paul Rockwell, showing the exact location of Kiffin's crash. The letter describes precisely where he had fallen and where a wooden cross had been placed to mark the spot. These documents, along with the many photos taken of the site, helped the author establish its location in 2014. *(Washington and Lee University Archives)*

Below: The tiny clearing in the midst of the corn stalks where Kiffin Rockwell crashed. *(Steven A. Ruffin)*

Above: Kiffin Rockwell's demolished Nieuport 17 N.1811 on September 23, 1916, only minutes after being shot down in aerial combat. His body, visible at the right, had not yet been removed. He landed behind the French trenches in a field of flowers just east of the Alsatian village of Roderen. *(Washington and Lee University Archives)*

Below: The same scene as it appeared in 2014. The crash site is just inside the field of corn near the center of the photograph. *(Steven A. Ruffin)*

Above: Archduke Franz Ferdinand and his wife, Czech Countess Sophie Chotek, as they leave the City Hall at Sarajevo on June 28, 1914. Only minutes later, they were shot and killed by a young Serb nationalist, Gavrilo Princip. The assassination of the heir to the Austro-Hungarian Empire led to a domino-like series of political events that culminated in the First World War. *(Steven A. Ruffin)*

Below: The blood-stained tunic that Archduke Franz Ferdinand was wearing on the day he was assassinated, as it appeared at Vienna's Military History Museum. *(Steve Miller)*

Above: The 43 members of the so-called "American Volunteer Corps" march through the Place de l'Opéra in Paris on August 25, 1914, on their way to the Gare Saint-Lazare train station. Leading the way and carrying the flag was René Phélizot, assisted by American poet Alan Seeger. They were on their way to Rouen to commence training as members of the French Foreign Legion. Among this group of men were William Thaw, Bert Hall, Kiffin Rockwell, and Robert Soubiran, all of whom would later become members of the Lafayette Escadrille. According to Paul Rockwell—also one of these volunteers and author of *American Fighters in the Foreign Legion*, of the approximately 90 Americans who volunteered to fight in the Foreign Legion during these early days of World War I, 38 were killed. *(Washington and Lee University Archives)*

Below: The same view as it appeared nearly a century later. *(Steven A. Ruffin)*

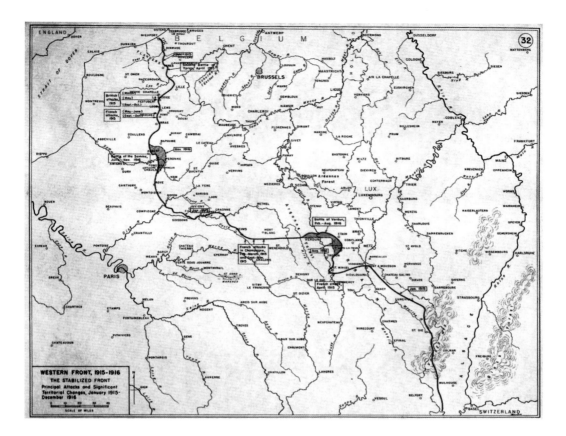

Above: The bold red line on this map represents the entrenched stalemate of the Western Front as it existed in 1915-1916. It extended southeastward from the North Sea, across France and Belgium, to the Swiss border. Despite numerous major battles and millions of casualties, it changed but little throughout the war. *(US Military Academy)*

Right: This Eugéne Courboin World War I-era lithograph portrays Uncle Sam shaking hands with the Marquis de Lafayette. It and other works like it exemplified the spirit and the motivation of many of the Americans who volunteered to fight for France. *(Library of Congress)*

Above left: The Rockwell brothers, Kiffin (left) and Paul, at Pérignon Barracks, Toulouse, France, September 1914. The two North Carolinians were among the first to volunteer to fight for France. (Washington and Lee University Archives)

Above right: A formal studio portrait of Legionnaire Paul Rockwell, April 1915. Of the two brothers, only Paul would survive the war. (Washington and Lee University Archives)

Left: This document, attesting to Kiffin Rockwell's status as an American citizen and signed by US Secretary of State William Jennings Bryan, was issued to Rockwell on August 6, 1914—the day before he sailed for Europe to volunteer for the French Foreign Legion. One of the biggest concerns of the men who traveled to France to fight was the possibility they would lose their US citizenship. (Washington and Lee University Archives)

Above: Hundreds of young American men saw posters such as this and answered the call, volunteering to drive during their summer vacation from college, while others stayed and served for the duration. Many of these healthy young men in search of adventure eventually volunteered for the air service. Nearly half of the 38 pilots who served with the Lafayette Escadrille started their wartime careers in this manner. *(Library of Congress)*

Above: World War I-era French Air Service insignia. It is displayed at France's Air and Space Museum, the Musée de l'Air et de l'Espace, located at Paris-Le Bourget airport. *(Steven A. Ruffin)*

Left and opposite: As a combat pilot, James McConnell was average, but as a writer, he excelled. He began writing articles while in the ambulance service and continued to write after transferring to aviation. While convalescing from a back injury suffered in a crash, he wrote his classic book *Flying for France* but did not live long enough to enjoy its success. *(Steven A. Ruffin)*

November 1916   25 Cents

THE
WORLD'S
WORK

The Authorized Life of
James · J · Hill

Universal Military Service
By
CHARLES·W·ELIOT

Flying for France
An American Aviator at Verdun
JAMES·McCONNELL

Above: Kiffin Rockwell proudly displaying his recently purchased uniform with newly acquired wings insignia. Mrs Alice S. Weeks, adoptive mother for many of the Americans serving in France and known as the "maman legionnaire" (Legionnaire Mom or Mother of the Legion), wrote in a letter on October 24, 1915: "Kiffin has come for six days' leave, and looks very handsome in his new uniform." Mrs. Weeks was an American expatriate living in Paris; she had lost her own son, Legionnaire Kenneth Weeks, on June 17, 1915. Rockwell's uniform is now on display at the Smithsonian Institution. *(Washington and Lee University Archives; Smithsonian National Air and Space Museum)*

Below left: Kiffin Rockwell's wing insignia and hat, as preserved at the Smithsonian Institution. *(Smithsonian National Air and Space Museum)*

Below right: This insignia, as displayed in the French Air and Space Museum at Le Bourget, is the type Westin Birch "Bert" Hall wore on his collar. *(Steven A. Ruffin)*

Above: The Hôtel de la Bonne Rencontre, was the abode of choice for many American pilots assigned to the Groupe des Divisions d'Entraînement (G.D.E.) at Plessis-Belleville. The G.D.E was the last stop before joining an active squadron. At this aviator pool, located a few miles northeast of Paris, pilots flew as much or as little as they wanted while waiting for a vacancy at the front. This hotel was conveniently located between the train station and the flying field, but all who stayed there agreed that it was anything but luxurious. Edmond Genet called it a "rotten little hotel," while James Norman Hall described it as a "ramshackle place, with beds on three legs... broken-down chairs, walls covered with hideous paper, and dust and grime over everything." *(Source Unknown)*

Below: The Hôtel de la Bonne Rencontre no longer exists, but the building still stands. Though obviously updated, it appears much the same today as it did 100 years ago. *(Steven A. Ruffin)*

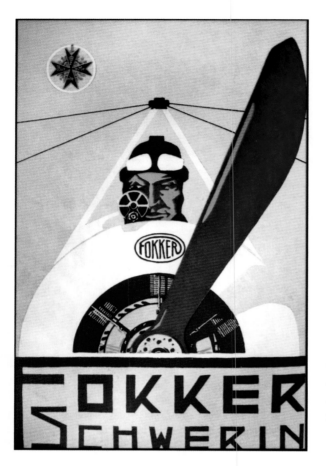

Left: A 1916 German poster touts the Fokker and its deadly machine gun. *(Artist Unknown)*

Below: A rare, original Nieuport 11 Bébé displayed at France's Air and Space Museum. This was the type first flown by Escadrille N.124 at Luxeuil in early May, 1916. Light and maneuverable, it featured a .303-caliber Lewis machine gun mounted atop the upper wing, which allowed the pilot to fire directly forward above the arc of the propeller. It was powered by an 80-horsepower Le Rhône air-cooled rotary engine, which rotated with the propeller. The lower wing was smaller than the upper one, making it, technically speaking, a "sesquiplane." Though this configuration improved the pilot's downward visibility, it also created structural problems that were never completely resolved. *(Steven A. Ruffin)*

Top: Kiffin Rockwell accomplished a rare feat on May 18, 1916, by downing an enemy aircraft in his first air-to-air combat—using only four rounds. Although undoubtedly as much luck as skill, it placed the squadron of all-American volunteers on the scoreboard on only its sixth day of wartime operations. On the right, we see the tunic Rockwell was wearing, courtesy of the North Carolina Museum of History. *(Washington and Lee University Archives; Eric Blevins, North Carolina Museum of History)*

Center: Rockwell's flying insignia, as it appears in color. *(US Air Force)*

Left: The "Bottle of Death" began life as a very old and rare bottle of whiskey that Paul Rockwell sent to Kiffin in honor of his aerial victory on May 18, 1916. It became a squadron tradition that a pilot who downed an enemy plane earned the right to take a swig from it. After the war, the empty bottle turned up in the estate of William Thaw and now resides in the American Friends of Blérancourt Museum in Blérancourt, France. *(Art Resource)*

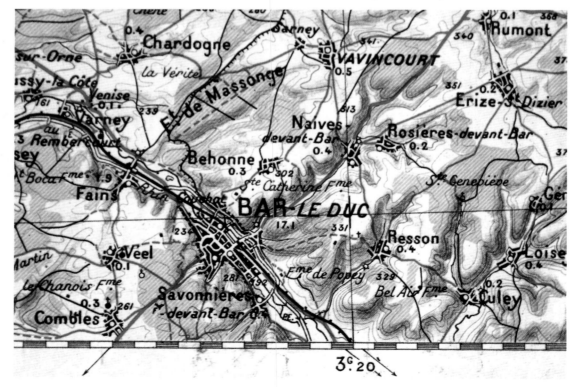

Indications de service.

N°................

Timbre
à date.

ORIGINE.	NUMÉRO.	NOMBRE DE MOTS.	DATE.	HEURE DE DÉPÔT.	MENTIONS DE SERVICE.

+   PARIS 3138) 12 20 14/ =

= MILLE FELICITATIONS POUR TON BOCHE = PRINCE :

Above: May 20, 1916: a telegram from Norman Prince to Kiffin Rockwell, wishing him "a thousand congratulations" for scoring the new all-American squadron's first aerial victory. Prince was in Paris at the time, waiting for a replacement airplane to take back to the squadron. *(Washington and Lee University Archives)*

Below: A World War I-era US Army map showing the location of the flying field at Behonne. Ferme Ste. Catherine was located on a high plateau above the city of Bar-le-Duc, adjacent to the village of Behonne. Verdun was some 30 miles to the northeast. *(US Air Force)*

Above and right: A Spad VII fighter, as displayed at France's Air and Space Museum. Note its complex design and beautiful lines. Famed French ace Georges Guynemer scored several confirmed victories in this original World War I fighter that he nicknamed *Vieux Charles*. (Steven A. Ruffin)

Bottom right: The internal construction of a Spad XIII fighter, which the Lafayette Escadrille flew in its final months of operation, as displayed at the French Air and Space Museum. This clearly shows the degree of design intricacy and workmanship seen in a typical World War I airplane. This disproves the standard contention that airplanes of this era were primitive or flimsy. In reality, they were—with few exceptions—rugged, beautiful machines with unprecedented performance. *(Steven A. Ruffin)*

Above: World War I began with the frontline use of relatively primitive aircraft like this Blériot, displayed at the French Museum of the Great War at Meaux. Nearly all aircraft in 1914 were underpowered and lacking in performance, and few carried any weapons at all. *(Steven A. Ruffin)*

Below: Examples of World War I flight suits used by French airmen, as displayed at the French Air and Space Museum. All were designed to keep the airman as warm as possible. *(Steven A. Ruffin)*

Above: Didier Masson was, like Raoul Lufbery, of French birth and a well-traveled man of the world. A famous pre-war exhibition pilot, he became one of history's first combat pilots in May 1913, when he flew bombing raids for General Álvaro Obregón in the Mexican Revolution. He reported to N.124 on June 19, 1916. The tie pin pictured here is identical to the one Masson is wearing. *(Washington and Lee University Archives; US Air Force)*

Below left: Fellow Legionnaires Paul Rockwell (left) and Paul Pavelka in Paris, November 1915. The exhausted Pavelka had come directly from the trenches to Alice Weeks' Paris apartment at 80 Rue Boissière. She wrote that he was "caked in mud and his coat nearly shot to pieces." Rockwell helped him pick nearly a pound of shrapnel out of the lining of the coat he was wearing in this photograph. Soon afterward, Pavelka—to his great relief—made the transfer to aviation. *(Washington and Lee University Archives)*

Below right: The same scene 99 years later—sans Rockwell and Pavelka. It is in front of the Jules Dalou statue, on the southeastern corner of the bridge Pont Alexandre III that spans the Seine River. *(Steven A. Ruffin)*

Above: Russell Smith's *Hostile Sky* depicts Victor Chapman's last flight on the afternoon of June 23, 1916. On the day of his death, he was carrying a package of newspapers, chocolate, and oranges to wounded comrade Clyde Balsley, who lay suffering in the hospital. *(Russell Smith)*

Below left: Victor Chapman's marker in the Meuse-Argonne American Cemetery, Romagne, France. The body lying under it was originally buried elsewhere by the Germans and erroneously labeled as that of Clyde Balsley— probably because a letter addressed to Balsley was found on Chapman's body. However, Paul Rockwell later examined the Graves Registration Service records and related in a March 6, 1929, letter that certain discrepancies he found were inconsistent with this being Chapman's body. Consequently, this body was never moved to the Lafayette Escadrille Memorial, and the sarcophagus there bearing his name remains empty. *(Steven A. Ruffin)*

Left, adjacent: A cenotaph honoring Chapman. It is located near the graves of his family members in the Saint Matthew's Episcopal Churchyard, Bedford, New York. *(Dana Garrow)*

Above: The old Ferme Ste. Catherine farmhouse, which was located just across the dirt road from the hangars at Behonne aerodrome. Note the damaged roof, which was probably caused either by a German aerial bombing attack or an airplane crashing into it. *(Willis B. Haviland Collection)*

Below: The farmhouse, as it appeared in 2014. The sagging roof visible on the left remains as evidence of the World War I-era damage. Of the nine different locations from which the squadron operated during its 22-month existence, its stay at Behonne was the longest—from May 20 to September 14, 1916—and one of the most photographed. *(Steven A. Ruffin)*

Bottom: The painted advertisement that is still visible on the farmhouse. *(Steven A. Ruffin)*

Above: William Thaw (far left) jokes with Charles Nungesser in front of the old Ferme Ste. Catherine farmhouse at Behonne, early July 1916. At the far right, Capitaine Georges Thénault stands with an unidentified fourth officer. *(Washington and Lee University Archives)*

Below: The same scene as it appeared in 2014. One can almost imagine the four long-dead aviators still standing there. Even the sagging roof at the upper right looks the same after nearly a century. *(Steven A. Ruffin)*

Above: Didier Masson's Nieuport 11 N.1314 "X" at Behonne with the Ferme Ste. Catherine farmhouse in the background. The circumstances of its demise are not known. *(Willis B. Haviland Collection)*

Below: There are no wrecked airplanes in this 2014 picture of the same spot, but the scene is otherwise similar to the above. *(Steven A. Ruffin)*

GRAND HOTEL DE LA POMME D'OR

A. GROSCOLAS — Luxeuil-les-Bains (Haute-Saône)

The men of the Escadrille Américaine stayed at the Grand Hôtel de la Pomme d'Or during their second stint in Luxeuil. The building looks much the same today, although the Pomme d'Or is now a café, rather than a hotel. *(Steven A. Ruffin)*

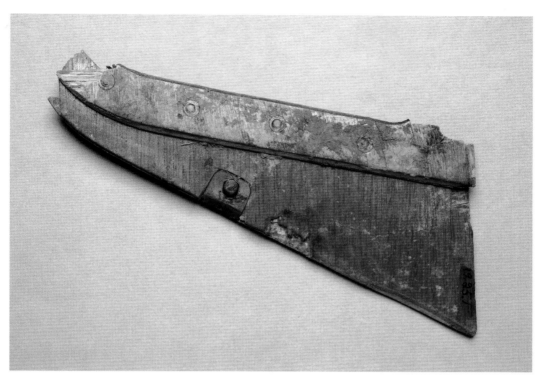

A piece of Kiffin Rockwell's crash wreckage from the North Carolina Museum of History (above) and a marker in a small memorial park dedicated to the fallen American aviator (below). The marker is located near his crash site, just outside of Roderen. On September 26, 1916, Paul Pavelka and Capitaine Thénault accompanied Paul Rockwell to the frontlines to see where Kiffin had fallen. Later that day, Pavelka wrote in a letter to James McConnell, "We did not see much, as the machine had been taken away, all there was left was a deep hole where his motor had embedded itself, and a few fragments ... most of which was covered by his blood...." *(Eric Blevins, North Carolina Museum of History; Steven A. Ruffin)*

Rockwell's grave, as it appears today in the Luxeuil city cemetery. With the possible exception of Victor Chapman, Rockwell was the only American killed while serving with Escadrille N/SPA.124 whose body has remained in its original burial site. Kiffin's family elected to honor his wish, which he related to Paul Pavelka the evening before his death, to be buried near where he had fallen. Several other markers in both France and the United States honor Rockwell's memory today. *(Steven A. Ruffin)*

Above: Capitaine Thénault addresses the mourners at Kiffin Rockwell's funeral, held in the cemetery at Luxeuil on the morning of September 25, 1916. He stated in his eulogy, "On the night of his death, when we were gathered together, I said to his comrades, 'the best and bravest of us all is no more.'" One person not in attendance was Bert Hall, who was—according to Paul Rockwell—in Paris "peddling" the story of Kiffin's death to the newspapers. True or not, Paul believed it and spent the rest of his life denigrating Bert's name. *(Washington and Lee University Archives)*

Below: Rockwell's grave appears at the lower left of this 2014 photograph just as it does in the one taken in 1916. *(Steven A. Ruffin)*

Above: The funeral procession for Norman Prince marches through downtown Luxeuil. It was a repeat of the one held for Kiffin Rockwell only three weeks earlier. Here, the camera is pointed northward up Rue de Grammont. *(Washington and Lee University Archives)*

Below: A similar camera view in 2014. *(Steven A. Ruffin)*

The brothers Prince of Escadrille N.124—Norman (left) and Frederick Jr. Exactly one week after Norman's death on October 15, 1916, Fred joined N.124 at Cachy. However, in spite of his best intentions, he was never allowed to fly patrols over the lines. His politically connected father, who did not wish to risk losing his only remaining son to the war, successfully pressured French military authorities to transfer Fred out of the combat zone. *(Smithsonian National Air and Space Museum)*

Yours sincerely Willis Bradley Haviland 1917

A signed photograph of Willis B. Haviland, who fellow squadron member Ted Parsons called "the handsomest man ... of the outfit." Haviland joined N.124 on October 22, 1916, and served with the Lafayette Escadrille for nearly a year. The collection of photographs he accumulated is one of the finest in existence relating to the famed squadron. The French pilot's badge pictured here and displayed at the French Air and Space Museum is identical to the one Haviland is wearing. The Aéronautique Militaire began issuing this insignia in September 1916, each with its own individual number stamped on the back. *(Willis B. Haviland Collection; Steven A. Ruffin)*

Above: Kiffin Rockwell's medals that his brother Paul donated to the North Carolina Hall of History in 1924. They are now located at the North Carolina Museum of History in Raleigh. At the far left is the Legion of Honor, which Rockwell received posthumously in 1922. His citation described him as, "an American pilot who never ceased to arouse the admiration of his commanders and comrades by his sangfroid, courage, and daring." *(Eric Blevins, North Carolina Museum of History)*

Right: A Savage Arms Company advertising logo. The men of the Lafayette Escadrille saw an image like this on an ammunition box and adopted it as their new squadron insignia. *(Willis B. Haviland Collection)*

Above: Russell Smith's *Mark of Distinction* portrays William Thaw presenting Escadrille N.124's new squadron insignia to Capitaine Thénault. The idea of using a Seminole Native American warrior to represent the newly named Lafayette Escadrille was inspired by a logo appearing on a Savage Arms cartridge box. The artist painting it onto the side of one of the squadron's Nieuport 17s based at Cachy was the mechanic Suchet. Meanwhile, Whiskey sits nearby, contentedly chewing on a paintbrush. *(Russell Smith)*

Below: *By the Dawn's Early Light*, by Russell Smith, depicts an early morning flight by pilots of the Lafayette Escadrille out of Cachy in the autumn of 1916. It shows William Thaw, flying Nieuport 17 N.1803, leading the flight. He is followed in the foreground by Raoul Lufbery in Georges Thénault's N.1844, which bears the three horizontal bars of a captain's rank. In the distance, Dudley Hill is flying his assigned aircraft, N.1950. Each fighter carries a Lewis machine gun affixed to the upper wing, in addition to the belt-fed Vickers gun mounted in front of the pilot and synchronized to fire through the propeller arc. The airplanes' silver appearance comes from the aluminum-based dope with which their fabric is painted. *(Russell Smith)*

A rare authentic example of the original Seminole Lafayette Escadrille insignia, as displayed at France's Air and Space Museum. It was taken from the fuselage of Raoul Lufbery's Spad S.238, pictured below. Traces of stains from the adjacent exhaust pipe are still visible on the displayed original. *(Steven A. Ruffin; Washington and Lee University Archives)*

Above: The funeral of Paul Pavelka at the French Military Cemetery at Zietenlick, Greece, November 13, 1917. After a lifetime of brushes with death, the world traveler and soldier of fortune met his end on the back of a bucking horse. *(Washington and Lee University Archives)*

Left: Paul Pavelka's burial site in Salonika. His remains were later transferred to the crypt at the Lafayette Escadrille Memorial. *(Washington and Lee University Archives)*

THE BEST AND THE BRAVEST

So stand to your glasses steady,
This world is a web of lies.
Then here's to the dead already,
And hurrah for the next man who dies!★

The rumor had long been that the Escadrille Américaine's next assignment would be somewhere on the Somme battlefront, a bloody battle of monumental proportions that had been raging since July. Like most rumors, however, it proved to be false. To everyone's surprise, the men of N.124 were headed back to Luxeuil and the Vosges sector. Exactly why, no one could guess, since the war's two biggest battles—Verdun and the Somme—were being simultaneously fought in locations other than Luxeuil.

They would soon find out the reason for this inexplicable move, but first, they would enjoy a rest that their arduous months at Behonne had earned them. The battle-weary pilots were to leave their equally battle-weary planes at Behonne and receive the newer and better Nieuport 17, a few of which had already arrived. While they waited for the replacement aircraft, Capitaine Thénault directed his pilots to leave immediately for Luxeuil—via the "scenic route" through Paris, some 125 miles in the opposite direction. For the tired and edgy American pilots, it was the place that, even in the midst of a world war, remained the "City of Light." It was where they would find friends, comfortable beds, good food, plenty of strong drink and adult entertainment—and more available and willing women than existed anyplace else on the face of the earth. Consequently, on September 14, they boarded the train in Bar-le-Duc and headed toward their idea of paradise.

★ From a WWI pilots' song made famous by the movie *The Dawn Patrol*. It was an adaptation of the Bartholomew Dowling poem, "The Revel."

Whiskey and another Rockwell

Thénault's dog, Fram, was loved by all the men, but she answered only to the Capitaine. The squadron needed a proper mascot, one that would reflect the character of the unique squadron, and this seemed the appropriate time to acquire one. While in Paris, one of the American pilots answered a newspaper ad placed by a Brazilian dentist trying to sell a four-month-old lion cub he had acquired for his office as a novelty. He had decided that it was getting too big and rambunctious to keep, so he was trying to unload it. The men decided that Escadrille N.124 would be the perfect home for it. After pooling their available resources, they acquired the little animal and brought him back with them on the train to Luxeuil. The unusual baby feline needed an equally distinctive name, and when he was observed lapping from a saucer containing a few drops of whiskey, the issue was settled.

Whiskey soon became the most famous and most photographed member of the Escadrille Américaine. The cute, gentle, and adorably playful cub went everywhere the men did and provided the type of companionship and distraction they needed. The exotic animal also added to the allure of the all-American squadron, bringing it even more into the public eye.

It was also during this period of R&R that the squadron's star pilot, Raoul Lufbery, managed to get himself into a bit of a jam. On September 16, he sent a telegram to Capitaine Thénault informing him that he was in jail! It seems that Luf had a difference of opinion with a train station official at Chartres. When the official made the mistake of getting physical with the stocky, tough-minded ace, Luf traumatically extracted several of the man's teeth—and ended up with a 30-day sentence in the stockade. Thénault quickly went to his rescue, making apologies and explaining that the man they had incarcerated was not a common criminal but rather, a decorated hero with four confirmed aerial kills under his belt. The authorities relented and released the pugilistic pilot to the custody of his Capitaine.

The escadrille also welcomed yet another new member to its fold while in Paris: a new American pilot to replace the fallen Victor Chapman.

15. CAPORAL ROBERT LOCKERBIE ROCKWELL, who happened to be a distant cousin of Paul and Kiffin Rockwell, was the 15th American to join the Escadrille Américaine. He was born in Cincinnati, Ohio, on March 28, 1892, to Marion and Mary Rockwell. In 1913, after two years of college, he entered New York University's school of medicine to become a physician. However, in early 1915, he decided to travel to France to serve as an intern at the American Hospital of Paris. He worked for the next year dressing wounds and performing other medical duties, before deciding to take a more active role in the war and volunteer for aviation. On September 17, 1916, Capitaine Thénault met with the newly winged pilot in Paris and selected him for Escadrille N.124. Caporal "Doc" Rockwell accompanied Thénault and the other pilots back to Luxeuil and would soon become an integral part of the squadron. He would never return to medicine.

Kiffin Rockwell, William Thaw, and Paul Pavelka in Paris, September 1916, playing with their new mascot, "Whiskey." The men of Escadrille N.124 acquired the four-month-old lion cub while there on leave. James McConnell called him a "cute, bright-eyed baby lion who tried to roar in a most threatening manner but who was blissfully content the moment one gave him one's finger to suck." This was Kiffin's final visit to Paris and the last time he would see his brother Paul. He had only a week longer to live. (Washington and Lee University Archives)

Kiffin Rockwell's Last Flight

The good life at Luxeuil resumed as it had before, only this time, the men boarded at Auguste Groscolas' elegant Grand Hôtel de la Pomme d'Or. After four long months of nearly daily combat in the deadly skies over Verdun, the pilots felt as though they were once again vacationing at a resort spa. Until the new airplanes were ready, they occupied themselves with such activities as trout fishing, gathering wild mushrooms, attending parties given by the airmen of the British Royal Naval Air Service, with whom they shared the airfield, and attending dances in town, where they taught the local girls the latest steps. It was, as James McConnell wrote, "about as much like a war as a Bryan lecture." Kiffin Rockwell noted that, "the same old girls are here but look a little worked out after the summer." His assessment was that, "from now on, it will be bad weather and no flying...." He was wrong about that. Two days later, he was back in the air, making the last flight of his life.

On September 19, six new Nieuport 17s—the latest in the rapidly evolving Nieuport series—arrived. These machines, powered by 110-horsepower Le Rhône rotary engines and fitted with larger wings, performed better than the old Bébé. More importantly, they were among the first to be equipped with Vickers belt-fed machine guns and synchronization gear. This allowed the men of N.124—like their German adversaries— to safely fire straight ahead through the spinning propeller. To increase their firepower, and also because the new Vickers still had a dangerously strong tendency to jam, most of the pilots also retained their Lewis gun mounted atop the upper wing. Now that they had the best flying weapon available, they waited impatiently as the mechanics readied the new planes for aerial combat.

The purpose for the move back to Luxeuil was eventually revealed: Escadrille N.124 had been sent there specifically to fly escort for the French Groupe de Bombardement 4, led by the famed—and infamously reckless—Capitaine Felix Happe. "*Le Corsaire Rouge*," as the bearded French pioneer of strategic bombing was known, had already lost an appalling number of his Maurice Farman and Breguet bombers and their crews. An upcoming operation, still in the planning stages, would be even more dangerous: Happe and his British Royal Naval Air Service counterparts would join forces to pound important munitions centers just across the German border with a series of bombing raids. Because the element of surprise was key, Happe requested that the men of Escadrille N.124 lay low for the time being, so as not to reveal their presence.

This proved to be an unrealistic request for the two aggressive pilots that Thénault called "fanatics"—Kiffin Rockwell and Raoul Lufbery. After languishing on the ground for more than a week, they finally had new fighting machines and were itching to get back into the fray. Consequently, they ignored Happe's request and began venturing out over the lines.

On the morning of September 23, 1916, Rockwell and Lufbery took off in search of trouble, and they found it. They engaged a flight of Fokkers, but when Lufbery's

Capitaine Felix Happe commanded the French Groupe de Bombardement 4 at Luxeuil that the men of Escadrille N.124 were sent to protect. The tall, bearded, and utterly fearless officer was one of France's most revered air heroes. The enemy also recognized his value by allegedly placing a 25,000 DM bounty on his head. (Washington and Lee University Archives)

machine gun became inoperable, they withdrew so he could land at the closest field—the aerodrome at Fontaine-lès-Luxeuil—and correct the problem. Rather than land and wait for Lufbery, the aggressive Rockwell decided to return to the lines alone. It was a dangerous thing to do, but as Thénault later wrote, "the blood of his soldier ancestors ran ever hot in his veins."

Upon reaching the lines, Rockwell sighted a lone German two-seater below him—a rare opportunity. The wiser, more cautious approach would have been to maneuver for an attack from behind and below. From that angle, the enemy rear gunner would be unable to fire his deadly swivel-mounted machine gun without shooting off his own airplane's tail. Instead, the impetuous Rockwell dove from directly above, guns blazing. It was a fatal mistake. French observers on the ground watched as he dove past the German two-seater, nearly colliding with it. As his plane continued downward, it dove ever steeper, eventually shedding one of its wings. The broken Nieuport then plummeted straight down until it impacted the ground at terminal velocity just behind the trenches, a few hundred yards east of the village of Roderen—and only a couple of miles from the spot where his first victory fell back on May 18. The crash was devastatingly violent, but it caused Rockwell no pain: the enemy gunner, who had been firing back at him the entire time, scored a direct hit. Rockwell's body was found lying next to the wreckage with a three-inch hole blown through his chest.

Rockwell's death was a devastating blow to the escadrille. The fearless fighter was seemingly invincible, with all he had been through, and it was hard to accept that he was gone. When the news reached the squadron, a visibly shaken Thénault gathered his pilots and announced that, "the best and bravest of us all is no more." James McConnell wrote about his fallen friend:

> No greater blow could have befallen the escadrille. Kiffin was its soul. He was loved and looked up to … by everyone who knew him. Kiffin was imbued with the spirit of the cause for which he fought and gave his heart and soul to the performance of his duty…. The old flame of chivalry burned brightly in this boy's fine and sensitive being.

An upset Paul Pavelka wrote to James McConnell in a September 26, 1916 letter:

> God almighty! Jim I feel terribly broken up about Kiffin's death. Today, Paul, the Captain and I went down to where he fell, and looked at that sacred piece of earth. He saw this boche bastard in our lines and attacked him at a height of about 3000 metres. Everything went fine in the fight, and it was a case of one or the other, and the boche mitrailleus [machine gunner] hit poor Kiffin in the breast, but the dirty son-of-a-bitch used an explosive ball, for the poor boy had a hole as big as your fist in his breast.

Lufbery expressed his sorrow in his own unique way: he took off alone and crossed the lines to the nearby German Flugplatz at Habsheim. There, he circled, with revenge in his heart, daring any German airman to come up and fight. Fortunately for either him or the enemy, no one responded to his challenge.

Rockwell had, on the night before his death, told Paul Pavelka that he wanted to be buried wherever he fell. Since the proximity of his crash to the frontlines made this impractical, he was buried at Luxeuil after a funeral that was, as James McConnell described it, "worthy of a general." On the morning of September 25, 1916, hundreds of mourners—including Paul Rockwell and practically all of Luxeuil's civilian and military population—accompanied his flower-covered coffin through the streets of Luxeuil to the town cemetery. Meanwhile, low-flying airplanes circled overhead and dropped more flowers. A few days afterward, Kiffin posthumously received an honor that had escaped him during his living years: a promotion—symbolic, though it was—to the officer rank of sous-lieutenant.

The only person missing from this elaborate event was Bert Hall. His absence would be duly noted and the repercussions from it would affect him for the rest of his life.

The Oberndorf Raid and another Empty Chair

For the next two weeks, bad weather prevailed, but Prince and Lufbery still managed to find trouble. On October 6, Prince was out on a solo patrol when he engaged enemy aircraft. In the ensuing fight, his plane was shot to pieces and he barely made it back home. On October 10, he achieved his third confirmed victory, when he downed a Fokker in the vicinity of Wittelsheim, France.

Meanwhile, on October 9, Lufbery had his closest call to date. It began with a long running battle with a Fokker manned by a German pilot of skill equal to his own—possibly the great Boelcke, himself. Each tried to outmaneuver the other but neither was able to gain an advantage. After several minutes of this aerial standoff, Lufbery detected an enemy observation plane in the distance, operating over French lines. He immediately waved to his worthy adversary and broke off the fight. He made a beeline for the impudent "big white two-seater of very substantial appearance," as he later described it, but in his eagerness to score an easy kill over friendly territory, he rushed his approach and missed his target altogether. Even worse, he exposed himself to the German rear gunner, in much the same way that Kiffin Rockwell had during his fatal last flight. Both Lufbery and his brand new Nieuport 17 were peppered with machine gun fire. His plane was shot to pieces, and some of the bullets passed so close to his body that they pierced his flight suit and ripped open one of his boots. With a dead engine and a badly damaged plane, he glided to the nearest available field and executed a hard crash-landing that demolished what was left of his fighter. He emerged unscathed from the wreck, lucky to be alive.

Finally, on October 12, the big event that had precipitated N.124's move back to Luxeuil came about. Participating, were more than 60 British and French bombers— Sopwiths, Breguets and Farmans—and escort fighters. Representing the Escadrille Américaine were Lieutenant de Laage, Prince, Lufbery, and Masson. The target was the Mauser arms works, located at Oberndorf, Germany. The date of the mission had been kept so secret that even Capitaine Thénault was unaware of when it would come about. Consequently, he was away on leave when the call came.

Allied fighters escorted the slow bombing machines as far as they could on the 100-mile flight to Oberndorf, before landing to refuel at an advance field. They would then rejoin the bombers on their return flight. German fighters and ground gunners fiercely defended their homeland by inflicting heavy casualties on the large formation and its fighter escorts. However, there were also some impressive Allied victories. Escadrille N.124, alone, accounted for three confirmed enemy fighters. Prince achieved his fourth aerial victory, while Lufbery downed his fifth, a Roland C.II. The Escadrille Américaine now, for the first time, had its own bona fide ace.

It was Didier Masson, however, who achieved the most impressive victory of the day—his first and only kill of the war. While engaging a Fokker, his engine suddenly quit dead. Whether from negligence or a punctured fuel tank, he had somehow managed to run out of fuel far over enemy territory in the midst of a dogfight. It was a very bad place to be. As he initiated a long shallow glide toward French lines, the Fokker came after him with a vengeance. The German pilot was so intent on downing the seemingly helpless Nieuport, that he became a little too bold. He apparently forgot that even with a dead engine, the top-mounted Lewis gun on Masson's Nieuport 17 could still be lethal. As the German carelessly pulled up in front of Masson to make another pass, Masson squeezed his Lewis trigger and shot his pursuer out of the sky. He then continued his dead-stick glide just past the French trenches, where he managed to get down in one piece. It was one of the most remarkable kills of the war.

The three victories scored by Escadrille N.124 that day, though impressive, would exact a heavy price. The October sky was darkening early as the fighter escorts scrambled for places to land. Lufbery and Prince chose the advance aerodrome at Corcieux, a small field located in a valley surrounded by hills. Lufbery landed first with some difficulty, but in the increasing darkness, Prince—whose vision was none too good, anyway—failed to notice a high tension wire, inexplicably strung across the approach to the field. As he glided in low and slow, his landing gear snagged the wire and flipped his fighter violently into the ground. Prince was thrown bodily from the cockpit, during which, he sustained two broken legs, along with undetermined internal and head injuries. Still, he retained his senses, and when Lufbery ran up to him, the conscientious Prince

French military personnel examining the crumpled wreck of Norman Prince's Nieuport 17 N.1790. After escorting Capitaine Felix Happe and his bombers back from their October 12, 1916, raid to Oberndorf, Germany, Prince tried to land at the small advance field at Corceiux. In the growing darkness, the astigmatic Prince flew into a high-tension wire stretched across the approach to the landing field. In the ensuing crash, he was thrown from the cockpit and severely injured. He died early on the morning of October 15 in the hospital at Gerardmer. (Source Unknown)

implored him to, "hurry and light the flares so another fellow won't come down and break himself up as I have done."

Luf accompanied his injured comrade on the long and bumpy ambulance ride to the hospital at Gerardmer, holding his hand and encouraging him the entire way. At first evaluation, the doctors believed he would recover, but he soon developed a fatal complication—a cerebral embolism, or blood clot to the brain. As he lay dying, his commanders solemnly awarded him, as a parting gesture of gratitude, the Légion d'honneur and promoted him to the commissioned rank of sous-lieutenant. On the Sunday morning of October 15, 1916, Norman Prince died.

★ ★ ★

After Prince had been laid to rest, it was again time for the men of the Escadrille Américaine to move—and none too soon. For even though they had been at Luxeuil for less than a month, they were more than ready to leave. In spite of comfortable

The men of Escadrille N.124, looking somber after the funeral of Norman Prince. Front row: Bert Hall, Lieutenant de Laage, Capitaine Thénault, William Thaw, the padre, and Chouteau Johnson. Back row: Laurence Rumsey, Paul Pavelka, Emil Marshall, Didier Masson, Dudley Hill, and Robert Rockwell. Thénault's inseparable dog Fram sits in the foreground. Marshall was an American volunteer mistakenly assigned to N.124 without any flight training. He remained with the squadron for several months, performing ground duties, before returning to the infantry. Raoul Lufbery was the only actively assigned squadron member absent from this photo. (Willis B. Haviland Collection)

accommodations in a beautiful setting, their stay there had been a depressing one, dominated by a frustrating shortage of available aircraft and ammunition made worse by battle damage and crashes, and equal measures of bad weather and bad luck. Worst of all, they had lost two of their comrades, both strong, idealistic leaders and founding members of the squadron. The next gig for N.124 would be 225 miles to the northwest, where another historic struggle was raging.

CHAPTER 8

MISERY IN THE SOMME

"We had … come to believe that we would wage only a deluxe war,
and were unprepared for any other sort of campaign."

On the morning of October 18, 1916, three Nieuport 17 fighters lifted off from the aerodrome at Luxeuil and turned to a northwesterly heading. These three aircraft, the only ones in Escadrille N.124 still airworthy, were piloted by Masson, Lufbery, and Capitaine Thénault. After a little more than two hours' flying time, the three arrived at their new base of operations. The large open field, bordered on one side by a dense wood, was located just north of the village of Cachy and 10 miles east of the larger city of Amiens. More importantly, it was only two miles from the banks of the River Somme.

The Somme Offensive, named after the river, had begun on July 1, 1916. In terms of sheer brutality and body count, this bloody battle was of a magnitude similar to Verdun. On the first day alone, the British army suffered some 57,000 casualties, a third of those killed outright. By battle's end in mid-November, British, French, and German combined casualties would total more than a million men.

The remaining pilots assigned to N.124, still grounded due to a lack of available airplanes, were compelled to make the trip from Luxeuil by rail—and as usual, via Paris. The rest of the escadrille's support personnel made their way cross-country in trucks packed with gear, tools, equipment, and supplies. This was a lengthy process, so it took until the end of the month for the squadron to become operational. In this new theatre of operations, N.124 was to be teamed with escadrilles de chase N.65, N.67, and N.112 to form Groupe de Combat 13, commanded by Capitaine (later Commandant) Philippe Féquant.

Another Prince of a Pilot

The Escadrille Américaine had taken some hard hits over the previous four months. Chapman, Rockwell, and Prince were dead; Cowdin had left the squadron; and the wounded Balsley would never return. Thaw had finally recovered from his elbow wound, but McConnell would not be back until November. As a consequence of this rapid attrition, the squadron was now down to only nine American pilots, two of which—as the next few days would prove—would also soon be leaving. Therefore, as the pilots passed through Paris on their way to Cachy, they picked up three new replacements—all officially assigned as of October 22, 1916.

16. CAPORAL WILLIS BRADLEY HAVILAND was born in Minneapolis, Minnesota on March 10, 1890, to Dr. Willis H. and Grace Haviland. In the autumn of 1915, he arrived in France and joined the American Field Service. In addition to having served a four-year stint in the US Navy and three years in the Illinois National Guard, he had completed two years of electrical engineering training at Iowa State College. Near the end of January 1915, he left the ambulance service and entered into aviation. After completing flight training, he reported to Escadrille N.124, which was just arriving at Cachy.

17. SERGENT FREDERICK HENRY PRINCE JR. was the older brother of Norman Prince, who had died only seven days prior to Fred's assignment to N.124. He was born on April 10, 1885, in Boston, and like Norman, attended Groton before becoming a member of

Robert Soubiran dressed in cold weather gear beside his Nieuport 17 N.1977 at Cachy, winter 1916-1917. Soubiran joined Escadrille N.124 on October 22, 1916, with Willis Haviland and Fred Prince Jr. The French-born Soubiran would become a well-liked and long-standing member of the squadron. Note the recently applied Seminole warrior insignia and Soubiran's personal marking, a dark vertical band. Like Haviland, he accumulated a large number of excellent Lafayette Escadrille photos, which can still be viewed in the archives of the National Air and Space Museum. (Smithsonian National Air and Space Museum)

the Harvard College Class of 1908. At brother Norman's urging, Fred sailed to France on January 4, 1916, on the *Rochambeau* with Norman, Elliot Cowdin, and William Thaw, who were returning to their French squadrons from Christmas leave. He joined the Foreign Legion on January 28 and began flight training at Pau on January 31 with fellow future Escadrille N.124 pilot Willis Haviland. Upon Norman's death in October 1916, Fred joined N.124 as his replacement.

18. SERGENT ROBERT SOUBIRAN was born on March 16, 1886, in Avallon, France, to Theodore and Clementine Soubiran. He thus joined Lufbery and Masson as a French-born American citizen serving in Escadrille N.124. Soubiran's mother died when he was very young, after which, his father moved his family to the United States. Robert grew up hustling on the streets of New York City as a newspaper boy before eventually landing a job as a mechanic for champion Italian-American racecar driver Raffaele "Ralph" De Palma. When his native country went to war, Soubiran joined the Rockwell brothers, Bert Hall, William Thaw, and the other American volunteers who marched through Paris to join the Foreign Legion on August 25, 1914. After serving more than a year in the trenches, he took advantage of a fortuitous knee wound to apply to aviation. He completed flight training just in time to join Willis Haviland and Fred Prince on their way to Cachy and Escadrille N.124.

The End of the 'Deluxe War'

The Somme offensive began with French and British domination of the skies over the battlefield. Allied leaders fully recognized the need for aerial reconnaissance and fighter protection, so they had committed the necessary resources to insure air superiority. However, by late October, when the Escadrille Américaine arrived at Cachy, the situation had changed. The German Air Service had responded with significantly greater numbers of aircraft, which they massed together into a large air fighting unit called a "Jadgstaffel," or "Jasta," for short. This meant that the day of lone wolf fighter patrols had come to an end for pilots on both sides of the lines. Surviving in the air now depended on teamwork, as well as individual skill.

Another change in the balance of air power that the pilots of N.124 were about to discover was that the Germans were developing improved aircraft to counter the excellent British and French fighting machines. The now-outdated Fokker Eindecker was being replaced by faster and more maneuverable machines, such as the new Albatros D-series of fighters. Their sturdy monocoque plywood fuselage construction—whose strength came from their outer wooden shell rather than internal bracing—and powerful Mercedes engines gave them much-improved performance. More importantly, this outstanding engine allowed them to carry two forward-firing, synchronized machine guns. As a consequence, the men of the Escadrille Américaine would meet with very stiff resistance in the skies above the Somme.

Captured German Albatros D.II 910/16. The Albatros D-series fighters were a vast improvement over the Fokker Eindecker and rivaled the best Allied counterparts of 1916 and 1917. Their success was primarily due to the outstanding Mercedes engine, which provided sufficient power for these fighters to carry two belt-fed, synchronized machine guns. This OAW-built example, flown by Leutnant Max Boehme of Jagdstaffel (Jasta) 5, was forced down and captured on March 4, 1917. The French later repainted it and used it for testing. (Greg VanWyngarden)

Life at Cachy was far more difficult for the men of N.124 in another way. Gone were the comfortable villas, hotels, and the excellent food they had enjoyed at Luxeuil and Behonne. Instead, they were quartered in cold, drafty, and leaky portable shacks located in a wind-swept environment James McConnell called "a sea of mud"—with a miserably cold and wet winter just about to begin. Moreover, because the squadron had, in the past, had such excellent accommodations, it arrived at Cachy without any stoves or other cooking and household utensils. As a consequence, the pilots had to impose on neighboring French squadrons for subsistence until they could get their own mess established. Lacking even such basic necessities as furniture and blankets, the pilots initially had to sleep on the floors of their huts in their flying gear. As James McConnell put it, "We had … come to believe that we would wage only a deluxe war, and were unprepared for any other sort of campaign." The good life that he and his colleagues had taken for granted had come to an end.

They immediately went to work, caulking cracks, papering walls, installing electrical lights and stoves, and making their living space as comfortable as possible. Some of the more artistically inclined even decorated the bleak walls with drawings of air combat scenes and other images of interest to men at war. Meanwhile, Thaw and the squadron "chef de popote" (mess officer), Didier Masson, took a truck to Paris, and after obtaining funds from the Franco-American Flying Corps Committee via Dr. Gros, purchased stoves and other necessary equipment to haul back to Cachy. Before long, N.124's austere living arrangements began to seem more like home.

Two Fewer "Bad Boys"

Other changes were also taking place during this time. The situation with Bert Hall had finally come to a head. Hall's biographer, Blaine Pardoe, discusses Bert's standing within the squadron, which was both complicated and controversial, in his book *The Bad Boy*. According to Pardoe, many of the offenses that authors have attributed to Bert over the past century were true: he probably was, in fact, "a liar and a scoundrel."

On the other hand, some of the more unsavory things generally ascribed to Hall were, according to Pardoe, exaggerations or out-and-out fabrications by his lifelong enemy, Paul Rockwell. The self-appointed squadron historian never forgave Hall for skipping out on Kiffin's funeral. Rockwell believed that Bert had, instead, scooted off to Paris to "peddle" the story of Kiffin's death to the newspapers. Because of this, the bitter elder Rockwell made it his life's mission to denigrate Hall in every way possible; and being the primary source of information about the squadron, Paul's assertions have generally been taken at face value and repeated verbatim by almost every author who has ever written about the Lafayette Escadrille. Thus, the historical picture of Bert Hall that resulted from this lifelong smear campaign is probably far worse than was really the case.

In spite of Bert's transgressions, either real or perceived, there is no evidence that he was "kicked out" of the squadron, as often alleged—neither Capitaine Thénault nor anyone else asked Bert to leave. It seems, instead, that his colleagues—led by James McConnell, who never liked Hall—reacted to his roguish behavior and rough manners by ostracizing him to the point where he no longer felt wanted. A few days after Kiffin Rockwell's death, he requested a transfer, and on November 1, left the squadron and reported to Escadrille N.103. After he left, McConnell made his feelings clear about Hall's departure when he wrote to Paul Rockwell, "I'm damned glad he's gone…." Bert also had a final comment, as remembered by Emil Marshall, an American non-pilot temporarily assigned to the squadron, who was present when Hall left. According to him, Hall shook his fist at his ex-friends as he walked out and shouted angrily, "You'll hear from me yet!" He proved true to his word.

The next "bad boy" to leave the squadron was Laurence Rumsey. Since reporting back in early June, he had flown only a few missions—his last one recorded in the squadron log was on September 9. Moreover, he had become so dependent on alcohol that he could no longer fly sober. On one notable occasion, he took off while in an excessively inebriated state and got completely lost. He was finally forced to land on a field he decided must be in German territory. Remembering the instructions that had been drilled into him, he promptly set his Nieuport on fire. Only too late did the muddle-headed pilot discover that he was on an Allied field several miles behind French lines.

Rumsey's heart had always been in the right place, and just to be where he was proved his exceptional courage and ability; but like a few of the other 38 men who eventually served with N.124, he was simply not cut out to be a fighter pilot.

The incident that sealed his fate occurred soon after the squadron arrived at Cachy. The beloved mascot Whiskey liked chewing on things, and when Rumsey—in a state of advanced intoxication—caught him eating his service cap, he grabbed a walking stick and clubbed the little animal in the head, blinding him in his right eye. Rumsey undoubtedly regretted this act, but it was just another indication that he was unraveling. Soon afterward, he broke out in a rash of painful boils and had to be hospitalized. By November 25, he was no longer with the squadron and was soon thereafter on his way back to the United States.

A Flashy New Insignia to Match a Flashy New Name

The squadron log indicates that the inclement weather and thick Somme River mist kept the squadron grounded for 51 of the 86 days they spent at Cachy. Consequently, significant operational events were few and far between during this period. However, other significant things were occurring within the squadron.

Germany continued to complain to the still-neutral American government about the outlaw "amerikanischen Piloten" opposing them. The much-publicized deaths of Rockwell and Prince highlighted to an even greater extent the role the Americans were playing in the war, and this only increased German outrage. It eventually became enough of a concern to the American government that on November 13, 1916, the French Minister of War ordered, "for diplomatic reasons," that the Escadrille Américaine henceforth be called the "Escadrille des Volontaires." This lackluster name appealed to virtually no one, so a new order, dated December 6, 1916, decreed that the new unofficial name for Escadrille N.124 would be "l'Escadrille Lafayette"—the Lafayette Escadrille. This new name did not solve the problem of pilots from neutral America serving in the French Air Service but it at least disguised the squadron's "national character" that had so offended the German government. Moreover, it was an appealing name that everyone could embrace.

To go with their catchy new name, the men of the squadron decided that they also needed their own unique insignia to distinguish them from other French squadrons. Since a US flag was out of the question, they had to find another, less obvious image to convey their national pride. When someone noticed a handsome Seminole Native American warrior logo on a case of Savage Arms Company ammunition, the issue was resolved. What could be more American than an American Indian? William Thaw then asked one of the squadron's more artistic mechanics, Caporal Suchet, to paint his interpretation of this image onto the fuselage sides of the squadron's aircraft. The Lafayette Escadrille now had its own unique logo. From now on, an Indianhead would adorn N.124 aircraft, and forevermore symbolize the Lafayette Escadrille.

Willis B. Haviland standing beside his Nieuport 17 N.1887 at Cachy, winter 1916–1917, ready for a patrol over the lines. Here, the plane is not yet fitted with an overhead Lewis gun. The white vertical band on the fuselage behind the newly applied Seminole warrior insignia was Haviland's personal marking. (Washington and Lee University Archives)

A Formidable New Mount

Another important development occurring during this period was the arrival of the squadron's first Spad VIIs. This highly acclaimed new fighter was in many ways a great improvement over the Nieuport 17, although the pilots did not universally welcome the change. Their beloved Nieuport was light on the controls, maneuverable, and easy to fly; whereas, the snub-nosed Spad—whose name was derived from the acronym of the company that built it, the Société Pour L'Aviation et ses Dérivés—had none of these characteristics. In fact, this thin-winged, inherently unstable machine seemed almost clunky by comparison.

The Spad, however, had some redeeming qualities that made it a better fighting machine than the Nieuport. Though more challenging to fly, especially from the small muddy fields so characteristic of WWI aerodromes, it was fast, incredibly sturdy, and it provided an exceptionally stable gun platform for the single .303-caliber Vickers machine gun mounted in front of the pilot. Thanks to its 140-horsepower Hispano-Suiza V-8 inline engine, it could cruise at 120 miles per hour and climb to an altitude of 6,500 feet in less than 5 minutes. Perhaps best of all, pilots could dive a Spad vertically to speeds approaching 250 miles per hour without fear of the wings shedding—a very useful feature during a diving attack or with an enemy fighter glued to their tail spitting hot steel into them. Even more so than the now-aging Nieuport, the Spad would become the favorite of the aces. The newly named Lafayette Escadrille would receive progressively more copies of this outstanding airplane in the ensuing weeks and months, until eventually, the official squadron designation of N.124 would change to SPA.124.

The remainder of 1916 progressed for the squadron at dreary, muddy Cachy with relatively few significant missions. One of the more noteworthy of these began in the early morning darkness of November 17, when German bombers attacked the aerodrome, set one of the hangars afire, and destroyed several airplanes. Paul Pavelka, who had been experimenting with night flying, took off in hot pursuit, aided by the light of the blazing hangar. He failed to encounter any bombers, and because his primitive signal system failed, he was unable to return for fear of being shot down by nervous French antiaircraft gunners. He wandered through the air for the next two and a half hours, becoming hopelessly lost in the blacked-out darkness of the Somme River haze. His engine eventually sputtered to a stop from fuel starvation, and he glided blindly down to a safe—and very fortunate—landing in a field some 25 miles from home. By the time he made his way back to the squadron, a new member had joined its fold.

19. CAPORAL RONALD WOOD HOSKIER was born on March 21, 1896, in South Orange, New Jersey. After completing a year and a half at Harvard, he decided to travel to France to join his father, Herman, who worked with the Norton-Harjes Ambulance Corps, and his mother, Harriet, an auxiliary nurse. Ronald drove an ambulance until entering into flight training in May 1916. He reported to the Lafayette Escadrille at Cachy on December 11, 1916. There, the intelligent and idealistic young aspiring author—seemingly poured from the same mold as the late Victor Chapman—would soon become a valuable and respected member of the squadron. Unfortunately, also reminiscent of Chapman, his time there would end tragically all too soon.

On January 19, 1917, another new man—the 20th American assigned to the squadron—showed up at Cachy, unexpected and unannounced. He had come from the GDE at Plessis-Belleville to retrieve a worn out Nieuport; however, since his assignment to N.124 was pending, he stayed. He later wrote, "Meals here are splendid, the service is excellent and everyone seems to be in unison from the Captain down to the last of us. It's fine."

20. CAPORAL EDMOND CHARLES CLINTON GENET, of Ossining, New York, had—like several other members of this elite squadron—an impressive pedigree. Born on November 9, 1896, to Albert and Martha Genet, he was a direct descendent of New York's first governor and two-time Vice President of the United States, George Clinton. He was also the great-great grandson of Edmond-Charles Genet, the French envoy to the United States, who in 1793, instigated the infamous "Citizen Genet" incident.

The small, cherubic Edmond, who attended church and wrote his mother faithfully, was the youngest pilot to fly for the Lafayette Escadrille—and he looked even younger than his 20 years. This prompted Edwin Parsons to refer to him as "the baby of the

Ronald Wood Hoskier reported to the Lafayette Escadrille on December 11, 1916. Here, he poses in early April 1917, wearing the horizon-blue greatcoat he had recently purchased in Paris. He stands in front of the squadron's recently acquired Morane-Saulnier parasol monoplane, MSP.1112, in which he would die a few days later. Courageous, idealistic, and a skilled pilot, the scholarly Harvard student exemplified the very best of the Lafayette Escadrille. (Washington and Lee University Archives)

The big 1916 Christmas bash at Cachy. Sitting near the stove in the front, James McConnell, Willis B. Haviland, and Dudley Hill. Back row: Paul Pavelka, unidentified British officer, Robert Rockwell (standing), Alfred de Laage, and Raoul Lufbery. The five men on the right, above Hill, were probably also British guests. McConnell noted the number of men present that evening and was heard to exclaim, "My God! Thirteen of us here. That's sure death. Wonder who'll be the next to get it?" On December 29, 1916, he wrote in a letter about this wild evening, "Lufbery and I got lit and pulled off a Wild West show. He held a basin while I shot holes in it. Fortunately the Captain took the revolver from me as I was to essay knocking a shaving brush out of our 'ace's' mouth." (Washington and Lee University Archives)

Lafayette," but he was no baby. In addition to having previously served in the US Navy, he had, before entering into flight training, completed 16 months of service with the Foreign Legion. Here, he had fought his way through some of the war's bloodiest battles. However, Genet's sterling qualities—his cheerful demeanor, impressive war record, and proven courage and flying ability—were offset by a darker side of his rather complicated personality. As is clear from his own writings, he was plagued by feelings of guilt and self-loathing, stemming in part from the fact that was a fugitive from the law in his own country—he had, before coming to France, deserted from the Navy. Equally burdensome was his love for a young woman back home who had long since lost interest in him.

Meanwhile, as the two new men were busy trying to adapt to the damp, cold climate pervading Cachy, the squadron's ace suffered from a painful bout of rheumatism. Even so, the irrepressible Raoul Lufbery continued his outstanding work. December 27 dawned a brilliantly clear day, and Luf made the most of it. He ended this very significant year in style by downing an Aviatik C two-seat observation plane, southeast of Chaulnes. Then, on January 24, he repeated this performance for his seventh confirmed victory.

Edmond Genet poses beside a Nieuport 17 fighter. Barely 20 years of age, he was the youngest pilot to fly for the Lafayette Escadrille, but his boyish appearance belied a fierce toughness and dedication to the cause. Plagued by a troubled past, a lost love, and a sense of guilt from losing a comrade in aerial combat, the emotional agony he felt may have contributed to his demise. (Smithsonian National Air and Space Museum)

Also on January 24, the popular and hard-working Paul Pavelka left the squadron. The wandering world traveler had grown weary of the miserable cold and dampness of the Somme and was anxious for a new environment. Both he and like-minded Willis Haviland had requested a transfer, but only Pavelka's was approved. He reported to the Armée de l'Orient in Salonika (Thessaloniki), Greece, where he saw a great deal of action and accorded himself well while flying for French squadrons on the Macedonian front.

His career came to a tragic end on November 11, 1917, after he volunteered to help an old Foreign Legion comrade—now serving in the English cavalry—break a wild horse. The former cowpuncher Pavelka mounted the vicious animal and somehow stayed with the bucking bronco until it wildly threw itself to the ground and rolled over on its human tormenter. Mortally injured, Paul Pavelka died the next day. It was as ironic as it was tragic for a man who had survived so many death-defying experiences—including months of desperate combat in the trenches and numerous deadly aerial dogfights and emergency landings—to die in such a way. He was buried with honors at Salonika, and in 1928, his remains were transferred to the crypt below the Lafayette Escadrille Memorial, located at Marnes-le-Coquette, on the western outskirts of Paris.

★ ★ ★

The much-anticipated Somme experience had been, for the most part, a bust for the squadron. They had arrived at Cachy just as the big offensive and the good flying weather were each drawing to a close. After huddling around a stove in their shack for three dreary months, they shed no tears when orders came to move again. On January 26, the pilots of the Lafayette Escadrille lifted off from Cachy and turned their planes south. Their new aerodrome—like Cachy, a field at the edge of a wood—was located between the towns of Ravenel and Saint-Just-en-Chaussée, 20 miles due south. They hoped the new location would bring with it more livable accommodations and better flying weather.

CHAPTER 9

MAC GOES WEST

"Wonder who'll be the next to get it?"

At just after noon on January 26, 1917, 11 warplanes bearing the colorful image of an American Indian warrior roared in from the north and buzzed low and fast over the makeshift aerodrome at Ravenel/Saint-Just. After the short 30-minute hop from Cachy, the pilots of the Lafayette Escadrille had fuel to spare; so in keeping with custom, some of them pulled up and went into a series of wild aerobatics in the sky above the field before side-slipping their motley collection of Nieuports and Spads in for a bumpy landing onto the rutted field of frozen mud and snow.

More Losses and More Replacements

One of the aircraft in the formation that flew in to Ravenel from Cachy on January 26 was manned by a new pilot who had just arrived from the GDE.

21. CAPORAL EDWIN CHARLES "TED" PARSONS was born in Holyoke, Massachusetts on September 24, 1892 to Frederick and Grace Parsons. Like most of the others who flew for this unique squadron of American volunteers, Parsons was a truly remarkable young man—a high-achieving, risk-taking adventurer. By the time he was 24, the slight, dapper pilot's biography already read like an adventure novel, and he was destined to distinguish himself even further before the end of his long and productive life.

After dropping out of the University of Pennsylvania, young Parsons headed west to America's land of opportunity. He worked at various pursuits, including cattle herding and gold mining, and somewhere along the way, made a brief and unsuccessful attempt at marriage. His life took a fateful turn in 1912 when he met famed aviation pioneer Glenn Curtiss, at Dominguez Field, near Los Angeles. Parsons immediately caught the flying bug and learned to fly a Curtiss pusher biplane.

Before long, the young pilot came into contact with an agent for the notorious Mexican revolutionary general, Francisco "Pancho" Villa. Anticipating fame and fortune, Parsons accepted a commission in Villa's División del Norte and delivered a Curtiss flying machine that Villa had purchased. In it, Parsons attempted to teach some of Villa's officers to fly. Ironically, he was making military aviation history at about the same time and location as fellow future Lafayette Escadrille member, Didier Masson, who was flying for General Álvaro Obregón. However, neither apparently knew of the other's role in the conflict until they later compared notes as squadron mates in France.

Eventually, Parsons wisely decided that working for Villa—who was by now planning raids into US territory—might not provide the kind of future he sought. Consequently, he made his way back home to Massachusetts but did not remain there for long. When he learned of an American flying squadron forming in France, he signed on as a veterinarian's assistant on the RMS *Carpathia* and waded his way to France in the manure of 2,200 horses. Upon arrival, he drove an ambulance until entering into the Aéronautique Militaire. He reported to the Lafayette Escadrille on January 25, 1917. The dashing Parsons was destined to become one of the squadron's most colorful and successful members.

★ ★ ★

A planned new spring offensive was the impetus for the Groupe de Combat 13 move from Cachy to Ravenel. French Général Robert Nivelle, of Verdun fame, hoped to inflict a fatal blow to the German army that would end the war. Until it came about, the pilots at Ravenel were instructed to remain incognito and refrain from crossing the lines.

The pain of this restrictive order was compounded by the abysmal living conditions at Ravenel. In spite of the men's high hopes, their new accommodations were even worse than at Cachy. Moreover, the foulest weather of this exceptionally bitter winter—which James McConnell called "the coldest since 1870"—was still to come. No barracks existed, and until they could be built, the men were forced to live underground "like moles," as Parsons phrased it, sleeping bundled up in their flight suits on dirt floors in a covered trench. It was so miserably cold that the oil in their aircraft engines congealed, their dampened hair froze into icicles before they could put a comb to it, and they suffered painful frostbite to fingers, toes, ears, and faces.

The American pilots did manage to become airborne on the few days in February that were fit for flying, but in keeping with their orders to lie low and fly only defensive patrols, they engaged little enemy opposition. They made good use of the down time, however, by once again getting their unfinished barracks in livable condition.

During this gloomy February, two members of the squadron managed to escape the misery—but neither by his own choice. Didier Masson was hospitalized with influenza. After he recovered, he was ordered to the flight training complex at Avord. Here, he served as an instructor until mid-June, before finally being allowed to return to the squadron.

Also leaving was Frederick Prince, who had joined the squadron back in October with the best of intentions. However, the unwanted intervention of his domineering father—who was understandably reluctant to lose his only remaining son in combat—forced Fred to leave N.124 without having flown a single patrol with it. Fred continued to serve in various French and American noncombat roles until the end of the war but never forgave his father for ending his combat career.

The Lafayette Escadrille had been in existence for several months but had never reached full operating strength. Wartime attrition throughout the French Air Service had been claiming pilots as fast as the schools could turn them out, so N.124 was only one of many squadrons with a manning shortage. By late 1916, however, this was changing. The rapidly expanding French training program was producing more new pilots than ever, so a steady stream of replacements began flowing to the front. Haviland, Prince, Soubiran, Hoskier, Genet, and Parsons had already arrived and more were on the way.

22. CAPORAL STEPHEN SOHIER BIGELOW reported to Ravenel on February 8, 1917, and flew his first combat patrol that same afternoon. He was born on March 18, 1894, in Boston, Massachusetts, to affluent parents, Joseph and Mary Bigelow. After graduating from Harvard in 1915, he attended the famous military training camp for civilians at Plattsburg, New York. When he heard of the new all-American flying squadron being formed, he sailed for France and entered into aviation training. His greatest attribute was that of a skilled pianist. In addition to flying patrols, he would keep the squadron entertained through some of its toughest months.

23. CAPORAL EDWARD FOOTE "POP" HINKLE was the oldest man to serve in the Lafayette Escadrille. He was born on May 22, 1876, in Cincinnati, Ohio, to William and Lucile Hinkle. After graduating from Andover Academy, followed by Yale and Cambridge Universities, he studied architecture and design in Paris at the prestigious École des Beaux-Arts. He practiced his profession in the United States until 1910, when he migrated back to Paris. When the war began, he volunteered for the air service but was rejected as being too old. In mid-1916 he finally succeeded in circumventing the age restriction and entered into flight training. On March 1, 1917, at the ripe old age of 40, Hinkle joined the Lafayette Escadrille at Ravenel.

24. CAPORAL WALTER LOVELL was born September 9, 1884, in Newton, Massachusetts, to Wallace and Josephine Lovell. The 1907 Harvard grad worked as a broker until 1914, when he joined the many other young Americans traveling to France to serve in the ambulance service. During his 16 months, he rose to the position of assistant section leader and earned the Croix de Guerre with star. In May 1916, he volunteered for aviation training and was formally assigned to the Lafayette Escadrille on March 1, 1917.

25. CAPORAL HAROLD BUCKLEY WILLIS was born in Boston on February 9, 1890, to John and Myrta Willis. Like eight previous other pilots belonging to the squadron, he was

Another member of the Lafayette Escadrille's "Harvard Club" was Walter Lovell, of Newton, Massachusetts—he was an '07 grad and classmate of Elliot Cowdin. Lovell joined the squadron on March 1, 1917, at the age of 32 and excelled as a combat pilot, just as he had as an ambulance driver. Here, he stands next to his Spad VII fighter, which is undergoing maintenance. The diagonal stripe was his personal marking. (Washington and Lee University Archives)

a Harvard man, graduating in 1912 with a degree in architecture. At the war's outset, he traveled to France to join the American Ambulance Field Service. Here, he earned the Croix de Guerre with star before giving up his noncombatant role and joining the air service. He reported to the Lafayette Escadrille with Lovell and Hinkle on March 1, 1917. He quickly became a valuable and reliable pilot and—like Bigelow—could, as Edwin Parsons put it, "make a piano do cartwheels and backflips."

One of the most important contributions the artistically talented architects Willis and Hinkle made to the squadron was their re-design of its trademark insignia. Hinkle noted that the Seminole Indian head copied from the ammunition case "looked like an old woman with a drooping bonnet…." Consequently, he and Willis teamed up to design a more ferocious-looking Sioux warrior that would also better display the French and American national colors of red, white, and blue. The men of the squadron enthusiastically adopted the new design, which would become the definitive insignia used by the Lafayette Escadrille.

On March 16, 1917, the squadron acquired yet another new member—though not a pilot. William Thaw went to Paris to pick up a new Spad, so he decided to take lion cub Whiskey along with him. Whiskey's blind right eye had taken on an unaesthetic, clouded-over appearance, and Thaw wanted to get the cub a new glass eye. Unfortunately, no eye doctor was apparently willing to risk such a procedure on

Harold Buckley Willis poses beside Nieuport 17 N.2551 with the original Seminole Indianhead insignia. Willis joined the Lafayette Escadrille on March 1, 1917, with Walter Lovell and Edward Hinkle. The 27-year-old Harvard-trained architect started his wartime career—like many of his colleagues—as an ambulance driver, before transferring into aviation. He and fellow artist Hinkle wasted no time in upgrading the squadron insignia to a more fierce-looking and colorful Sioux Indianhead. (Smithsonian National Air and Space Museum)

a half-grown lion cub, so Thaw did the next best thing: he somehow acquired a little female lion cub as a companion for Whiskey and shipped the two animals back to Ravenel. It did not take the men long to come up with a name for the new mascot: the Lafayette Escadrille now had "Soda" to go with its Whiskey.

The men of the Lafayette Escadrille continued to battle the elements at Ravenel. The changing weather of approaching spring transformed the field from a frozen, rutted wasteland that burst tires upon landing to a melted quagmire of gumbo, so soft and gooey that men and planes, alike, mired to a standstill in it. Meanwhile, new pilots continued to stream into the squadron.

26. CAPORAL KENNETH ARCHIBALD MARR was born on June 10, 1885, in Oakland, California, to Archibald and Alberta Marr. Soon after the war began, Marr was on his way from Alaska to France, delivering 300 Alaskan malamute sled dogs to the French army for use in the Vosges Mountains. This task completed, he decided to stay and see the war. He joined the ambulance service and served in the same section as future squadron mates McConnell, Lovell, and Haviland. He later followed their lead into aviation, and on March 29, 1917, into the Lafayette Escadrille. Because of Marr's experience with Alaskan natives, his fellow pilots called him "Siwash"—a nickname he kept for the rest of his life.

27. SERGENT WILLIAM EDWARD DUGAN JR. was born on Long Island, New York, on December 1, 1889, to William and Sally Dugan. After dropping out of MIT, young Dugan caught a

Whiskey, with his clouded-over blind right eye and his new little mate, Soda. Whiskey was friendly and playful, and according to Edmond Genet, "just loves to be rolled on his back and tickled." Soda, on the other hand, was "rather snappy" and proved to have a less amicable temperament. (Washington and Lee University Archives)

tramp steamer to Nicaragua, where he signed on with a fruit company, overseeing a Costa Rican banana plantation. When war clouds formed over Europe, he sailed for France to be a part of the "great adventure." On September 19, 1914, he joined the Foreign Legion and, for the next horrendous year and a half, fought nearly nonstop in all the major battles on the Western Front. In so doing, he served with fellow future Escadrille N.124 members, Thaw, Rockwell, Chapman, Hall, Genet, Pavelka, and Soubiran. Dugan's hellish ground war finally ended when a wound landed him in the hospital. While there, Dr. Edmund Gros personally intervened to have him transferred into the air service. He reported to the Lafayette Escadrille on March 30, 1917. Having already more than proven his mettle under fire, the diminutive Dugan accorded himself well in the skies above France.

28. CAPORAL THOMAS MOSES "JERRY" HEWITT JR. was born on December 21, 1894, in Westchester, New York, to Thomas and Sarah Hewitt. In December 1915, he worked his way to England on a tramp steamer and tried to enlist in both the Royal Flying Corps and Naval Air Service but was rejected because of citizenship issues. He then crossed the Channel to France and signed on with the Norton-Harjes Ambulance Corps, where he served until entering into aviation training. Hewitt had established a good training record, so Capitaine Thénault chose him—along with Marr and Dugan— for his squadron. Hewitt reported on March 30, 1917, but unlike the other two men, failed to live up to expectations.

The Death of James McConnell

As the bleak winter weather in Northern France began to improve in March 1917, Général Nivelle finalized preparations for his upcoming April offensive. The operation, which would become known as the Second Battle of the Aisne, was destined to fail— though not for lack of effort by the pilots of Groupe de Combat 13. The assault was to be launched along a front extending from Soissons to Reims, toward the German-held Chemin des Dames ridge. However, in spite of precautions to the contrary, the upcoming offensive had become one of the war's best-known secrets. Consequently, the Germans had already begun a strategic withdrawal northeastward to their highly fortified defensive position, the Hindenburg Line.

This rapid enemy movement made accurate and timely aerial reconnaissance critical, so the men of the Lafayette Escadrille finally had a job to do. Not only were they tasked with harassing enemy troops on the ground and providing protection for reconnaissance aircraft, they were ordered to observe and report enemy movements. During the month of March, the squadron logbook—the *Journal des Marches et Opérations*—indicates that they flew approximately 160 sorties. As they began to rack up flight hours, encounters with enemy ground fire and aircraft also increased.

Monday, March 19, 1917, dawned cool, cloudy, and windy—but suitable enough for flying. With 17 sorties in the making, it would be the Lafayette Escadrille's busiest day of the month. Included in the day's itinerary was a three-plane reconnaissance

The 28th member of the Lafayette Escadrille, Thomas Hewitt Jr., could fly and he looked sharp in his crisp new uniform. Unfortunately, he lacked the "right stuff" to become a successful fighter pilot. Early missions unnerved him to the point where he became overly reluctant to fly. He served without distinction, earning from Ted Parsons the disparaging nickname "Useless," before Capitaine Thénault finally removed him from the squadron roster. His life after the war continued in a tragic downhill spiral. (Smithsonian National Air and Space Museum)

patrol assigned to James McConnell, Edmond Genet, and Ted Parsons. Soon after taking off from the aerodrome at Ravenel just before 9 a.m., Parsons dropped out of the formation with a dud engine and returned to the airfield. McConnell and Genet continued on toward enemy territory, which at that time was some 30 miles to the northeast. As they crossed the lines, they encountered two enemy aircraft. During the ensuing melee, the two men became separated, each involved with his own adversary.

Genet squared off with an aggressive two-seater and exchanged machine gun fire with the enemy gunner until the two nearly collided. Both scored hits, but Genet received the worst of it. Bullets severed one of his control rods and a main upper wing support, while a metal fragment flew into his left cheek, cutting a deep gouge in it. With a severely shot-up airplane and a bleeding face, he finally managed to escape back to friendly territory. In spite of the damage and painful wound, he circled over Ham for 15 minutes, waiting worriedly for Mac to join back up with him. As he circled, he tried to stem the flow of blood and prayed that his weakened top wing would not go sailing off into the slipstream. When Mac failed to show, Genet reluctantly turned and limped his way back to Ravenel, where he landed and relayed the disturbing news to his squadron mates. Two hours later, Lieutenant de Laage and Raoul Lufbery took off and patrolled the area where Genet had last seen Mac, looking—unsuccessfully—for any trace of him. Meanwhile, the men back at the aerodrome waited anxiously, watching and listening for any indication of their friend's return, but it never came. Where he had gone, no one knew, but they braced for the worst.

Not until four days later, March 23, did the truth become known. That evening Groupe Commandant Féquant received a call from a French cavalry commander, whose unit had been operating in an area recently vacated by the Germans. A local woman had led them to the smashed wreckage of a Nieuport, serial number N.2055, and a bullet-ridden body lying beside a road, near the village of Petit-Détroit, a mile south of Flavy-le-Martel. The body had been stripped of everything—personal effects, papers, even outer clothing and shoes—but there was no doubt as to the dead pilot's identity: it was McConnell.

According to the woman, he had been bounced from behind as he dove toward his intended quarry. Why this experienced pilot allowed himself to be surprised in this manner will never be known. It could have been carelessness, but another reason is more likely. He was still disabled with his injured back when he took off on his last mission. Only six days before his death, he had written in a letter to Paul Rockwell, "I'm worse off than when I went to Hospital and feel damned discouraged. Don't know what to do about it. Seems hopeless." Because of his severely restricted mobility, he was probably unable to turn and look behind him as his killer, Leutnant Heinrich Kämmerer of Jasta 20, approached. McConnell's plane was seen diving straight down into an apple orchard that had been recently destroyed by the retreating Germans.

Some of the men of the Lafayette Escadrille remembered back to the Christmas evening dinner at Cachy, when McConnell had suddenly looked around and exclaimed, "My God! Thirteen of us here. That's sure death. Wonder who'll be the next to get it?" Perhaps he had a premonition, much like the one Kiffin Rockwell had the night before he died when he gave Paul Pavelka his burial instructions. Presentiment or not, McConnell had answered his own question. The squadron had lost the fourth of its seven founding members: Chapman, Rockwell, Prince, and now Mac. The only original member now still with the squadron was the ever-resilient Bill Thaw.

McConnell was buried without ceremony where he fell, in a coffin made from the door of a nearby pillaged house. It was as he had requested in a letter he left for his comrades. Written with his typically sarcastic wit, the letter ended:

> My burial is of no import. Make it as easy as possible for yourselves. I have no religion and do not care for any service. If the omission would embarrass you, I presume I could stand the performance. Good luck to the rest of you. God damn Germany and vive la France.

On April 2, 1917, a memorial service was held for McConnell at the American Cathedral of the Holy Trinity, also called the American Cathedral in Paris. It was well-attended by fellow pilots, ambulance service members, friends, and at least three women who believed they had been engaged to the handsome flier. In 1928, his remains were transferred from his wartime grave at Petit-Détroit to the crypt at the Lafayette Escadrille Memorial, where they rest today.

Edmond Genet was devastated. Still barely 20 years old and already suffering the guilt from his Navy desertion and grief for his lost love, he blamed himself for McConnell's death. He wrote his mother on the day after Mac went missing, "I'll avenge him if it costs me my own life." The next day, Genet wrote to McConnell's good friend, Paul Rockwell, that he felt "utterly miserable over the whole affair," and in his diary, he wrote, "I feel horribly depressed over it. If I had only been able to get to him and save him from his fate! ... I'm out after blood now in grim earnest to avenge poor McConnell."

A few days later, on March 27, Genet received what for him must have seemed the final blow. A letter from his mother informed him that his beloved Gertrude, the girl back home who had stopped writing him months earlier, had become engaged to another man. The comment he wrote in his diary that day was telling: "It won't make much difference after all, tho. I don't expect to live thru to the end of the war." He would soon fulfill his own morbid prophecy.

★ ★ ★

Even with the departure of Masson, Fred Prince, and now McConnell, the Lafayette Escadrille had finally, by the end of its ten-week stay at Ravenel/Saint-Just, reached full manning. Along with the new pilots came more of the new Spad VII fighters to replace the aging Nieuports. With this increased warfighting ability, the squadron prepared to

One of the happiest occasions for the men of the Lafayette Escadrille was when the United States declared war on Germany on April 6, 1917. Finally, the American pilots were fighting for their homeland as well as their adopted France. Pictured here with mascots, proudly displaying the Stars and Stripes, are, from left, Harold Willis, William Dugan, Georges Thénault, Thomas Hewitt, William Thaw, Raoul Lufbery, Alfred de Laage, Kenneth Marr, Edwin Parsons, and Edward Hinkle. (Washington and Lee University Archives)

move with the other escadrilles of Groupe de Combat 13 to a location 30 miles to the northeast. It was a recently abandoned German flying field on the western outskirts of Ham. Here, the men of the Lafayette Escadrille would encounter some of the most intense enemy opposition yet. It would test their endurance and courage, and it would exact yet more of their precious blood.

At about the same time the squadron departed Ravenel a very significant international development occurred that bolstered morale like nothing else could have. On April 6, 1917, the reluctant US government finally ended its strict 20-month neutrality posture and formally declared war on Germany. This meant that the American "mercenaries" of the Lafayette Escadrille were now flying and fighting for their own country, as well as France. Perhaps now, the question of their loyalty and their citizenship status would cease to be an issue. In time, they might even find themselves wearing the uniform of a US Air Service officer.

CHAPTER 10

THE HEARTBREAK OF HAM

"… a rendezvous with death"

On Saturday, April 7, 1917, the planes and pilots of the Lafayette Escadrille winged their way, in small groups, to their new airfield at Ham. Here, they were lucky enough to occupy an abandoned house near the flying field, but there was little time to unpack or otherwise settle into the new space. Wartime events were happening so fast that patrols continued uninterrupted. To complicate the men's transition to their new home, a German welcoming committee of marauding aircraft bombed the airfield only hours after their arrival and destroyed five hangars.

The squadron soon got some measure of revenge, however. On April 8, its rapidly rising ace, Raoul Lufbery, forced an enemy two-seater down east of St. Quentin. Like many of his victories, it went down too far behind enemy lines to be officially confirmed, but no one doubted the veracity of his claim. Meanwhile, the hard-working Lieutenant de Laage had even better luck. That afternoon, he downed an enemy Albatros D.III single-seater that fell in French lines, and an hour later, a two-seater, for his second and third confirmed kills. This rare double victory earned him a well-deserved Legion of Honor, which was officially awarded two weeks later. As tragic events would soon prove, this prestigious award came none too soon.

On April 13, Raoul Lufbery destroyed another enemy plane, a camouflaged two-seater northwest of Saint-Quentin. This one was confirmed—his eighth. His less successful fellow pilots continued to marvel at his skill and phenomenal success in the air. They knew painfully well just how difficult it was to shoot another airplane out of the sky *and* receive confirmation for it, yet he had now accomplished it not once, but eight times—and he was far from finished.

On the afternoon of April 15, a new pilot arrived at Ham to replace the fallen James McConnell. His presence brought the squadron roster back up to full strength—but only temporarily.

A typical scene with the Lafayette Escadrille at Ham. The men lived in a house adjacent to the flying field, possibly one of those visible in the background. It was here that the squadron first flew the Stars and Stripes. In the left foreground, Raoul Lufbery stands in flying gear, supervising the maintenance of a Spad VII. (Washington and Lee University Archives)

29. CAPORAL ANDREW COURTNEY CAMPBELL JR. was born on November 19, 1891, in Kenilworth, Illinois, to wealthy parents, Andrew and Cornelia Campbell. As a youth, he developed a reputation as a daredevil, by racing around in fast boats and cars. In 1910, he enrolled in the University of Virginia but dropped out to become a professional dancer. In June 1916, he sailed for France, and soon afterward, entered into aviation training. He reported to the Lafayette Escadrille at Ham on the afternoon of April 15, 1917. Though a skillful and fearless pilot, his devil-may-care attitude and cavalier approach to the very serious business of combat flying quickly earned him a reputation as a "wild man," to whom, according to Ted Parsons, "trouble gravitated as naturally as iron filings to a magnet." He would become a squadron legend for pulling off a seemingly impossible life-saving feat—as well as another so foolhardy that it drove a fellow pilot from the squadron. Not surprisingly, his days among the living were numbered.

Let the Funerals Begin

The eight weeks the men of the Lafayette Escadrille spent at Ham were hectic, reminiscent of its hard-fought days at Behonne in the Battle of Verdun. The weather had finally improved, so that patrols were near-daily occurrences. In addition, there was enough enemy presence to keep the pilots busy, not only countering their aircraft, but also dodging ground fire while flying low to observe troop movements. This environment afforded the squadron plenty of opportunity for success but it also greatly increased the danger.

A distressing event, occurring the day after the men arrived at Ham, set a somber tone that would remain for their entire time there. Early on the Easter Sunday morning of April 8, the pilots were lounging in their house next to the aerodrome, when their attention was drawn to a bizarre occurrence outside. As Ted Parsons later described it, they looked through their window to see a French Farman "flaming like a torch, appear like a ghost ship out of the mist and crash onto the field, burning its occupants to a crisp." They had no idea who it was, where it came from, or why it was on fire. It was not the first—or last—fatal crash to occur before their eyes on one of their aerodromes, but to the superstitious pilots of the Lafayette Escadrille, it was a bad omen. Upcoming events would bear that out.

Monday, April 16, 1917, would be yet another black letter day for the squadron. Young Edmond Genet was still suffering from his facial wound—and even more so from the emotional agony of McConnell's death, coupled with the loss of his beloved sweetheart and the stigma resulting from his desertion from the US Navy. Somewhat prophetically, he had written in his diary only 12 days earlier:

> Somehow I've given away completely this evening. I feel sure there is something very serious going to happen to me very soon. It doesn't seem any less than Death itself. I've never had such a feeling or been so saddened since coming over to battle for this glorious France.

All of the emotional baggage that 20-year-old Genet carried was apparent to his fellow pilots—and, at least as it appears now, should also have been to Capitaine Thénault. Yet, though Genet was tired, depressed, and sick in both body and spirit, he continued to fly relentlessly and—by his own admission—ever more dangerously. As he wrote his mother after McConnell's death, "I've already been told I was reckless in the air over the lines, but after this I vow I'll be more than reckless, come what may." Clearly, he needed a long rest, but it was not to be.

On April 16, Genet was scheduled to fly two missions. The first was a 7:00 a.m. morning patrol with Walter Lovell and Jerry Hewitt, which lasted an hour and 15 minutes. During this patrol, flown at low level because of the cloud cover, Genet became separated from the rest of his flight and came under heavy ground fire, one shell barely missing the tail of his Nieuport fighter. The constant evasive action he was forced to take made him violently airsick. After landing, he looked so worn out that his fellow pilots urged him to take a rest. That afternoon, Willis Haviland, whose airplane was temporarily inoperable, asked to borrow Genet's for a patrol he was scheduled to fly with Raoul Lufbery. Young Edmond—never a shirker and not particularly keen to allow others to fly his airplane—insisted he was feeling better and would fly the mission himself. Consequently, at 2:30 p.m., the two pilots lifted off and headed for the lines. Half an hour into the flight, Lufbery saw three enemy antiaircraft shells burst near Genet's fighter. Genet immediately turned toward friendly lines and Lufbery, seeing no apparent damage to Genet or his airplane, continued the patrol alone. However, soldiers on the ground saw Genet's machine eventually fall into a spiral that progressively tightened until a wing ripped loose and fluttered away. They watched in horror as his machine smashed headlong into the ground at full speed near the village of Clastres. It was not far from where James McConnell had fallen exactly four weeks earlier. Had Genet—probably still feeling ill—fainted, or had a shell fragment wounded him or disabled his airplane? No one knows, for the resulting crash was so devastating that no determination was possible. Both plane and pilot were completely obliterated. Some of the men who helped retrieve his body were appalled by the sight. Walter Lovell later wrote that he had never seen so complete a crash and Ted Parsons reported that Genet's plane had bored five feet deep into a hard-packed dirt road, with no piece of the wreck "bigger than a match." According to Parsons, "Every bone in his body was broken, and his features were completely gone."

Reminiscent of Rockwell and McConnell seemingly sensing their own impending death, Genet had made clear in his letters and diary his premonition that he too would soon die. After attending church in Ham on the day before his death, he had—for reasons known only to himself—walked all the way across town to visit the town cemetery. Did he somehow sense that he was about to occupy one of the newly dug graves he saw there?

Genet was buried in that cemetery with full military honors. In a letter he had left behind, he had written, "If I die, wrap me in the French flag, but place the two colors upon my grave to show that I died for two countries." Accordingly, his casket was draped with both the French Tricolor and the Stars and Stripes of the United States. He had the unenviable distinction of being the first American to die in combat after the United States entered the war.

Courageous, sincere, and passionately idealistic, the conflicted young warrior had, during his three months with the Lafayette Escadrille, gained the respect and affection of his fellow pilots—and he fulfilled his destiny by dying for the cause in which he so ardently believed. He would have been gratified to know that soon after his death, Secretary of the Navy Josephus Daniels officially cleared his name by declaring that, "the record of Edmond Genet, ordinary seaman, United States Navy, shall be considered in every respect an honorable one."

Unlucky Monday Strikes Again

Both McConnell and Genet had died on a Monday, and the pilots of the Lafayette Escadrille began to take notice. Like most men subjected to the utter randomness so characteristic of war, the pilots coped with their fears, in part, by indulging in superstitions. Each man had his own good luck charm he carried with him while flying—for example, a trinket or piece of intimate apparel given to him by a lady friend—and each came to believe that certain occurrences or actions brought either glad tidings or disaster. Now, it was Mondays they feared, and future events would further substantiate that feeling. Exactly one week after Genet's death, the Angel of Death paid yet another Monday visit to the squadron.

The burial of Edmond Genet at Ham. Genet died on April 16, 1917, after diving into the ground—for reasons still not clear—during a combat patrol. He was the first American killed in combat after the United States entered the war. As he had previously requested, he was buried under both French and US colors. The ceremony occurred on a dark, cloudy day, but at the conclusion of the final remarks, the sun broke through and, according to Ted Parsons, "pierced the clouds for an instant and illuminated the bier like a benediction from heaven." The civilian in the dark coat, standing between Lieutenant de Laage and William Thaw, is William's brother, Benjamin Thaw Jr. He was there representing the US Consulate. (Washington and Lee University Archives)

Young Ronald Hoskier had by now established himself as a dependable pilot and a good comrade who flew often and effectively. As such, he was liked and respected by his squadron mates. He was also apparently something of a tactician. Based on his experiences over his last four months with the squadron, he had developed the notion that a two-seat airplane, properly flown and manned, could outfight a single-seater. Though a two-seater was generally not as fast or maneuverable, its extra swivel-mounted gun with its wide arc of fire and the additional set of eyes provided by the gunner/observer gave it indisputable advantages. Hence, Hoskier had begun experimenting with the squadron's lone two-seat airplane, an old Morane-Saulnier parasol monoplane the pilots used for gunnery training and transport. When he flew it, he took along with him, as his gunner, Caporal Jean Dressy, a Frenchman assigned as Lieutenant de Laage's orderly. Dressy was, however, more than just an orderly to de Laage. He was also an old family friend and fellow Dragoon who had, during his fateful August 31, 1914, cavalry charge, rescued de Laage after he was wounded and knocked off of his horse.

On April 23, 1917, Hoskier and Dressy strapped themselves into the Morane and took off on a patrol. The old parasol was to have been retired from service after this mission. The formation in which they flew that day consisted of Harold Willis in the lead, followed by William Thaw and Willis Haviland, with Hoskier and Dressy bringing up the rear. At some point during the patrol, the slower Morane became separated in the clouds from the other three fighters. When it emerged, Hoskier and Dressy found themselves perfectly positioned above a lone enemy aircraft. Undoubtedly thanking their lucky stars at such good fortune, they dove on it to attack. As they did so, however, they were immediately ambushed by three Albatros D.III fighters that had been lurking in the distance. It was a classic trap the Germans employed throughout the war and Hoskier had fallen into it.

The two airmen fought valiantly against their adversaries, nearly proving Hoskier's pet theory about the superiority of two-seat fighting aircraft. In the end, however, they ran out of ammunition and luck at about the same time: Hoskier was struck in the head by a bullet, and the inherently unstable Morane—now with a dead man at the controls—entered into a death spiral. The doomed Dressy could do nothing other than watch in horror as he plummeted 8,000 feet downward to his death. Eventually, the parasol's wing collapsed, and the fuselage—now, a two-man projectile—dove at terminal velocity into a field on the side of Hill 62, just inside French lines east of the town of Grugies. The German airman credited with their destruction was Jasta 20 pilot, Leutnant der Reserve Wilhelm Schunke. It was Schunke's first victory, and it would be his last: a month later, he too would die in combat.

Late that night, Ted Parsons, Dudley Hill, and Robert Rockwell traveled up to the lines to retrieve the crushed bodies of their two fallen comrades. After returning, they placed the remains into pine coffins at a small mortuary in Ham. They were to be buried in the same cemetery where Hoskier's friend, Edmond Genet, had been interred a week earlier. Attending the funeral were Hoskier's parents, Herman and Harriet, both of whom were working and living in France. Before the burial, Parsons accompanied Herman to the chapel to view Ronald's closed casket. As Parsons described it, they stood there, alone and in sadness, for a few minutes before turning to leave. When they did, a "weird and inexplicable" incident occurred:

> For almost three days, Ron's cold, stiffened, battered body had lain untouched in the pine coffin supported on trestles. As we started to go out, I heard a faint sound and, turning back, saw a steady stream of blood dripping slowly from one corner of the plain box, each drop echoing with a hollow noise as it struck the uncarpeted cement floor. It gave me a cold shock, for it seemed as if it were a sign from the dead to the living loved ones.

After the war, the bodies of the gallant Hoskier and Genet were moved to an American cemetery, and in 1928, to a place of honor beneath the Lafayette Escadrille Memorial, where they rest today.

Another Tragic Rendezvous

The painful losses the Lafayette Escadrille had recently suffered did nothing to slow down the war. Flying and fighting was as intense and deadly as ever, but with the

The beginning of the dual funeral procession for Hoskier and Dressy at Ham. This sad reenactment of the scene that had occurred only a few days earlier with Edmond Genet must have given those in this photograph a distinct feeling of déjà vu. Unfortunately, they were destined to relive it yet again a few days later. (Washington and Lee University Archives)

Hoskier and Dressy's burial ceremony in the cemetery at Ham. Capitaine Thénault and Lieutenant de Laage are standing near the caskets, next to the padre, while Hoskier's father Herman is standing, hat in hand, on the right, near the far end of the open grave. Ronald's mother is also present but hidden behind her husband. Several other pilots of the Lafayette Escadrille also appear in this photograph. The valiant de Laage, who grieved every loss, was particularly devastated by the death of his faithful orderly and lifelong friend, Dressy. (Washington and Lee University Archives)

casualties came some successes. On April 24, 1917, the day after Hoskier and Dressy fell, the unrelenting Raoul Lufbery obtained some measure of revenge by downing his ninth confirmed enemy airplane east of the village of Cerizy. Two days later, Chouteau Johnson finally got—after nearly a year of continuous service in the squadron—his first confirmed aerial victory. That same day, Bill Thaw and Willis Haviland teamed up to claim yet another.

The escadrille's mounting successes did not go unnoticed. In part, due to their recent successes, Johnson and Willis were promoted to the rank of adjudant and Thaw received yet another citation. In addition, the French Aero Club honored several of the men from the squadron—in particular, Raoul Lufbery, who became the first American to receive their Gold Medal—at an awards ceremony in Paris. Luf was still waiting for his long-overdue promotion to sous-lieutenant, but his September 16, 1916, encounter with the train station official at Chartres continued to haunt him. Fortunately, he would not have to wait much longer.

The recent losses had another effect, besides spurring the remaining pilots of the Lafayette Escadrille on to greater success: it created a need for more replacement pilots.

30. CAPORAL RAY CLAFLIN BRIDGMAN became, on May 12, 1917, the 30th American to fly for the Lafayette Escadrille. He was born in Lake Forest, Illinois, on May 31, 1895, to Walter and Leoline Bridgman. In spring 1916, near the end of his junior year at Yale, Bridgman abruptly quit school and sailed for France. Though a dedicated pacifist who hated war and all it stood for, he decided to enlist in aviation. After completing flight school, he flew briefly for Escadrille N.49 before reporting to the Lafayette Escadrille at Ham on May 1, 1917. Because of his strict moral convictions, he found it difficult to fit in with this diverse group of rough-and-tumble combat pilots. Still, he managed to earn their respect with his courage and aggressive spirit in the air.

31. CAPORAL CHARLES HEAVE "CARL" DOLAN JR. was born on January 29, 1895, in Boston, Massachusetts, to Charles and Anne Dolan. He studied electrical engineering for a year before traveling to Europe in 1914. He was employed first in England as an aircraft magneto inspector before moving to Paris to work for the Sperry Gyroscope Company. While there, he became acquainted with members of the Lafayette Escadrille. In August 1916, he quit his job and entered flight training—like every other American, via the Foreign Legion. He joined the Lafayette Escadrille at Ham on May 12, 1917.

32. CAPORAL JOHN ARMSTRONG DREXEL was born in Philadelphia on October 24, 1891, to wealthy parents Anthony and Margarita Drexel. He was attending the prestigious English public school, Eton, when he became fascinated with aviation. He learned to fly from British aviation pioneer, Claude Grahame-White in 1909, and soon became the eighth pilot—just behind Glenn Curtiss and the Wright Brothers—to earn a flying certificate from the Aero Club of America. Flying a Blériot, Drexel went on to set

Charles Heave "Carl" Dolan, Jr. was working for the Sperry Gyroscope Company in Paris when he decided to join the Aéronautique Militaire. He reported to the Lafayette Escadrille at Ham on May 12, 1917. (Washington and Lee University Archives)

a series of world altitude records. In 1916, he joined the French Air Service and was officially assigned to the Lafayette Escadrille on May 12, 1917. He flew his first patrol two days later and continued to fly for the next month before leaving the squadron.

33. CAPORAL HENRY SWEET "HANK" JONES reported to the Lafayette Escadrille on May 12, 1917, the same day as Dolan and Drexel. He was born on June 6, 1892, in Harford, Pennsylvania, to Edward and Hattie Jones. He briefly attended Lehigh University before traveling to France in 1916 and joining the American Ambulance Field Service. After serving for several months, he applied to aviation and began training on November 28, 1916. He would serve with distinction in both the Lafayette Escadrille, and its US Air Service successor, the 103rd Aero Squadron.

The Lafayette Escadrille's days at Ham had already been unlucky, claiming the lives of three men. However, as the squadron's time there neared the end, its pilots began to think they might escape Ham without further tragedy. Unfortunately, they were wrong. On May 23, 1917, the universally beloved Lieutenant Alfred de Laage—the courageous and aggressive fighter, mentor, and inspirational leader—died the worst way possible for a combat pilot: in an accident.

Henry Sweet "Hank" Jones poses at Senard on the wing of Capitaine Thénault's Spad VII S.1417, bearing Thénault's butterfly insignia. Jones reported to the Lafayette Escadrille with Carl Dolan and John Drexel on May 12, 1917. (Washington and Lee University Archives)

Late that day, he took off in a new Spad VII for a test flight. He held the airplane on the deck, building up speed, and then abruptly pulled up into a chandelle. This steep climbing turn is a beautiful maneuver to watch from the ground, but this time something went wrong. The fighter's new high-compression Hispano-Suiza engine sputtered just as he began his climb. Pointing almost straight up with no power, altitude, or airspeed, he had no chance to recover. The heavy, thin-winged Spad fighter fell—as if pushed off the top of a 250-foot skyscraper—and crumpled straight into the ground. De Laage was instantly killed.

The loss of this respected, admired, and beloved veteran of so many deadly combats— right before his pilots' eyes—distressed them and rattled their confidence like nothing else could have. If a superman like de Laage could not survive, what chance did they have? The Lieutenant's last written words were simple but eloquent:

> Since the formation of the American Escadrille, I have tried to exalt the beauty of the idea which brought my American comrades to fight for France. I thank them for the friendship and confidence they always showed me. If I die, do not weep for me. It is not good that a soldier should let himself give way to sorrow; and now, Vive la France!

The feelings the men of the Lafayette Escadrille had for de Laage cannot be exaggerated. Ted Parsons spoke for one and all when he wrote, "With him went the soul of the Escadrille, for no truer, finer gentleman ever existed, and his friendship was more precious than almost any other gift that life had to offer." The loss of this fine officer left a void in the squadron that needed to be filled, so no time was wasted in replacing him.

LIEUTENANT ANTOINE ARNOUX DE MAISON-ROUGE reported on May 28, 1917. Born on December 24, 1892, he had—like his predecessor de Laage—started his military career as a cavalry officer before transferring into aviation in 1915. The son of a distinguished French general, Maison-Rouge was a highly competent pilot and professional officer, but he had very big shoes to fill. It would have been virtually impossible for anyone to adequately replace the fallen de Laage, so Maison-Rouge had his work cut out for him.

★ ★ ★

After the rapid-fire loss of McConnell, Genet, Hoskier and Dressy, and now de Laage, the men of the Lafayette Escadrille were in an understandably somber mood. In their grief and their concern for their own future, they might have remembered a recently published poem that was popular at the time and that would become a literary classic. Alan Seeger, a brilliant young American serving in the French Foreign Legion—and an acquaintance of several of the men in the squadron—had written *I Have a Rendezvous with Death* shortly before his own July 4, 1916, demise in the Battle of the Somme. After this latest tragedy, every pilot in the squadron may rightfully have felt that his own "rendezvous with death" was just around the corner.

However, there was little time to reflect on such matters. A new assignment was once again in the making. Ham had been a place of tragedy and, as far as the men were concerned, anywhere else would be better. That anywhere else was a large open field some 30 miles to the southeast. Chaudun aerodrome was located a mile and a half southwest of the village of the same name and five miles southwest of Soissons. Here, near the Chemin des Dames area of the Aisne Sector, the men of the Lafayette Escadrille hoped for better days.

CHAPTER II

CHAUDUN AND BEYOND

"Luck Be a Lady"

As evidenced by the "Monday hex" which plagued the men of the Lafayette Escadrille, the topic of "luck" was a recurring theme in it and many other World War I flying squadrons. These young American pilots, like most other combat airmen, considered luck—they might have called it chance, fate, or the grace of God—to be an important factor in their day-to-day lives. This is not surprising, given the many perils to which they were exposed that were completely beyond their control. To them, luck was a fickle lady that sometimes smiled on them, and other times, not. During their time at Chaudun, they would see their fair share of both her good and bad side.

The pilots of the Lafayette Escadrille made their way to the new location on June 3, 1917, with few problems—in spite of this particular aerodrome's confusing assortment of names. The Americans called it Chaudun, after the closest town, while the French referred to it as "Maison-Neuve"—the farm on which it was located. The Germans, on the other hand, called it "Beaurepaire," after the cluster of farm buildings that sat on the adjacent farm. All three names referred to the same flying field.

The large, smooth, rolling field of grass was an ideal place from which to fly, except for one hazard: a deep drainage ditch at the far border. All the pilots had been made aware of this obstacle and were easily able to avoid it, except for one particular pilot. On the day of the move from Ham to Chaudun, Jerry Hewitt did a low, slow flyby of the field in order to locate the offending ditch. He then proceeded to land and roll directly into it, almost as if had been aiming for it. His overturned Spad was a write-off. An angry Capitaine Thénault punished Hewitt by sending him back to Ham in an automobile—a long, arduous journey over shell-torn roads—to bring another airplane back. When Hewitt finally returned, he once again landed—and once again rolled into the ditch at almost the same place as before. The luckless—and hapless—Hewitt, who had by now acquired the disparaging nickname "Useless," would continue his mostly ineffective service with the squadron for a few weeks longer before Thénault lost patience with him and cut him from the roster. His last recorded combat mission was on August 5, 1917, and on September 17, he was sent to the rear.

The Lufbery Phenomenon

Escadrille N.124, soon to be re-designated SPA.124 because it now had more Spad VIIs than Nieuports, would spend the next six weeks at Chaudun. During this time, pilots of the Lafayette Escadrille would take advantage of the long summer days and good weather by flying some 400 sorties of all types: escorting reconnaissance and bombing aircraft, attacking enemy observation planes and enemy troops, and occasionally flying reconnaissance missions themselves.

On June 12, Raoul Lufbery became a "double ace" by achieving his 10th confirmed victory, a German two-seater he picked out of a formation and sent down in pieces. This earned him a sixth palm to his Croix de Guerre, and yet another citation—this one describing him as a "marvelous fighter pilot" and "living example of audacity, coolness, and dedication." More importantly, it paved the way for his belated promotion nine days later to sous-lieutenant. His phenomenal success in the air had finally overcome his career-retarding encounter with the station attendant at Chartres. He and William Thaw were destined to be the only Americans ever to fly with the Lafayette Escadrille as commissioned officers.

The skillful Lafayette ace was making the fine art of shooting down enemy planes look easy; however, it was anything but. Although a certain measure of luck was always a necessary ingredient, Luf minimized the need for it by laboring diligently for each of his victories. He spent hours on the ground maintaining his airplane to keep it in top shape. He even measured and polished each machine gun round to minimize victory-killing jams. Otherwise, he practically lived in the air, methodically stalking his prey like a big game hunter. As with most of the successful aces of this war, he made his move only when he was perfectly positioned for a lightning-quick surprise attack and an equally quick diving escape.

However, even with this systematic—almost scientific—approach, coupled with his superb eyesight, quick reflexes, and brilliant flying and shooting skills, Lufbery failed to score in at least a dozen attacks for each time he succeeded in bringing down an enemy plane. Air combat was an ultra-challenging endeavor that might be compared, in baseball terms, to hitting a 90-mile-per-hour fastball. Just as the great Babe Ruth hit a homerun only once in every 12 times at bat, even the highest-ranking aces in World War I failed far more often than they succeeded. Perhaps their biggest distinction from less successful pilots was that they possessed the confidence and drive to keep trying until they found the right combination—or until they were, themselves, killed.

The stringent requirements for confirming victories made running up victory scores even more difficult. Most aces never received official credit for many of the aircraft they

A dapper Edwin C. "Ted" Parsons posing with his medals. Like several other of his squadron mates, he learned to fly before the war. He achieved one confirmed kill with the Lafayette Escadrille and would later score seven more while serving with French Escadrille SPA.3. *(Washington and Lee University Archives)*

Ted Parsons' uniform and medals are displayed at the Smithsonian National Air and Space Museum's Steven F. Udvar-Hazy Center. The medals, displayed below, are (l–r) the Legion of Honor, Médaille militaire, French Croix de Guerre with eight palms, Belgium Croix de Guerre, and the Belgian Order of Leopold. *(Smithsonian National Air and Space Museum, Steven A. Ruffin)*

Above: An iconic shot of the men of the Lafayette Escadrille as they prepare to take off on a mission. Conferring in the foreground, from left to right: Walter Lovell, Edmond Genet, Raoul Lufbery, and James McConnell. This photo was taken at Ravenel in early March 1917, only days before McConnell's death. Pictured right is McConnell's hat—a little worse for wear—as displayed at the University of Virginia. *(Smithsonian National Air and Space Museum; Steve Miller)*

Right: A surviving example of a Lafayette Escadrille Sioux Indianhead insignia, taken from Spad VII S.1227 that was wrecked by Harold Willis at Ham on May 21, 1917. It now resides at the American Friends of Blérancourt Museum. Note the fierce visage and the brilliant red, white, and blue colors representative of both the United States and France. Willis and Edward Hinkle designed the image so as to be visible in the air from a great distance. *(Art Resource)*

Within months of McConnell's death, French soldiers built a more elaborate memorial for the fallen aviator, as seen here. His machine gun remained at the site. *(Washington and Lee University Archives)*

Top right: Friends of the fallen James McConnell congregate outside the American Cathedral of the Holy Trinity in Paris, following his memorial service on April 2, 1917. Edmond Genet, Chouteau Johnson, and Robert Soubiran were the only Lafayette Escadrille pilots able to attend. Pictured from left to right are Robert Donze and Granville Pollock (both American pilots assigned to other French squadrons), Fred Prince, Paul Rockwell, Chouteau Johnson, and Robert Soubiran. Partially visible at the far right is Didier Masson. Prince and Masson were, at this time, no longer with N.124. Genet later complained that the service "was too long and badly arranged." He also took exception to the "vast array of American Ambulance Corps fellows" that filled the church, writing that they were "entirely too much of an eyesore for us all."

Bottom right: The same scene, as it recently appeared. (Steven A. Ruffin)

Above: The James McConnell crash site and marker as it appears today at Petit-Détroit, one mile south of Flavy-le-Martel (Aisne), France. A local French woman planted these flowers in 1917, vowing they would never die. A hundred years later, they still thrive, thanks to the efforts of local French citizens who still remember McConnell's contributions. His body was transferred to the Lafayette Escadrille Memorial in 1928. *(Steven A. Ruffin)*

Below: Artifacts from the James McConnell crash site, as displayed at the University of Virginia. At left, a piece of shrapnel from his plane and a button from his uniform, and on the right, a strip of fabric removed from his aluminum-painted Nieuport 17 by a French soldier after it crashed on the outskirts of Petit-Détroit. *(Steve Miller)*

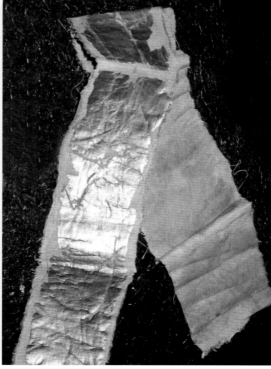

Another significant monument to James McConnell is "The Aviator," which stands on the campus of his alma mater, the University of Virginia at Charlottesville. Inscribed at the statue's base is the phrase, "Soaring like an eagle into new heavens of valor and devotion". The University established this memorial soon after McConnell's death; the sculptor was a then relatively unknown Gutzon Borglum, who would later gain fame as the creator of the presidential faces on Mt. Rushmore. *(Steven A. Ruffin)*

Above: Mishaps in the squadron continued to be an almost–daily event. Here Nieuport 17 N.2297 "ECP", formerly flown by Edwin C. Parsons, lies on its back on the railway embankment at the northern edge of the aerodrome at Ham. On April 8, 1917, Ken Marr had engine problems and overshot the field while trying to land. This may have been that accident. *(Washington and Lee University Archives)*

Below: The scene of the mishap revisited nearly a century later. *(Steven A. Ruffin)*

Above: The devastating crash of Ronald Wood Hoskier and Jean Dressy. The two were shot down on April 23, 1917, during a vicious dogfight with three German fighters. They were flying the obsolete Morane parasol MS.1112, trying to prove the superiority of a two-seater. The translated inscription on the cross reads, "Here Sergeant-Pilot Ronald Hoskier and Machine Gunner Jean Dressy fell on 23-4-16, Lafayette Escadrille. Died for France." In the top photo, looking on with unidentified French personnel are Robert Soubiran (second from the left) and Edward Hinkle (wearing the beret). *(US Air Force)*

Below: The field just east of Grugies, where Hoskier and Dressy crashed, as it appeared recently. The point of impact was near the center of the photograph. The rise in the distance was called Hill 62. *(Steven A. Ruffin)*

Herman and Harriet Hoskier outside of the cemetery in Ham, following the burial of their son, Ronald. They are talking with William Thaw (partially hidden), as Capitaine Thénault (just to the left of Thaw) looks on. Below, we see the same scene nearly a century later. *(Washington and Lee University Archives; Steven A. Ruffin)*

IN REVERENT MEMORY
OF
RONALD WOOD HOSKIER,
BORN 21 MARCH 1896. FELL 23 APRIL 1917
IN THE GLORY OF HIS YOUNG MANHOOD, BEFORE S⸀ QUENTIN
IN DEFENCE OF RIGHT AND LIBERTY.
HE WAS THE SECOND AMERICAN AVIATOR WHO GAVE HIS LIFE
AFTER THE U.S. ENTERED THE WORLD-WAR.
A VOLUNTEER, ABANDONING HIS COLLEGE COURSES AT HARVARD EARLY IN
1916, HE TRAINED IN FRANCE AND AFTER 5 MONTHS AT THE FRONT WITH THE
ESCADRILLE LAFAYETTE (WHERE HE GREATLY DISTINGUISHED HIMSELF) HE FELL
IN GLORIOUS BUT UNEVEN COMBAT AGAINST THREE ENEMY AEROPLANES.

IN THE WAY OF RIGHTEOUSNESS IS LIFE; AND IN THE PATHWAY THEREOF
THERE IS NO DEATH." PROV. XII. 28.

THIS TABLET WAS ERECTED BY THE MEMBERS OF SECTION SANITAIRE AUTOMOBILE
AMERICAINE N⸀ XI, OF WHICH HIS FATHER WAS LEADER.

Above left: After the war, this monument, honoring the memory of Ronald Hoskier and Jean Dressy, was placed at the crash site, just outside of Grugies. However, the owner of the land grew tired of plowing around it and threw it down a dry well. The townspeople of Grugies eventually retrieved it and placed it in their cemetery, where it can be seen today. Its inscription translates to, "Here on the afternoon of April 23, 1917, after a hard fight against three enemy aircraft, Sergent Ronald Wood Hoskier, aged 21, American volunteer pilot of the Lafayette Escadrille, fell with his gunner, French Adjudant [sic] Jean Dressy, aged 28." *(Steven A. Ruffin)*

Above right: This brass etching, honoring Ronald Hoskier, hangs inside the American Cathedral in Paris. *(Steven A. Ruffin)*

Below: A view from the rear of Lieutenant de Laage's funeral procession marching through the town square of Ham. The statue of Général Foy still overlooks the scene today. *(Washington and Lee University Archives; Marc Roussel)*

Above: A front view of the funeral procession through Ham for Lieutenant de Laage. *(Washington and Lee University Archives)*

Below: The same street in Ham, as photographed in 2014. *(Steven A. Ruffin)*

One of the most famous of all the Lafayette Escadrille fighters, Spad VII S.1777, at Chaudun, with Didier Masson at the controls. Records indicate that 10 different pilots flew this much-photographed airplane a total of 89 patrols during its exceptionally long operational period of June 28 to December 19, 1917. However, only Raoul Lufbery engaged in combat in it—nine times, during the course of which, he downed two of his last three enemy aircraft. The airplane's fabric was clear-doped and varnished to give it the typical light yellow appearance, while the swastika emblem—later made infamous by the Nazis—was, in 1917, nothing more than a good-luck symbol. *(Washington and Lee University Archives)*

Above: On July 4, 1917, Capitaine Thénault granted his pilots 48-hour leave to celebrate American Independence Day in Paris. While there, some of them gathered to pose for a photograph on one of the historic cannons near the north front of the Hôtel des Invalides. From left to right, Robert Rockwell, Chouteau Johnson, Dudley Hill, Edgar J. Bouligny, Didier Masson, William Thaw, Raoul Lufbery, Robert Soubiran, and Paul Rockwell. Bouligny had been among the first Americans to join the Foreign Legion in August 1914 and was the first American wounded in the service of France. At the time this picture was taken, he had only recently transferred to the Aéronautique Militaire. *(Washington and Lee University Archives)*

Below: The same scene outside the Hôtel des Invalides, as it appeared in 2014. *(Steven A. Ruffin)*

Above: Another spontaneous July 4, 1917, gathering of Americans in Paris occurred at Place des États-Unis, near the statue of Lafayette and Washington. Most of the men pictured here—including Andrew Walbron, standing at center—were Legionnaires. The three fliers were Frederick Zinn (standing far left) and Raoul Lufbery and Willis Haviland (sitting on either side of Paul Rockwell). *(Washington and Lee University Archives)*

Below: Raoul Lufbery roughhousing with his beloved "Whiskey-man." Luf had a special relationship with Whiskey, probably because he spent more time with the gentle lion cub than anyone else in the squadron. On June 12, 1917, Lufbery became a "double ace" when he downed his tenth German airplane. The other pilots liked and admired the enigmatic ace, but none could say they really knew him. *(Washington and Lee University Archives)*

A striking artistic rendering of Raoul Lufbery in flying helmet, by famed French World War I pilot and aviation artist Henri Farré. *(National Archives)*

Above: The aerodrome at Senard, as it appeared during World War I, and the same scene today. Only a solitary bird flies through the airspace once occupied by the Spads of the Lafayette Escadrille. Both photographs were taken looking south-southwest from D151, which leads into the town from the east. *(Steven A. Ruffin)*

Below: Major Raoul Lufbery smiling as he poses with a Nieuport 28 fighter on April 18, 1918. Lufbery left the Lafayette Escadrille with 16 confirmed victories on January 5, 1918, to accept a commission with the US Air Service. After several weeks of flying a desk, he eventually made his way back into combat with the 94th Aero Squadron. *(US Air Force)*

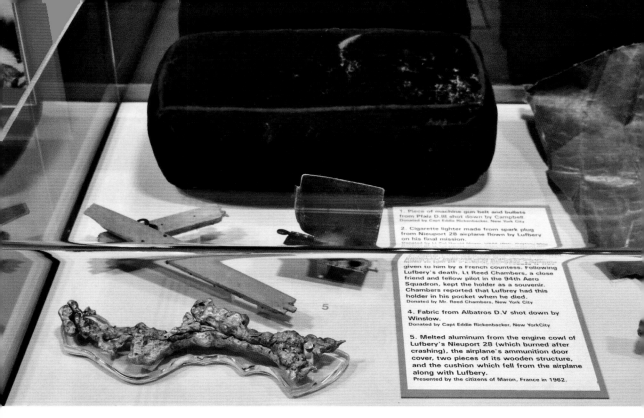

1. Piece of machine gun belt and bullets from Pfalz D.III shot down by Campbell.
Donated by Capt Eddie Rickenbacker, New York City

2. Cigarette lighter made from spark plug from Nieuport 28 airplane flown by Lufbery on his final mission.
Donated by Lt Col Harold Meun, USAF (Ret), Dayton, Ohio

3. [...] given to him by a French countess. Following Lufbery's death, Lt Reed Chambers, a close friend and fellow pilot in the 94th Aero Squadron, kept the holder as a souvenir. Chambers reported that Lufbery had this holder in his pocket when he died.
Donated by Mr. Reed Chambers, New York City

4. Fabric from Albatros D.V shot down by Winslow.
Donated by Capt Eddie Rickenbacker, New York City

5. Melted aluminum from the engine cowl of Lufbery's Nieuport 28 (which burned after crashing), the airplane's ammunition door cover, two pieces of its wooden structure, and the cushion which fell from the airplane along with Lufbery.
Presented by the citizens of Maron, France in 1962.

Above: Artifacts from Raoul Lufbery's last flight of May 19, 1918, as displayed at the National Museum of the US Air Force. In the top photo: a cushion of some sort that fell with Luf from his Nieuport 28; the plane's ammunition door cover; part of his plane's wooden structure; and a piece of melted aluminum cowl taken from his plane after it crashed and burned. *(Steven A. Ruffin)*

Left: The picket fence on which Raoul Lufbery fell after he exited his Nieuport 28 fighter on May 19, 1918. Lufbery fell just behind the building seen here at the left of the color photo. He died on, or very soon after, impact. It will never be known, conclusively, why he fell from his Nieuport 28 fighter. The Moselle River lies straight ahead, just behind the nearest line of trees. The view here is toward the southwest. *(Washington and Lee University Archives; Steven A. Ruffin)*

It was behind the house on the far right in the photograph above—41 Rue de Toul, Maron—that Raoul Lufbery fell. Soon afterward, the small marker seen on the right was placed, in honor of the great ace. The bronze plaque on the marker was later moved to a war memorial at the town center, in front of the church, where it is today. Lufbery's Nieuport continued on after he exited it, and crashed on the distant hillside.
Below: The same view in 2014. *(US Air Force; Steven A. Ruffin)*

Above: Raoul Lufbery's body lying in repose with an honor guard at the Red Cross Evacuation Hospital at Toul, May 20, 1918. *(US Air Force)*

Below: The bronze plaque previously displayed at 41 Rue de Toul was moved to the war monument at the town center of Maron. It was in need of polishing when this photo was taken. *(Steven A. Ruffin)*

Jerry Hewitt's life continued to decline after leaving the Lafayette Escadrille. Even with a law degree, he was unable to avoid serving prison time for a long list of white collar offenses. He died alone and penniless in a cheap Washington, DC, hotel room, with no one to claim his body. It was only through the efforts of a group of concerned citizens that the way was finally cleared for his burial at Arlington National Cemetery. His marker is located in Section 18, Grave 5652. *(Washington and Lee University Archives; Steve Miller)*

Chris Ford flew for the US Air Service 103rd and 213th Aero Squadrons after leaving the Lafayette Escadrille. He was credited with three official victories before being brought down by ground fire on October 15, 1918, and taken prisoner. In the 1919 photo on the right, taken shortly after he returned to the United States, he is wearing the insignia of a major. Below, we see the identity card Captain Christopher Ford carried while serving with the US Air Service in France. *(US Air Force)*

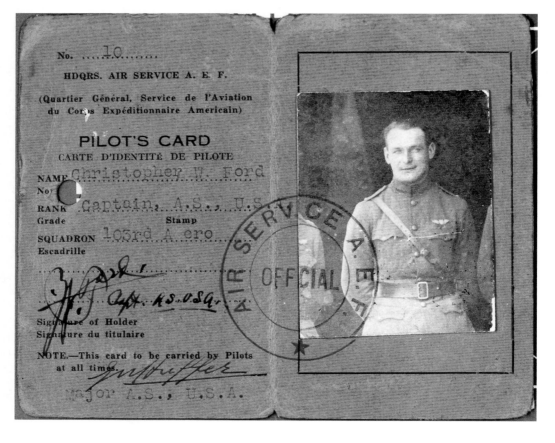

Right: Major William Thaw, US Air Service. At the time this photograph was taken, he was the commander of the 3rd Pursuit Group. *(US Air Force)*

Below: *4 Down for Thaw* depicts a December 3, 1917, dogfight in which Lt. William Thaw claimed a German Rumpler C two-seat observation plane. It was Thaw's fourth claim of the war—made on his second of four patrols he flew that day. He was flying one of the squadron's new Spad XIIIs. These bigger, heavier, and more powerful fighters, equipped with two machine guns, had begun arriving at Chaudun in early October, 1917, replacing the seven Spads that were destroyed in the bombing raid at Senard. *(Russell Smith)*

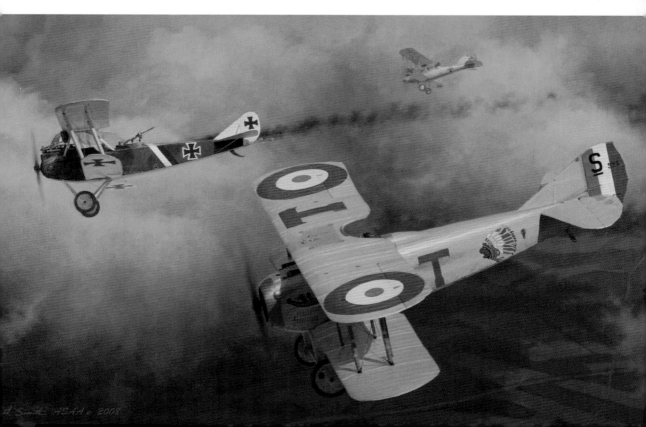

A Henri Farré depiction of Thaw. *(US Air Force)*

Above: Edwin C. Parsons and an unidentified officer lighting the flame of France's Tomb of the Unknown Soldier, as Georges Thénault looks on. This photograph was taken on July 4, 1928, the same day the Lafayette Escadrille Memorial was dedicated at Marnes-la–Coquette. *(Washington and Lee University Archives)*

Below: The same scene in 2014, far more striking in full color. As evident here, the flame still burns. This sacred monument is located in the heart of Paris at the base of the Arc de Triomphe. *(Steven A. Ruffin)*

Above: The dedication of the Lafayette Escadrille Memorial at Marnes-la-Coquette, France, on July 4, 1928. *(Washington and Lee University Archives)*

Below: The same view of the Memorial in 2014. Though in need of extensive renovation, it retains its original splendor. *(Steven A. Ruffin)*

Above: The walls of the monument are literally covered with names, places, and symbolic references to the young Americans who flew and fought for France in World War I. *(Steven A. Ruffin)*

Right: Even today, the sight, as one approaches the front of the monument, is nothing less than spectacular. *(Steven A. Ruffin)*

Bottom right: Even after eight-plus decades of wear and exposure, this mosaic located on the floor of the monument is still striking. The planners of the memorial seemed confused as to whom the monument was intended to honor. Its very name and its images, like the one pictured here, implied that it specifically commemorated the Lafayette Escadrille. However, the identities of those lying in the crypt and of those whose names are carved into the sides of the monument demonstrated that it was actually meant to honor all the Americans who had flown for France. This mixed message caused some misunderstanding and resentment among the surviving pilots. *(Steven A. Ruffin)*

Above: A confusing aspect of the Lafayette Escadrille Memorial lies in the contents of its crypt. In spite of the names inscribed on the 68 sarcophaguses, only 49 are actually occupied. For example, all four of those pictured here are empty. Victor Chapman's body was never positively identified, so it lies elsewhere; Dennis Dowd is buried in an unmarked grave in the cemetery of Saint Germain-en-Laye; Kiffin Rockwell's remains are in Luxeuil; and Norman Prince's body rests in the United States. *(Steve Miller)*

Below: Norman Prince's sarcophagus at the National Cathedral in Washington, D.C. After the war, his body was moved from Luxeuil to the American Cathedral in Paris. However, in April 1929 Prince's father refused to allow his son's body to join those of his fallen comrades in the crypt of the newly built Lafayette Escadrille Memorial, despite the wishes of the surviving members. *(Steve Miller)*

Above: A memorial tablet commemorating the formation of the Lafayette Escadrille was presented to the city of Luxeuil-les-Bains and displayed at the Hôtel de Ville on June 19, 1932. *(Washington and Lee University Archives)*

Below: The original plaque was later replaced by these stone tablets, seen here in 2014. *(Steven A. Ruffin)*

Another impressive monument in France to the Americans who fought under her colors during World War I is this memorial to the American volunteers. Located in Paris at Place des États-Unis, it was dedicated on July 4, 1923. The soldier standing at the top was patterned after American Legionnaire Alan Seeger, who was killed on July 4, 1916. Inscribed on the back of the monument are the names of Americans who died for France in World War I. *(Steven A. Ruffin)*

Above: French and American citizens pay homage to all the men of the Lafayette Flying Corps during a Memorial Day ceremony on May 23, 2009, as a missing-man formation of US Air Force F-16 Fighting Falcons flies overhead. The Lafayette Escadrille Memorial has remained an important symbol of Franco–American cooperation and friendship. *(US Air Force, Master Sergeant Scott Wagers)*

Below: A US Air Force color guard presents the flags of the United States and France during a Memorial Day ceremony on May 26, 2012, at the Lafayette Escadrille Memorial. *(US Air Force, Tech. Sergeant Markus M. Maier)*

Above: An important part of the Lafayette Escadrille's legacy is the squadron of the same name perpetuated by the French Air Force ever since its American pilots transferred to the US Air Service on February 18, 1918. Pictured here is a World War II-era Curtiss P-40 Warhawk belonging to the French Lafayette Escadrille. The squadron's chaplain stands in front of the airplane, greeting two US Army Air Forces officers. Note the Sioux Indianhead painted on the fuselage. *(Library of Congress)*

Below: This French Mirage 2000N, bearing the iconic Sioux Indianhead insignia, is a direct descendant of the Lafayette Escadrille. Today, Escadron de chasse 2/4 La Fayette, is based at Base aérienne 125 Istres-Le-Tubé, France. Researcher and author Alain Vezin has traced the lineage of the squadron in his *Escadron de chasse La Fayette, 1916–2011: Du Nieuport au Mirage 2000N. (Alain Vezin)*

Raoul Lufbery beside a Spad VII, looking every bit the highly decorated ace that he was. With 10 confirmed kills as of June 12, 1917, there seemed to be no stopping him. (Library of Congress)

legitimately brought down. For example, most of Lufbery's contemporaries agreed that he had far more victories than the number with which he was officially credited. For every claim, one or more independent witnesses on the ground or in the air had to see the aircraft go down in flames, break up in the air, or crash; otherwise, credit could not be granted; and if a different pilot operating in the area also put in a claim, as sometimes happened, credit could wrongly be assigned to him.

Clearly, Raoul Lufbery's success was a phenomenon that only a tiny fraction of even the most outstanding pilots in World War I were able to achieve, and as time passed, he was getting more deadly. He was also becoming more famous. Like most of the aces of World War I, his visage routinely appeared in newspapers and magazines, along with accounts of his latest successes. Newsmen hounded him and beautiful women shamelessly threw themselves at him wherever he went, hoping to be seen with the great American ace. Parents named their babies, and chefs their newest culinary creation, after him, and he drove a sleek sports car that the Hispano-Suizo company provided him for free. It was extremely difficult to become a World War I ace, but for those few who succeeded, it paid handsome benefits.

More Tragedy on the Aerodrome

On the same day that Luf was blasting his 10th enemy plane out of the sky, "Pop" Hinkle left the squadron to report to the hospital with pneumonia. He had, in spite of his advanced age, flown with the squadron for more than three months and established a solid flying and fighting record.

Three days later, on June 15, 1917, the men of the Lafayette Escadrille were witness to another tragic crash occurring out on the field before their eyes. Herman "Lincoln" Chatkoff, an American who had been employed washing automobiles in Paris before the war, had served in the Foreign Legion before entering into aviation. After completing training, he was assigned to a French Caudron squadron, Escadrille C.11, based near SPA.124. On this day, he had flown over to Chaudun with a passenger, a young American ambulance driver named Benjamin Woodworth, to visit his comrades in the Lafayette Escadrille.

During lunch, Chatkoff was the butt of a fair amount of good-natured ribbing about the slow, clumsy "truck" that he flew. Feeling slightly insulted, he decided to show the hotshot Lafayette fighter jocks what he could do. He took off in his big, twin-engine Caudron and proceeded to attempt a series of low-level aerobatics over the field—maneuvers this lumbering observation and bombing machine was never designed to do. The men on the ground watched in horror as the inevitable occurred: the big plane stalled and plunged into the ground, from an altitude of 200 feet. Woodworth was killed instantly, his skull crushed and body cut in half. Chatkoff was barely alive but horribly injured with multiple fractures of the skull and legs and massive internal injuries. He would eventually survive but never fly or live a normal life again. The effect this inane

Herman Chatkoff's tragic June 15, 1917, crash at Chaudun. This American pilot, assigned to Escadrille C.11, was trying to impress his Lafayette Escadrille friends in his lumbering Caudron bombing/observation airplane when he stalled and crashed out on the field, as they watched. His passenger, a young American ambulance driver, was killed instantly. Chatkoff barely escaped the same fate to become, instead, a lifelong invalid. The US Congress later passed a special law under the World War Veterans' Act of 1924 to provide hospitalization benefits and compensation to Chatkoff. (Washington and Lee University Archives)

performance had on the men watching below was sobering. Ted Parsons admitted that it, "cured forever my desire to indulge in low-level aerobatics." Raoul Lufbery had no sympathy for Chatkoff or his ill-conceived actions and considered what he had done to poor Woodworth little less than murder. Only the carefree Courtney Campbell seemed unaffected by the incident, as he would dramatically demonstrate only three weeks later.

Meanwhile, more personnel changes were occurring within the squadron. At about the same time that Chatkoff was pulling off his fatal stunt, John Drexel departed, with very little fanfare, for greener fields. His influential father had arranged for him a commission in the US Air Service. He flew his last patrol with the Lafayette Escadrille on June 14, 1917, and left the squadron the next day.

At about the same time, an old friend returned. The popular and highly competent Didier Masson finally escaped his onerous training duties and joined back up with his comrades at the Lafayette Escadrille. With him, came three new replacements.

34. CAPORAL JAMES NORMAN HALL was born on April 22, 1887, in Colfax, Iowa, to Arthur and Ella Hall. Though one of the last men to join the Lafayette Escadrille, he was destined to become one of its most popular and distinguished members. Of all the

inimitable individuals in this highly unique squadron, Hall stands out. Growing up in the Midwestern town of Colfax, Iowa, he graduated from Grinnell College in 1910, before entering into a series of endeavors that found him, in 1914, in England. The aspiring writer was bicycling through the British countryside when World War I erupted and changed the course of his life, along with millions of others. On August 18, he joined the British Army, claiming Canadian citizenship, as a private in the Royal Fusiliers, with

James Norman Hall poses in front of a Blériot trainer. Hall distinguished himself by fighting under the flags of three different nations during World War I. Serving first as a soldier in the British army, he later flew for the French Aéronautique Militaire and the US Air Service. The many adventures and close calls he suffered during these years were the stuff of novels—literally. The talented writer was already on his way to becoming a world-renowned author when he joined the Lafayette Escadrille on June 16, 1917. (US Air Force)

whom he served for more than a year—much of it fighting in France. He returned to the United States in late 1915 and began writing of his experiences. These efforts culminated in the publication of his first book, *Kitchener's Mob*. With his reputation as an author firmly established, he accepted an assignment from the *Atlantic Monthly* to travel to France and write a series of articles about the newly formed American flying unit operating there. After meeting with Paul Rockwell, and Dr. Edmund Gros, he was told, "Good heavens, man, you don't want to write about them, you want to fly with them." Hall took their advice and signed up for aviation on October 11, 1916. After completing training, he joined the Lafayette Escadrille at Chaudun on June 16, 1917. Starting almost immediately, his next year and a half would bring thrills, adventures, and life-and-death experiences that even a creative writer like himself could never have imagined.

35. CAPORAL DOUGLAS MACMONAGLE was born in San Francisco, California on February 19, 1982, to Dr. Beverly and Minnie MacMonagle. After leaving Berkeley in 1915, he traveled to France to serve with the American Ambulance Field Service. He served there for nine months, earning the Croix de Guerre with star, at Verdun for rescuing wounded men at an advanced post under fire. He enlisted in aviation in October 1916, and joined the Lafayette Escadrille on June 16, 1917.

Coffee time for the men of the Lafayette Escadrille at Chaudun, as photographed by Paul Rockwell during his June 27 to July 6, 1917, visit. This is one of a series of snapshots he took, the original negatives of which, still exist. Visible from far left: Walter Lovell, Harold Willis, Didier Masson, Chouteau Johnson, and Willis Haviland. Leaning on the pole, facing the camera are William Dugan and Ted Parsons. (Washington and Lee University Archives)

An informal gathering of Escadrille SPA.124 pilots in front of William Thaw's Spad VII S.1456 at Chaudun. From left: Robert Soubiran, Willis Haviland, Kenneth Marr, Thaw, unidentified mechanic, and at far right, new arrival David McKelvey Peterson. Peterson reported with Douglas MacMonagle and James Norman Hall on June 16, 1917, and would prove to be a solid addition to the roster. Levelheaded and fearless, he had the ideal personality for a fighter pilot, which would contribute to his future successes. Here, it appears that the casually dressed pilots must have been saving their good uniforms for, as Ted Parsons later phrased it, "adventures in Paris, which, after all, we considered the most important part of the war." (Washington and Lee University Archives)

36. CAPORAL DAVID MCKELVEY PETERSON was born on July 2, 1894, in Honesdale, Pennsylvania, to Dr. Person and Louise Peterson. After graduating from Lehigh University in 1915 with a degree in chemical engineering, he worked for a time at the Curtiss aircraft factory in Buffalo, New York, where he also learned to fly. In September 1916, he traveled to France and completed the flight training curriculum, during which, he proved to be a talented and exceptionally even-keeled pilot. He reported to the Lafayette Escadrille with Hall and MacMonagle on June 16, 1917.

James Hall's Lucky Escape

On June 26, new pilot "Jimmy" Hall was scheduled for an eight-plane sunset patrol over the lines. It was only his second combat patrol. Taking off at around 8:00 p.m., as the sun was almost ready to touch the horizon, were Lufbery, Willis, Johnson, Dugan, Bigelow, Lovell, Hall, and MacMonagle. Hall's mechanics had difficulty getting his Spad—Ken Marr's old S.1386—started, and by the time he got off the ground, the other members of the patrol were out of sight.

Hall climbed for altitude and headed straight for the lines, hoping to catch up with his departed comrades. To his joy, he caught sight of the seven-plane formation three miles inside German lines, so he hurried to join it. However, as he approached, he was horrified to see one of the biplanes from the formation suddenly turn toward him and open fire. In the dusky sky, he had mistaken a German formation for his own, and now there was no escape. As Ted Parsons vividly described Hall's ordeal, "Machine guns tapped at him from every angle. Tracer bullets left a tangled cobweb of phosphorescent blue smoke in the clear air, holding the little Spad in the center like a fly in a spider's web." Several enemy bullets found their mark. One of them knocked the goggles off of Hall's face and creased his forehead, and another slammed into his left shoulder. The German fighters continued their deadly assault until the seriously wounded Hall lost consciousness. He tumbled from an altitude of 14,000 feet in his stricken Spad, completely out of control.

The only bit of luck Hall had that day saved his life: before impact with the ground, either he—or a divine guiding hand—directed his plummeting Spad into a trench, lengthwise, so that most of the impact was absorbed by the wings as they collapsed against the parapets on either side. Thanks to his sturdy Spad, Hall miraculously survived what should have been certain death. No other airplane could have made such a dive without shedding its wings. He was rushed, badly injured, to the nearest aid station and eventually ended up at the American Hospital at Neuilly-sur-Seine, on the northwestern outskirts of Paris. He had barely survived his very short air combat career but would live to fight again. Meanwhile, he would, as James McConnell had earlier, put his recovery time to good use. He began writing a semi-fictional account of his experiences that became, upon its publication in 1918, his second book—and in time, an aviation classic: *High Adventure: A Narrative of Air Fighting in France.*

There were many admiring witnesses to Hall's disastrous fight and, though his performance was hardly anything he cared to brag about, French military authorities appreciated his aggressive spirit, his sangfroid under fire—and most of all, his ability to survive. On July 9, they awarded him the Médaille militaire for his "courage and purest spirit of sacrifice." With Hall's violent and abrupt departure from the squadron, new talent was needed to replace him and it arrived less than a week later.

37. CAPORAL JAMES RALPH DOOLITTLE—not to be confused with James Harold "Jimmy" Doolittle of World War II fame—was born in Chicago, Illinois, on January 6, 1894 to James and Frances Doolittle. Doolittle left Columbia University in 1916 to serve in France with the Norton-Harjes Ambulance Corps. He entered the French aviation program in October 1916, but on May 2, 1917, while at the GDE at Plessis-Belleville, he crashed his Nieuport and received serious injuries. Not until eight weeks later, on July 2, 1917, did the young pilot with a newly scarred face join the Lafayette Escadrille at Chaudun.

More Lady Luck and More New Horizons

On July 4 and 5, Capitaine Thénault granted the men of the Lafayette Escadrille a much-appreciated 48-hour leave to participate in the American Independence Day festivities. These included a ceremony held in Paris near the statue of Washington and Lafayette at Place des États-Unis. Given the recent US declaration of war, this most patriotic of all American holidays had far more meaning and appeal to the pilots than in past years. The last part of the celebration involved an impressive military parade at Chaudun on Saturday, July 7, during which, the squadron was presented a silk flag stitched by President Woodrow Wilson's daughter, Mrs. William Gibbs McAdoo, and other women representing the US Treasury Department.

Though the flag presentation was an important occasion, July 7 was equally remembered for another extraordinary event that was not on that day's agenda. Early that morning the irrepressible daredevil, Courtney Campbell, returned to Chaudun from a patrol and decided to treat the visitors congregating below to an impromptu aerobatic display. After overstressing his Nieuport 23 fighter with a series of violent maneuvers, he was hanging upside-down at the top of a loop when his lower left wing simply separated and fluttered to the ground below. It should have been sure death—no airplane is designed to fly without one of its wings—but Campbell somehow found a way to keep it under control as he glided down to a perfect landing in a beet field some five miles away from the aerodrome. Rather than being scared witless at his near-death experience, like any normal person, the insanely fearless pilot considered it all good fun. Riding in the ambulance that was dispatched to retrieve his smashed remains, he made the rounds at several local drinking establishments, toasting to his close call with the Grim Reaper. He received the Croix de Guerre with star, for miraculously cheating death, but for him, the clock was ticking. Only once more would he successfully defy the odds before his amazing luck would finally desert him.

On July 17, the squadron was abruptly ordered to move again—this time to Saint-Pol-sur-Mer. This airfield was located just outside of Dunkirk, only two miles from the beach. The assigned task was to support the British Flanders offensive, known as the Third Battle of Ypres or the Battle of Passchendaele.

The flight from Chaudun to Saint-Pol was anything but smooth, with several pilots becoming lost in the misty overcast. Haviland and Peterson crash landed, while Parsons and Willis nearly collided with an observation balloon that suddenly appeared before them. The pilot who encountered the most trouble, however, was the new man, Doolittle. While winging his way to Saint-Pol, he became disoriented in the soup. Lost and alone, he descended to an airfield he spotted below to get his bearings but discovered, to his chagrin, that it was an enemy field. As machine gun fire from the ground began zipping all around him, he ducked back into the clouds.

A few minutes later, he again cautiously emerged from the overcast, only to see a Royal Flying Corps Nieuport battling a German fighter that had attacked a British observation balloon. He immediately went to the aid of his ally, but was promptly attacked by two other German fighters that had escaped his notice. In the ensuing melee, he was hit in the leg by German machine gun fire and his own Nieuport 24 peppered with enemy slugs. As he tried to escape the relentless attack, British antiaircraft fire opened up on the Germans but managed to hit only the unlucky Doolittle. He finally crash landed in a field behind British lines, during which his recently healed face wound was reopened. He spent weeks recovering from his multiple injuries before being released from service to return to the United States. For his courageous actions, he was awarded the British Military Medal and the French Croix de Guerre with palm.

Doolittle's post-Lafayette Escadrille luck continued to let him down. After returning to the States, he signed on as a civilian instructor with the US Air Service. On July 26, 1918, he and his observer died after crashing near Kenilworth Field, Buffalo, New York. Doolittle, who was scheduled to be married only six days later, thus joined the ranks of Lafayette Escadrille pilots who failed to survive the war.

The carefree Andrew Courtney Campbell stands next to his broken Nieuport 23 N.3578 and laughs after his death-defying flight of July 7, 1917. After reporting to the Lafayette Escadrille on April 15, 1917, he became infamous for his bizarre flying antics. In this case, while stunting over the field at Chaudun early that morning, his lower left wing ripped loose and flapped away in the slipstream. Campbell kept his head and somehow managed to bring his crippled bird down for a successful landing in this beet field. (Washington and Lee University Archives)

Right after Courtney Campbell's July 7, 1917, miracle, the men of the Lafayette Escadrille were treated to an impressive ceremony on the airfield at Chaudun. A regiment of elite French Chasseurs Alpins presented the squadron with an American flag stitched and donated by the women of the US Treasury Department. Here, Lieutenant William Thaw, holds the hand-made silk flag. As Ted Parsons described it, "poor Bill Thaw had to dress up, stagger out and accept it with a delightful speech which no one could hear or understand." (US Air Force)

This Paul Rockwell photograph, taken at Chaudun on July 7, 1917, shows all but four of the assigned pilots posing with the newly presented flag. Sitting: Dudley Hill, Didier Masson (holding Soda), William Thaw (petting Fram), Georges Thénault, Raoul Lufbery and Chouteau Johnson (holding Whiskey), Stephen Bigelow, and Robert Rockwell. Standing: Robert Soubiran, James Doolittle, Courtney Campbell, Ted Parsons, Ray Bridgman, William Dugan, Douglas MacMonagle, Walter Lovell, Harold Willis, Hank Jones, Antoine de Maison-Rouge, and David Peterson. MacMonagle, Doolittle, and Peterson had only recently joined the squadron, as had Lieutenant de Maison-Rouge, who was Lieutenant de Laage's replacement. Missing from this photo were Jerry Hewitt, Willis Haviland, Carl Dolan, and Ken Marr. The squadron roster was at this time at its peak, with a total of 24 pilots. (US Air Force)

★ ★ ★

While at Saint-Pol, the men of the Lafayette Escadrille managed to fly patrols most days, during which they encountered some enemy opposition. In addition, they experimented with the new and dangerous art of ground assault. Fortunately, however, the weather did not cooperate enough for them to get into any kind of routine, and this afforded them some much-needed downtime. A third of the 24 days they operated from there were nonflying. Even when the weather was fit for flying, the pilots were unable to achieve any significant results. Ted Parsons later remembered Saint-Pol as a "continuous round of sea bathing, poker, and drinking parties...." Even the hard-driving ace Lufbery appreciated the more relaxed lifestyle, stating in an August 1, 1917, letter to Paul Rockwell that, "we never enjoyed ourselves so much."

On August 11, 1917, the men of the Lafayette Escadrille were once again ordered to move, this time back to the Verdun sector. After their pleasant interlude on the beaches of Saint-Pol, their new assignment was a large field just outside the village of Senard, 185 miles to the southeast. Here, they would find an abundance of good weather and intense air fighting that would bring them additional victories—along with more losses.

CHAPTER 12

HARD TIMES AT SENARD

"… I just let him have it. He came all to pieces in the air."

The quiet little town of Senard sits in a clearing at the lower edge of the Argonne Forest, and on the town's southern outskirts is a sprawling pasture where cows now graze. In August 1917, that pasture, through which the emergent Aisne River still meanders, was a busy aerodrome, housing the planes and pilots of the Lafayette Escadrille and its sister squadrons of Groupe de Combat 13. At that time, this area was part of the now-relatively quiet Verdun sector, but it was about to become much more active. French Général Philippe Pétain was about to launch a new offensive, which would ultimately push the German Army back to where it had begun its massive February 1916 attack on Verdun.

As was now abundantly evident on both sides of the trenches, aerial superiority was a critical element to success on the ground. Commanders needed their eyes in the sky—their two-seat photo reconnaissance airplanes and observation balloons—to keep them apprised of enemy movements and help direct artillery fire. In order for these aircraft to operate effectively, control of the skies was a must, and this was the responsibility of the pilots of Groupe de Combat 13. In addition, they would be called on to support bombing missions into enemy territory. Thus, the men of the Lafayette Escadrille had their work cut out for them.

Harold Willis down, but Not Out

It was not until August 16 that SPA.124 was ready to commence flight operations from Senard. With the generally good weather and long summer hours of daylight, the pilots began racking up flight hours and filling their logbooks, diaries, and letters with accounts of deadly encounters with exceptionally hostile enemy airmen. The pilots of SPA.124 would remember their seven weeks here as some of the most intense and exhausting of all the campaigns in which they had participated.

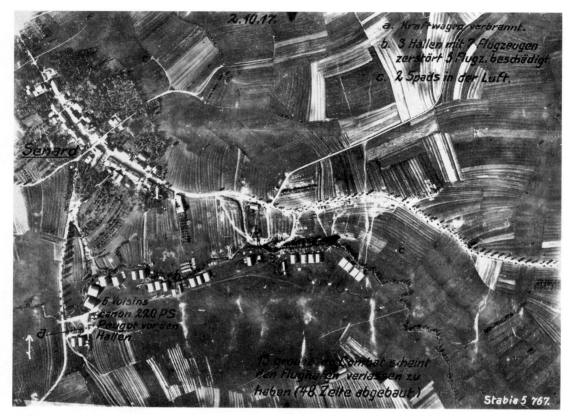

A German reconnaissance photograph of the aerodrome located on the southeastern edge of Senard. Note the numerous hangars lined up along the Aisne River, which ran through the field. The Lafayette Escadrille and other squadrons belonging to Groupe de Combat 13 arrived at Senard on August 11, 1917. (Source Unknown)

August 18, the squadron's third operational day at Senard, brought with it an abundance of action. The mission that day for Escadrilles SPA.124 and SPA.65 was to protect a group of 13 Sopwith bombers from Escadrilles SOP.66 and SOP.111. Their objectives, all several miles inside enemy-held territory, included the railroad yard at Dun-sur-Meuse and munitions depots at Banthéville. After crossing the lines at about 12,000 feet altitude, the large formation came under a series of running attacks by formations of determined German fighters. During one of these melees, Walter Lovell downed an enemy Albatros fighter, which he shared with a SPA.65 pilot, for his first and only confirmed kill of the war. However, that welcome event was offset by some very bad news involving Lovell's friend, Harold Willis. The Spad VII flown by the highly competent architect-pilot Willis, vanished from the scene. None of his fellow pilots saw what had happened to him, and though they hoped for the best, they feared the worst. The men of SPA.124 grieved the popular pilot's loss. He had been a good friend and a valuable pilot who had done stellar work in the five months he had served with the squadron. On the day Willis went missing, Walter Lovell wrote about him in a letter to Paul Rockwell:

> Right from the start, his work was characterized by a conscientious and a thoroughness second to none. His reconnaissance work on which he specialized always proved to be of great value.

Raoul Lufbery sitting on the edge of the cockpit of Capitaine Thénault's Spad S.1417 at Senard. On September 4, 1917, Luf downed his 11th enemy aircraft while flying this plane. The camera is pointing north towards the road in the background, which leads into Senard. (Chuck Thomas)

> On account of his splendid work, he was proposed for sous-lieutenant about two weeks ago. Willis was one of the most valuable men in the escadrille and his loss is going to make a tremendous hole.

It would take several weeks, but Willis' friends would eventually learn—to their great relief—that his loss was not quite as final as they feared. He was, in fact, very much alive, and though no one yet knew it, his adventures in the Great War were far from over.

Willis later related what had happened. During one of the attacks, enemy bullets from an attacking German fighter had disabled his airplane, forcing him to begin a violent descent to the ground, two miles below. The pursuing German fighter, accompanied by two of his comrades, stayed with him all the way down, spraying machine gun fire at him the entire time. During the course of this prolonged attack, his Spad was shot to pieces. Bullets whizzed past Willis so close that, reminiscent of James Hall's close call, one well-aimed bullet knocked the goggles off of his head. Though his engine was dead, he executed every diving aerobatic maneuver he had ever learned and probably invented some new ones, as he tried to evade the streams of hot steel emanating from the Germans' twin Spandau machine guns.

As the beleaguered Willis approached the ground, he desperately used the last of his airspeed to hop a clump of trees, before plunking his broken Spad down onto the top of a hill overlooking Dun-sur-Meuse. The German pilot who, only seconds before, had been doing his level best to kill Willis, now flew over his vanquished enemy and cheerfully waved. He and his two comrades circled and then landed on the slope below him. They strode up to him, and as Willis later recounted, "They all saluted very

Harold Willis' Spad VII S.1615, after being forced down in enemy territory on August 18, 1917. He descended from an altitude of 12,000 feet with a dead engine, while under attack by his German pursuer, Jasta 16b Leutnant Wilhelm Schulz. In spite of that, he managed to execute a flawless dead-stick landing on the crest of this hill overlooking Dun-sur-Meuse, France. It earned him the unenviable honor of being the only pilot captured while flying for the Lafayette Escadrille. Note the bullet exit hole on the cowling, just behind the propeller. Jasta 16b later repaired this airplane, only for one of its pilots to overturn it in a marsh. (Greg VanWyngarden)

properly as they came up—young chaps, perfectly correct. My machine was a wreck: thirty bullets in the engine, radiator and fuselage; exactly half of the cables cut, tires punctured, wings riddled."

It was not uncommon for combat airmen of this era to land beside their downed opponent. To bring an enemy pilot down alive in friendly lines was a rare event, so it was a thrill for the victor to meet—face to face—the man with whom he had just bested in mortal combat. It was also an opportunity to examine the downed enemy plane, to obtain the witness signatures needed for official confirmation, and to take some photographs and collect a few souvenirs.

Another reason pilots sometimes landed next to their helpless adversary was to personally take charge of him—ostensibly, for interrogation—but in reality, to protect him from unfriendly ground troops. Almost without exception, the downed pilot was then escorted back to his victor's aerodrome to begin his life as a prisoner of war in the least painful way possible—with a belly full of good food and liquor. In keeping with this chivalrous routine, the hosts typically considered it impolite to ask any questions about operational matters. Intelligence officers would interrogate the prisoner later.

Accordingly, Willis' captor, Leutnant Wilhelm Schulz, whom he described in a 1961 interview as "a very decent fellow and a good sport," placed him into an automobile that took him straight to his pilots' mess. Here, Willis and the German aviators shared a congenial breakfast—and probably also a few glasses of schnapps. He was then marched off to a prison cell, wearing only his pajamas and a sweater under his flight suit—and no money, cigarettes, or identification. Only then did the reality of the situation hit him. He had just become the first and only pilot to be captured while flying for the Lafayette Escadrille. He sat down on his bare cot and wept like a baby at the sudden and unhappy turn of events. However future actions would prove that the gritty Willis had not yet thrown in the towel.

Strike Two for Courtney Campbell

Back at Senard, the torrid pace continued, with patrols going out from sunup to sunset and some pilots flying several "shows" a day. Soon after Willis went missing, the piano-playing Stephen Bigelow engaged a formation of German Albatros fighters that were attacking one of the Sopwith bombers he was assigned to protect. In the ensuing fight, a bullet smashed into his windscreen, sending metal and glass fragments into his face, just as had previously happened to both Edmond Genet and Kiffin Rockwell. However, because of the intensity of the flying at this time and the need for every available pilot, Bigelow declined any time off for medical treatment. His decision to remain with the squadron was a testament to his dedication but not to his good judgment. His wounds became infected—a serious condition in this pre-penicillin era—and he was forced to enter the hospital. His recovery was slow, and by January 1918, he was declared physically unfit for further service and discharged from the air service.

Not all the news at Senard was bad. Lovell had already scored on August 18, and before long, some of his squadron mates also found success. One of these was Ted Parsons, who had flown his fair share of combat over the past seven months without a confirmed victory. This changed on September 4, 1917, when he downed a Rumpler two-seater. According to the ever-self-deprecating Parsons in a 1961 interview, this victory was more accidental than intentional. As Parsons was executing a climbing turn, the Rumpler—which he had not even seen—suddenly appeared in front of him. "There he was, as big as a house and right in my machine gun sights. I guess it was just nervous reaction or something, but I just let him have it. He came all to pieces in the air."

That same day, Raoul Lufbery claimed his 11th confirmed enemy airplane, which he sent spinning down in flames near where Parsons' victim had fallen. Then, on September 19, David Peterson and Ken Marr teamed up with the three crewmembers of a French Escadrille F.44 reconnaissance plane, to shoot down an Albatros near Montfaucon. And finally, on September 22, Luf scored yet again, for his 12th confirmed victory.

On September 12, a ceremony was held out on the flying field, during which the Lafayette Escadrille was presented with a rare and unexpected unit citation. Groupe de

Raoul Lufbery, holding Whiskey, as Ted Parsons looks on. On September 4, 1917, both pilots succeeded in downing an enemy plane. It was Parsons' first confirmed and Luf's eleventh. (Willis B. Haviland Collection)

Combat 13 Commandant Féquant had, weeks earlier, proposed the squadron for the award, and it was formally approved by Général Pétain. According to this document, the volunteer Americans who had traveled to France "in the spirit of purest sacrifice" had, "excited the profound admiration of the officers who have had it under their command and of the French escadrilles who, fighting by its side, have striven to vie with it in valorous deeds."

During this period, the somewhat bloated squadron roster was being diminished by other losses besides those resulting from combat. Thomas Hewitt, who flew his last recorded patrol on August 16, finally left the squadron on September 17. The harrowing intensity of the missions the squadron was flying when he first arrived may have been too much, too soon for the new pilot. His courage and confidence seemed to evaporate, and his consequent lack of aggression rendered him unpopular and ultimately, unfit for combat. Ted Parsons later wrote, rather unkindly, about "Useless" that he, "showed a marked preference for making all his patrols either in the bar or, in the rare cases when he was in the air, behind our balloon lines." Soon afterward, long-standing squadron member Willis Haviland also transferred out—ultimately, to accept a commission as a US Naval Aviator.

On September 19, the same day that Peterson and Marr shared their first confirmed victory, the lucky Courtney Campbell—of lost-wing fame—made yet another entry in the Lafayette Escadrille book of legends. The fearless thrill seeker was a good pilot and a dependable man in a scrap, but his almost-pathological need to push the limits alarmed his fellow pilots. Ted Parsons, who considered Campbell a "pain in the neck on patrols," described how Campbell would—just for the fun of it—try to see how close he could fly to other squadron members' planes without hitting them—sometimes with his whirring propeller only three feet from the other plane's tail. Needless to say, such behavior was potentially fatal to both pilots, but, according to Parsons, "no amount of pleadings, coercion, or threats of physical retaliation was sufficient to make him desist from his distressing tactics in the air."

On the day in question, Campbell was up to his usual antics, this time with the nervous, no-nonsense squadron second-in-command, Lieutenant Maison-Rouge. Campbell positioned himself just above the French officer's plane and, ignoring his angry gestures to back off, lowered his Spad to where his wheels were only inches above Maison-Rouge's top wing. What happened next was almost predictable: either a slight misjudgment by one of the pilots or a bump in the air drove the wheels of Campbell's Spad down into Maison-Rouge's top wing. They punched through the fabric, and embedded themselves into the wing. Locked together, as Parsons described it, "like Siamese twins," they made two very careful circuits of the field, as those watching in horror below alerted the ambulances. Finally, Campbell decided to end it, one way or another: he hauled back on the stick. His luck held and his Spad broke free, allowing the petrified and enraged Maison-Rouge to glide in for a safe landing. Campbell then proceeded to put on an aerobatic display that Parsons said "nearly took off the tops off

On September 18, 1917, Willis B. Haviland left the Lafayette Escadrille, after nearly a year with the squadron. He served briefly in Escadrille SPA.102, before becoming a US Naval Aviator. By war's end, he was one of the most decorated former Lafayette Escadrille pilots. (Washington and Lee University Archives)

of the hangars before he landed without even a flat tire." The carefree daredevil had just had his second brush with death in as many months. He would not have to wait long for his third and last strike.

The harrowing experience traumatized Maison-Rouge, who was already unhappy—and unpopular. He angrily lashed out at the Americans, calling them "sauvages" and, within a matter of days, Capitaine Thénault removed him from the squadron roster and sent him to the rear for reassignment. Eventually, the high-strung Frenchman was reassigned to another squadron and on May 31, 1918, was shot down and killed. Meanwhile, his replacement at SPA.124, who would soon arrive, would be a much better fit with the "savages" of the Lafayette Escadrille.

A Mother's Heartbreaking Visit

Despite the regrettable combat losses of Willis and Bigelow, the pilots of the Lafayette Escadrille were feeling in justifiably high spirits over their recent successes in the air: five confirmed and several unconfirmed kills in less than three weeks. However, another sobering loss, occurring under particularly tragic circumstances, would soon bring their spirits back down again.

Douglas MacMonagle had been with the squadron for just over three months and, during that time, had established a solid record that gained him the respect of his fellow airmen. At 7:35 a.m. on the morning of Monday, September 24, 1917, MacMonagle took off on a patrol with Raoul Lufbery and Robert Rockwell. Also assigned was Ted Parsons, but he had trouble starting his engine and was forced to take off a few minutes later. The three Spads were climbing in a V-formation over the lines, when Luf spotted a large formation of German fighters above them. He immediately began maneuvering to bring his flight into a more advantageous position.

Unfortunately, the aggressive MacMonagle missed or ignored Luf's signal and turned his Spad directly into the attacking formation of enemy fighters. They swarmed over him like angry hornets, and before Lufbery or Rockwell could intervene, it was all over. MacMonagle's Spad spiraled straight down into a wood near the town of Triaucourt. He was dead at the controls, with a bullet through his head.

It was Carl Dolan's depressing task to retrieve his friend's body and bring it back to the aerodrome. Then, he had to go to the train station to meet Mac's mother, Minnie, a volunteer Red Cross nurse who was working in Paris. She had just arrived at Senard to visit her son, but instead, had to hear the heartbreaking news that he had just been killed. Douglas MacMonagle had, like several of his fallen squadron mates before him, predicted his own death. According to Dolan, in a 1962 interview, MacMonagle had confessed to him that his number was up and that he was certain he was about to die. Another premonition had come true—and once more, "Bad Luck Monday" had claimed a victim from the Lafayette Escadrille.

Douglas MacMonagle (right) and a colleague stride across the aerodrome at Senard, with a Nieuport fighter in the background. On September 24, 1917, he took off on a patrol with Raoul Lufbery and Robert Rockwell and, during an ensuing dogfight, was shot down and killed. He died at about the same time his widowed mother arrived at Senard to visit him. Instead, she spent her time there attending her son's funeral and settling up on his hefty bar bill. (Washington and Lee University Archives)

The men of the squadron grieved the loss of the popular MacMonagle. Ken Marr wrote of him in an October 31, 1917, letter to Paul Rockwell that, "Mac was a boy with courage and that's about the best thing I know of these days." His body was buried at the cemetery at Triaucourt and later moved to the Meuse-Argonne American Cemetery in Romagne. In 1928, his remains were transferred, for the last time, to the crypt at the Lafayette Escadrille Memorial.

Dissension in the Ranks

The men of the Lafayette Escadrille had yet another reason to feel disheartened during these turbulent times. Dr. Edmund Gros, now a major in the US Air Service, had recently visited the squadron and urged the American pilots to apply for commissions in their own country's still mostly nonexistent air service. The United States had entered the war completely unprepared, and its infant air arm was in the process of being built from the ground up. Gros felt that the dozens of veteran American airmen serving throughout the French Air Service—including the pilots of the Lafayette Escadrille—were best suited to form the core of the US combat squadrons currently being formed. Warning that those who chose to remain with the Aéronautique Militaire would cease to receive financial support from the Franco-American Flying Corps (now called Lafayette Flying Corps) Committee, he even went so far as to suggest that they replace the French roundel insignia they proudly displayed on their Spad fighters with ones painted in American colors.

None of this sat well with the American pilots. First and foremost, they were loyal to France, the country that had trained and treated them so well. Further, none of them relished the idea of serving under superior officers with no combat experience, as would be the case if they joined the US Air Service. Besides, there were only vague promises—and no guarantees—that they would be accepted and commissioned at an appropriate rank. The ridiculously stringent physical, mental, and educational requirements, in place at the time for entering the US Air Service, were daunting. Postwar statistics show that only a small percentage of the tens of thousands of applicants could pass muster, and many of the pilots of SPA.124—accomplished combat veterans though they truly were—were well aware that they would never qualify without a generous allowance of waivers. The French had accepted these men—most of whom were considerably older than the average US Air Service applicant—with their defective eyesight, hearing, sense of balance, and other defects. After months of stressful combat flying, some were now in even worse shape.

All of this uncertainty affected morale within the squadron, and it also began to affect the men's performance. Groupe de Combat 13 Commandant Féquant, who only three weeks earlier had recommended the Lafayette Escadrille for a citation, penned a contrasting memorandum. In it, he noted "an uneasiness pervading the Escadrille Lafayette," in which "the majority of the pilots seem to be disinterested in maintaining the high reputation of their unit." Charging that the squadron's "soul has fled," he attributed this negativity to the uncertainty they felt about their future and suggested that it was damaging the excellent reputation the squadron had established over the past 16 months. He therefore recommended that the Lafayette Escadrille be "cleanly and quickly" eliminated and its pilots disseminated throughout other squadrons in the Aéronautique Militaire. This was serious stuff, and clearly, drastic changes were in the making.

★ ★ ★

Meanwhile, it was time for the Lafayette Escadrille to move again, and the German Air Service provided an explosive sendoff. On the evenings of September 25 and 27, 1917, German bombers attacked the aerodrome at Senard, setting fire to a hangar and destroying at least seven SPA.124 aircraft. As they flew over, Lieutenants Raoul Lufbery and William Thaw entertained themselves on the ground by blasting away up into the darkness with ground-mounted machine guns. They did no apparent damage but were gratified the next day when someone found a blood-spattered German map and helmet lying out on the field. Their aim had apparently been better than they imagined.

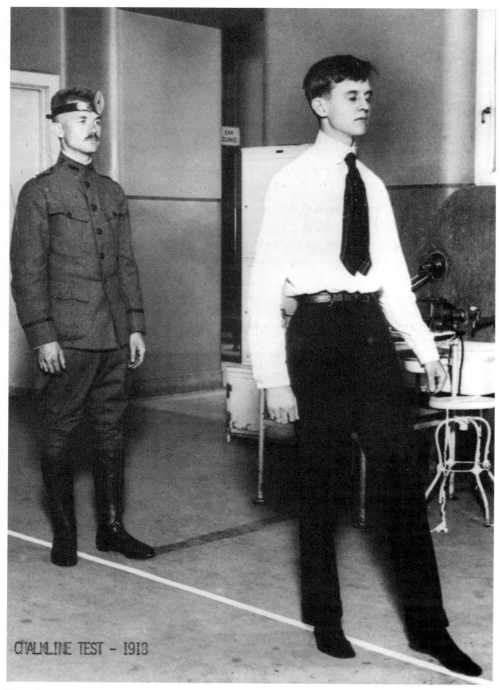

CHALKLINE TEST - 1918

A candidate for the US Air Service takes the "Chalkline Test," which SPA.124 ace Raoul Lufbery would probably have failed. Men of the Lafayette Escadrille were skeptical of ever obtaining US commissions, mainly because of the notoriously stringent physical requirements. US Army doctors had the luxury of far more applicants than they could accept, so they applied screening requirements to extremes. Many of the pilots of the Lafayette Escadrille were—in the eyes of US Air Service flight surgeons—too old, too blind, too deaf, or otherwise unfit to fly. In the end, wisdom prevailed and nearly all received waivers. (US Air Force)

The extensive damage the German night-bombing attacks of September 25 and 27, 1917, did to the aerodrome at Senard. In addition to the obliterated hangars, at least seven SPA.124 fighters were destroyed. (Washington and Lee University Archives)

In seven weeks of heavy fighting, the squadron had collected five confirmed kills in 150 aerial combats—but at the cost of one man killed, one wounded, and another shot down and captured. It had been a strenuous and dangerous time, and the men were ready for a new hunting ground. On September 28, they were in the air heading back to a slightly less hostile environment and a place that already seemed like home. They were going back to Chaudun.

CHAPTER 13

FROM FALCONS OF FRANCE
TO AMERICAN EAGLES

"Glory to all these volunteers. Glory to all these noble heroes, these noble forerunners."

The men of the Lafayette Escadrille and Groupe de Combat 13 resumed operations at Chaudun two days after their September 28, 1917, arrival date. Their mission was to provide aerial support for what would be the last major French attack of 1917, the so-called Malmaison offensive. This, like the recent Verdun offensive, was limited in scope. French Général Paul Maistre and elements of the French 6th Army sought to push the Germans back from the heights of the Aisne River. Ultimately, the French would succeed in capturing the fort at La Malmaison and take control of the Chemin des Dames ridge.

The men of the Lafayette Escadrille may have been briefed on the ground strategy, but to them, it mattered only slightly. Their role in the battle was more or less the same it had always been: to clear the skies of enemy aircraft. They faced opposition in this sector—but thankfully, not as much or as aggressive as at Senard; however, as they would soon find out, the skies around Chaudun were still deadly.

Courtney Campbell Strikes Out

The men of the Lafayette Escadrille got off to a very bad start at their newest assignment. On Monday, October 1—their second operational day at Chaudun—Hank Jones and Courtney Campbell took off to patrol the area between Craonnelle and Berry-au-Bac. The two pilots attacked four enemy two-seaters flying low inside French lines, and during the hectic fight, Jones had part of his flight controls shot away. In the process, he lost contact with Campbell and never saw him again. Later, the men back at Chaudun learned that ground observers reported a French plane falling inside German lines, but did not see it crash.

The last pilot to die flying for the Lafayette Escadrille was Andrew Courtney Campbell Jr. He is seen here on the left, posing with Kenneth Marr in front of Spad VII S.1777. Campbell was killed in aerial combat on October 1, 1917—the sixth straight man from SPA.124 to die in combat on unlucky Monday. He fell behind German lines. His remains now rest in the crypt of the Lafayette Escadrille Memorial. (Washington and Lee University Archives)

IN · MEMORY ·
OF
· ANDREW · COURTNEY · CAMPBELL · JR ·
· SERGEANT · PILOT · LAFAYETTE · ESCADRILLE ·
· BORN · CHICAGO · NOV. · 19TH · 1891 ·
· STUDENT · UNIVERSITY · OF · VIRGINIA · 1914 ·
· VOLUNTEER · IN · FRENCH · ARMY · 1916 ·
· DECORATED · WITH · CROIX · DE GUERRE · PALM AND STAR ·
· KILLED · IN · AIR · BATTLE · WITH · THREE · GERMAN · PLANES ·
· · · OCTOBER · 1ST 1917 · · ·
"I · CHOOSE · TO · SERVE; THERE · ARE · WORSE · FATES · THAN · DEATH"

The plaque pictured here is displayed in the chapel of Campbell's alma mater, the University of Virginia. The last line of the inscription seems especially appropriate for the risk-taking Campbell. (Washington and Lee University Archives)

Jon Guttman, author of *SPA124 Lafayette Escadrille: American Volunteer Airmen of World War 1*, reveals that Campbell was the victim of Kurt Andres and Karl Ritscherle, a German observation aircraft crew. Campbell lived a charmed life, defying the odds in cars, speedboats, and airplanes, but it was a German bullet that finally ended it. His unfortunate distinction was to be the last pilot to die while flying for the Lafayette Escadrille. In 1928, his body made its final journey to the crypt of the Lafayette Escadrille Memorial.

It is one of those interesting but inexplicable ironies of war that the last six men from the squadron to die in combat met their fate on Monday: McConnell, Genet, Hoskier and Dressy, MacMonagle, and now Campbell. Whatever sinister meaning this may have had is lost to history, but if the pilots of the Lafayette Escadrille had developed an aversion to flying on that day of the week, who could have blamed them?

Arrivals and Departures

On October 3, 1917, the men of the Lafayette Escadrille welcomed back an old friend in the form of the resilient James Norman Hall. He had recovered from his injuries of

June 26 and returned to SPA.124 at Chaudun. The highly popular, multi-talented pilot was welcomed back with open arms. Paul Rockwell captured the general feeling the men had for him when he wrote that Hall, "was one of the finest all-around persons I have even known, and an honorable man in every way." He was now back to stay and would soon make his mark with the squadron.

A new French pilot arrived on October 6 to replace Lieutenant de Maison-Rouge, who flew his last patrol on October 1 and had only recently left the squadron.

LIEUTENANT LOUIS VERDIER-FAUVETY was born in Paris on February 4, 1886. Like each of his two French predecessors, Lieutenants de Laage and Maison-Rouge, Verdier-Fauvety had started his military career as a cavalryman. After recovering from a serious wound, he had transferred into aviation and was serving in Escadrille N.65, one of SPA.124's sister Groupe de Combat 13 squadrons, when Capitaine Thénault invited him to join the Lafayette Escadrille. Because Verdier was a known quantity—already liked and respected by the American pilots of the Lafayette Escadrille—he was the obvious selection. He proved to be the same type of man as the beloved de Laage and soon became just as popular. His superb leadership, both in the air and on the ground, was the exact opposite of the more aloof management style that both Maison-Rouge and Thénault displayed. As a result, Verdier-Fauvety almost immediately turned the dispirited squadron around. Under his guidance, their effectiveness in the air improved and casualties dropped to zero. This outstanding officer would remain with the squadron for as long as it remained under French control.

There were other losses during this period, although not from casualties. Rumors were flying back and forth like artillery shells about the impending dissolution of the Lafayette Escadrille. In fact, its days were numbered, and it was only a matter of time before the US Air Service would take it over. For that reason, many of the American pilots were proactively lobbying for US Army officers' commissions. The pay would be far better and it might provide a postwar future for them in the new field of aviation.

On October 8, the venerable Didier Masson departed. The popular and highly competent pilot had flown steadily with the squadron—with a four-month break earlier in 1917—since June 1916. He had achieved only one confirmed victory, but his unbelievable feat of downing an enemy fighter, in spite of having a dead engine, was legendary. By now, he was simply worn out and in need of a rest. He eventually reported to the large American flight training complex at Issoudun for instructor duties and would survive the war.

Other departures were in the making, as well. On October 24, 1917, Walter Lovell left the squadron after eight months of distinguished service and one confirmed victory. Well liked and highly respected as a flight leader, he was sorely missed. He accepted a commission in the US Air Service and served—to his chagrin—in various administrative positions until the end of the war. In spite of his impressive record, he never again flew combat.

Old hand Didier Masson departed for greener fields on October 8. He had been with the Lafayette Escadrille most of the time since June 1916 and needed a rest. Here, he is seated in a Nieuport 11, spring 1917, when serving temporarily as an instructor at Avord. He would finish the war instructing at the US flight training complex at Issoudun. He left the squadron with one confirmed kill. (Willis B. Haviland Collection)

The next pilot to jump from what must have seemed like the sinking ship of the Lafayette Escadrille was long-standing squadron member Charles Chouteau Johnson. He departed on October 31, 1917, to accept a commission in the US Air Service. Only Raoul Lufbery and William Thaw had been with the squadron longer than Johnson. Never a particularly aggressive pilot—and considered by at least one squadron mate, the late Edmond Genet, to be something of a shirker—he had, nevertheless, been steady. He had been good enough to not only survive 17 continuous months of aerial combat, but also bag one confirmed victory. He had also, like several other of the "older" members of the squadron, shown a great deal of fortitude in another way. He had continued to fly after seeing at least 10 of his close friends die in the most violent way possible. It was a fate, he had once confided in a letter to Paul Rockwell, that he believed he too would inevitably suffer. Yet, he continued to fly and he survived.

Two other important departures occurred during this period that particularly saddened the men of the Lafayette Escadrille. The two beloved squadron mascots, Whiskey and

Another old timer transferring out during this period was Charles Chouteau Johnson. Though not an aggressive pilot, he had managed to survive for 17 months and acquire one confirmed victory. He left on October 31, 1917, and reported as a first lieutenant flight instructor in the US Air Service. He was later promoted to captain—the insignia he is wearing in this photograph. (US Air Force)

Soda, departed Chaudun and their human friends of the Lafayette Escadrille on October 15, 1917. The two cubs were growing ever larger, and though generally well behaved for lions, they were rambunctious. On one unfortunate occasion a few days earlier, Whiskey noticed the gold braid on a man walking across the aerodrome at Chaudun. That man was none other than Groupe de Combat 13 Commandant Féquant. Whiskey playfully knocked the officer to the ground and proceeded to chew up the brightly colored braid he was wearing. The enraged Féquant ordered both lions shot, but later granted them a reprieve. Instead, he ordered the men of SPA.124 to get rid of them. Sadly, they put the two cubs into their open touring car and transported them, with their ears flapping in the breeze, to a Paris zoo. They had been the heart of the squadron and now they too were gone. The eloquent Ted Parsons aptly penned their epitaph:

> To all those dumb friends of ours, I, for one, am deeply grateful. They deserved a citation every bit as much as we humans for they were our constant companions and comforts in all the black hours and endured every hardship with us cheerfully and uncomplainingly. Knowing that we loved and appreciated them, may their souls rest peacefully in the animal heaven.

Even with the revolving door of arrivals and departures, and rumors of the squadron's impending demise running rampant, flight operations at Chaudun continued, uninterrupted. The October weather remained relatively good, as the men of the Lafayette Escadrille patrolled the skies, in search of enemy aircraft. They were helped, in this regard, by another

Men of the Lafayette Escadrille bidding farewell to Whiskey and Soda. By the autumn of 1917, more and more squadron members were leaving for other assignments, but no departure was more painful than this one. On October 15, 1917, James Norman Hall, William Thaw, Dudley Hill, Kenneth Marr, David Peterson, Raoul Lufbery, Robert Rockwell, Ray Bridgman (partially visible), and Dr. Manet, the squadron physician, gathered to say goodbye at Chaudun before delivering their beloved mascots to a Paris zoo. (Washington and Lee University Archives)

significant new arrival: the new Spad XIII—larger, heavier, more powerful and with twice the firepower of the Spad VII—had begun to make its appearance at Chaudun.

Not surprisingly, the pilot that capitalized the most on the favorable conditions of this period was the fearless and talented squadron ace, Raoul Lufbery. On the morning of October 16, he downed his 13th, a two-seater, near Vauxaillon. Walter Lovell, who was writing Paul Rockwell often during this period, keeping the war correspondent friend of the Lafayette Escadrille up to speed on squadron events, described Luf's victory:

> Today was very clear and the boche were out in force. Lufbery, who was flying alone, attacked a boche biplace [two-seater] at a very high altitude. It must have been a great scrap. Luf received several bullets in his machine but finally succeeded in bringing the boche down. It has just been confirmed making thirteen for Luf. One of the bullets that hit Luf's machine pierced the radiator and lodged in the carburetor. It was a most fortunate thing for Luf it was not an incendiary bullet. Luf was just able to make the nearest aviation field before his motor stopped.

As impressive as this difficult performance was, it was nothing compared to the Lufbery show of October 24, 1917. In his greatest display of talent ever, he flew three grueling patrols that morning, and incredibly—within the space of six hours—claimed six enemy airplanes down. Most of these were not observed by the rapidly moving army below, so only one could be confirmed, but no one ever doubted a Lufbery claim. Unlike some pilots, he did not file a claim unless he was sure it was a kill. Dishonesty simply had no place in his mental and emotional makeup. Besides, by this time, he was so incredibly deadly that if the opportunity presented itself, he could very well have done what he claimed. When fellow pilot Carl Dolan once asked Luf how failing to receive confirmation for so many of his claims affected him, Luf simply replied, "What the hell do I care. I know I got them." His score now stood at 14, but he was not quite yet finished.

During the first week of November 1917, as the enemy opposition slowed and the winter weather of Northern France began to make its cold and foggy appearance, a new face showed up at Chaudun. The man belonging to that face had the distinction of being the 38th and last pilot ever assigned to the Lafayette Escadrille.

38. CAPORAL CHRISTOPHER WILLIAM FORD was born on October 2, 1892, in New York City to immigrant parents Christ and Anna Ford. Unlike most of the other men to serve with the Lafayette Escadrille, Ford did not come from a family of wealth. Orphaned at an early age, he was forced to work his way up in the world, eventually becoming a reporter for the *Wall Street Journal*. He soon developed an interest in aviation and, in 1916, traveled to San Antonio, Texas. Here, he learned to fly at the school the famed flying Stinson family was operating south of town. In 1917, he traveled to France, enlisted in the Aéronautique Militaire, and recorded his first flight with the Lafayette Escadrille on November 8, 1917. Initially, this pilot of modest beginnings seemed out of place in a squadron of millionaires, but he quickly became a highly capable pilot and a welcome addition to the squadron.

The 38th and last American to join the Lafayette Escadrille was Christopher William Ford. He made his first flight on November 8, 1917, and remained with the squadron until its February 18, 1918, transfer to the US Air Service. Ford established a solid record with SPA.124 and later, the US Air Service, before being brought down by ground fire on October 15, 1918, and finishing the war in a German POW camp. (US Air Force)

The End of an Ace and an Era

On December 2, 1917, the highly touted "Lufbery Show" made its final performance, and it was a good one. On this morning, in two separate patrols, the great ace achieved his 15th and 16th confirmed kills. The first of these he scored while flying one of the squadron's new Spad XIIIs, S.1970. He and four pilots from Escadrille SPA.88 shared the two-seater. Then, during a second patrol later that morning, Luf downed his second of the day, also a two-seater—this time, unassisted. No one could have guessed it, but this rare double victory—which marked the pinnacle of Lufbery's career and occurred on the three-year anniversary of the death of his friend Marc Pourpe—would constitute the last two confirmed aerial kills of his life.

On January 5, he too would leave the squadron to accept a commission in the US Air Service—appropriately, as a major. After languishing behind a desk for several weeks, he eventually found a way to resume flying combat missions with the 94th Aero Squadron. However, even the great Lufbery's luck had its limits, and it was about to run out.

On May 19, 1918, Major Raoul Lufbery, US Air Service, watched from his American airdrome near Toul, as one of his young pilots botched an attack on a nearby German two-seater observation plane flying low inside Allied lines. Luf hurriedly jumped into the closest available Nieuport 28 and took off to intercept the impudent Germans. He quickly caught up with the airplane and engaged it. His first attack was thwarted by a gun jam, which forced him to pull away and clear it. As he began his second attack, witnesses saw Lufbery's plane suddenly flip upside-down and, to their horror, saw his body exit the plane and began falling to the earth. He landed in the backyard of a house in the village of Maron, a few hundred feet from the banks of the Moselle River. He fell on a picket fence, part of which penetrated his throat, and died soon after impact. Only one battle-related injury was noted: his right thumb had been shot off.

No one knew exactly what had happened. Some claimed that Lufbery's airplane was on fire and that he jumped to escape the flames. The pilotless Nieuport did definitely burn after it crashed on a distant hillside, but witnesses watching from the town below swore that it was not burning when Lufbery fell from his airplane. Another possible scenario is that he took off in an unfamiliar plane in a great hurry and failed to properly secure his seatbelt, or perhaps had loosened it to clear the gun jam. As he violently maneuvered the Nieuport—maybe when his thumb was hit—he was accidentally ejected from the cockpit. Regardless of the cause, it was an ignominious end to a courageous man and his brilliant career.

On December 7, 1917, the men of the Lafayette Escadrille made their final move. They took off from the aerodrome at Chaudun, turned their Spad fighters to an east-southeast heading, and flew for 60 miles, before landing on a large grass field. The new aerodrome was Ferme de la Noblette, located on the southwestern outskirts of the town of La Cheppe.

The purpose of the move was to help counter an anticipated German attack—which, as it turned out, never materialized. Consequently, opposition there was light and the

Raoul Lufbery's grave after his body was moved, in 1919, from the Sebastopol cemetery, near the Toul aerodrome, to the St. Mihiel American Cemetery at Thiaucourt. It was later transferred one final time, to the Lafayette Escadrille Memorial. (US Air Force)

winter weather often unsuitable for flying. As a result, little of significance occurred in the squadron during this period—with two exceptions: first, almost all the American pilots eventually decided to apply for releases from the Aéronautique Militaire in preparation for being accepted as officer pilots in the US Air Service. The only exception was Ted Parsons, who was on leave in the United States. When the requests were processed and accepted, the pilots remained in place "sans statut official"—without official status. Though still flying combat patrols, they were technically civilians.

The second exception to this otherwise stale period involved one of these "civilians." Budding author James Norman Hall celebrated New Year's Day 1918, by downing an Albatros fighter, for his first confirmed victory. The German pilot, who must have been feeling the effects of the previous night's celebration, never saw Hall diving on him. It was the last victory ever credited to the Lafayette Escadrille.

Finally, on February 18, 1918, the event the men of the Lafayette Escadrille had been both dreading and anticipating occurred. After much high-level, behind-the-scenes negotiating, the squadron was officially transferred to the US Air Service and designated the 103rd Aero Squadron. Capitaine Thénault was re-assigned to other duties, as was Lieutentant Verdier-Fauvety. The valiant lieutenant was destined to die on the evening of August 21, 1918, when the French escadrille of which he was in command came under attack by German night bombers. He was killed by a bomb explosion while attending to his men.

Twelve of the remaining American pilots—Bridgman, Dolan, Dugan, Ford, Hall, Hill, Jones, Marr, Peterson, Rockwell, Soubiran, and Thaw—stayed with the 103rd, with Major William Thaw in command. Within months, however, most of these men were dispersed to other units throughout the US Air Service. The wealth of knowledge and leadership these combat veterans would provide to the inexperienced young US Air Service pilots was incalculable. Meanwhile, Escadrille SPA.124 remained on the books and continued to operate with Groupe de Combat 13 as a French squadron.

★ ★ ★

With the stroke of a pen, the Lafayette Escadrille passed into history. During its 22 months, its 38 American pilots had left an indelible mark, as they swept across the skies of the Western Front. They had flown a total of some 3,000 combat patrols in every major sector of the war and destroyed, in all likelihood, far more enemy aircraft than the 33 with which they were officially credited. Eight of these young American volunteers had lost their lives in aerial combat, one had become a prisoner of war, and several others had sustained crippling wounds.

In tribute to these men, their commanding officer, Capitaine Georges Thénault, wrote, "Let us bow low before them and salute them very respectfully. Glory to all these volunteers. Glory to all these noble heroes, these noble forerunners." French Général Henri Gouraud also expressed a feeling that many of his countrymen shared for the Americans of the Lafayette:

> When men who have no obligation to fight, who could not possibly be criticized if they did not fight—yet nevertheless decide upon their own individual initiative to risk their lives in defense of a cause they hold dear—then we are in the presence of true heroes, and France owes them all the homage that word implies.

As the past 100 years have shown, neither France nor the United States would soon forget the dashing young men of the Lafayette Escadrille, their exploits, or their sacrifices.

CHAPTER 14

AFTERMATH

"… swallowed up in the disenchantment of the Lost Generation"

On November 11, 1933, a 48-year-old arms peddler was sentenced to two and one-half years in Federal prison. On May 24, 1936, a 41-year-old alcoholic ex-convict died in a Washington, DC, flophouse of acute congestive heart failure. No one claimed his body. On November 9, 1951, a depressed 56-year-old college professor fell, or more likely jumped, from the deck of a New York ferry and drowned. These three men had absolutely nothing in common, except for one thing: all had once flown for the World War I fighter squadron known as the Lafayette Escadrille.

Twenty-seven of the thirty-eight Americans who had served with the escadrille survived the war and most spent the remainder of their lives basking in the glory that attended it. The group of young Americans who had voluntarily risked their lives flying for an ideal in which they believed was the stuff of legends. To be one of these pilots was a distinction the world never forgot. It was so appealing that, in the years following the war, an estimated 4,000 men—according to historian Philip M. Flammer—fraudulently claimed to have served in the Lafayette Escadrille. These "ringers," as they were derisively called, who attempted to exploit its name seemed to crop up everywhere, and they became a very sore subject to the surviving Americans who actually had flown for Escadrille 124. This fact serves only to demonstrate just how prestigious it was to be a bona fide member of this unique flying unit.

Most of the Lafayette Escadrille survivors successfully adapted to the peacetime environment and went on to enjoy happy and productive lives. Even so, all suffered in one way or another from their traumatic experiences. Like most men returning from war, they had seen horrors—as ambulance drivers, soldiers in the trenches, and combat airmen—that no amount of time could let them forget. The nightmarish images etched into their brains were memories that would continue to haunt them for the remainder of their lives.

Compounding this mental trauma were the unhealthy habits the pilots picked up during the war and retained afterward. Most of them had learned to offset the tremendous stresses that daily combat patrols imposed on their nervous systems with regular doses of alcohol and nicotine. Most of the pilots in the Lafayette Escadrille had used these substances as tonics to settle their nerves, help them forget, and give them the strength and courage to carry on with their often terrifying duties. For some, these vices became demons that possessed them, destroyed their lives, and helped send them to early graves.

Another, entirely different set of memories these men brought back with them from the war also may have adversely affected their later lives. Their carefree sprees in "Gay Paree" were legendary. They lived for the moment when they could steal away to the City of Light for a few hours to eat, drink, party, and carouse. Ted Parsons was not entirely joking when he wrote that he and his comrades returned to the front from a typical binge in Paris only to get some rest. Paris in World War I was a place unique in all of history. Even during the war's darkest days, it was a lively city packed with good restaurants, bars stocked with the best liquor, and limitless numbers of lonely, willing women in need of a man. The town belonged to the heroic American airmen who strutted down the Champs-Élysées with their pockets stuffed with francs, their medals and aviator's insignia gleaming in the sunlight, and a beautiful woman hanging on each arm. For the world-famous "rock stars" of the Lafayette Escadrille, a visit to Paris was a visit to paradise, an experience they would always remember and long for again. Unfortunately, it was also an experience that could never be re-created. Never again would these men find themselves in such an exalted position. When the war ended, some of them felt—at the delicate age of 20-something—that life as they knew and loved it, had also forever ended. It left them with a feeling of emptiness. How could they ever again be content with an ordinary job or the girl back home, when they had once owned the world?

Thus, the men of the Lafayette Escadrille ended the war mentally and physically scarred by some of the best and worst memories imaginable. They were addicted to stimulants, sex, celebrity, and perhaps most damaging of all: the euphoric adrenalin buzz they had daily experienced from defying death in the clear blue sky. They had seen and lived it all at a very young age, and life would never be the same for any of them. Most would cope, but a few would be swallowed up in the disenchantment of the Lost Generation.

★ ★ ★

The Rest of the Story

GEORGES THÉNAULT will always be remembered as the only commanding officer of the Lafayette Escadrille. Though his sometimes ill-disciplined young American pilots did not always see things his way, they rarely failed to pay him the respect he had earned

Major Georges Thénault (right) standing outside the White House on October 29, 1925, with the leading Allied ace of World War I, French Capitaine René Fonck. Thénault served as the air attaché at the French Embassy in Washington, DC, from 1920 to 1933. Fonck finished the war with 75 officially credited victories. (Library of Congress)

and deserved. After the war, he served as the air attaché to the French embassy in Washington, DC, and in 1921, published his classic book *The Story of the Lafayette Escadrille*. In 1925, he married Sarah Spencer, of St. Joseph, Missouri, with whom he had two children. Thénault retired from the French Air Service in 1935, after which, he entered into business. Living in Paris during World War II, he suffered through the years of Nazi occupation, and on December 17, 1948, died of a stroke, at the age of 61. His remains lie in the crypt at the Lafayette Escadrille Memorial next to those of the men he considered, "the honor of my life to have commanded…."

CHARLES NUNGESSER, who lived and flew with N.124 in July 1916, finished the war as France's third-ranking ace, with 43 confirmed victories. Though physically debilitated from all the injuries and wounds he suffered during the war, he continued to fly afterward. He ran a flying school, flew exhibitions, and performed as a stunt pilot in Hollywood—in 1925, he even starred as himself in the silent movie *Sky Raider*. Still, this was insufficient for a man who was used to taking big chances and being idolized by an adoring public. On May 8, 1927, he and fellow Frenchman François Coli, took off from Paris' Le Bourget field in a big white biplane they named *l'Oiseau Blanc*—the white bird. They headed west, hoping to make history's first nonstop flight from Paris to New York City. Soon after takeoff, they disappeared and were never seen again.

WILLIAM THAW was the only pilot to serve with the Lafayette Escadrille for its entire span of existence. As the ranking American and most long-standing member, he, more than anyone else, was the heart of the squadron. After it disbanded on February 18, 1918, Thaw accepted a commission as a major in the US Air Service. He first had to obtain a waiver from American Expeditionary Forces Commanding General John J. Pershing, for defective hearing and vision, a bum knee, and a bad elbow. He was named the commanding officer of the 103rd Aero Squadron, and later, promoted to command the 3rd Pursuit Group. He was credited with five confirmed aerial victories—two with the Lafayette Escadrille and three with the 103rd Aero Squadron. Lieutenant Colonel William Thaw was discharged from the Air Service in 1919. In the postwar years, he engaged in various business pursuits but eventually began to suffer from the effects of his wartime experiences and years of heavy drinking. He passed away on the morning of April 22, 1934, from pneumonia. He was 40 years old.

ELLIOT COWDIN spent only a short time with the squadron and flew but a few missions. He left under a dark cloud but managed to secure a commission as a major in the US Air Service Bureau of Aircraft Production. After the war, he unenthusiastically continued to play polo, but never married or worked at any particular profession. He died on January 6, 1933, at age 46 of complications from influenza.

BERT HALL left the Lafayette Escadrille on November 1, 1916, also under less than happy circumstances. After transferring to Escadrille N.103, he achieved, on November 26, 1916, his fourth and last aerial victory. He went on to write two books, produce and star in two Hollywood movies, marry at least four beautiful women—and serve time in a federal penitentiary for illegal arms transport. The "lovable old rogue" died of a heart attack on December 6, 1948, at the age of 63. His ashes were scattered from an airplane over his hometown of Higginsville, Missouri.

CLYDE BALSLEY had a long and painful road to recovery after his disastrous, first and only aerial combat of June 18, 1916. For two weeks, he lay in the filthy, crowded French evacuation hospital, only a few miles from the front. Virtually unattended by an overworked staff, he was delirious with pain and on the verge of death when finally transferred to the American Hospital at Neuilly-sur-Seine. Here, he received the care he needed. Six surgeries and a year and a half later, he had recovered to the point where he could walk with a cane. He joined the US Air Service and was working in recruiting and war bond drives, when he met and married silent screen star actress Miriam MacDonald. In the years that followed, he involved himself in various business enterprises. He died in Los Angeles on July 23, 1942, four days shy of his 49th birthday.

CHOUTEAU JOHNSON served as an instructor in the US Air Service until the Armistice. Afterward, he became a stock broker in San Francisco and married. He and his wife had one daughter, before they divorced—largely, because of Johnson's addiction to alcohol. He eventually moved to New York and remarried, but soon afterward, developed throat cancer, from which he died on October 10, 1939. He was 50 years old.

LAURENCE RUMSEY returned to the United States, after his rather lackluster performance with Escadrille N.124. He enlisted in the US Army and ended the war as an artillery lieutenant. After the Armistice, he resumed his polo career and lived off of his family's wealth. For the remaining 50 years of his life, he avoided further association with his former squadron mates, but to his credit, also refrained from exploiting his status as a pilot in the Lafayette Escadrille. He died in Buffalo, New York, on May 11, 1967, at the age of 80.

DUDLEY HILL joined the 103rd Aero Squadron, thanks also to a vision waiver that General Pershing approved. He eventually transferred to the 139th, and then the 138th Aero Squadrons, the latter as squadron commander. He was later elevated to command the 5th Pursuit Group. He finished the war with an aversion to flying and never flew again. Similarly, he left his memories in France and avoided talking about them, even to his family. He worked in various business pursuits over the years, married, and in 1942, was blessed with a son. He died of a heart attack on June 30, 1951, at his home in Peekskill, New York, at age 57.

DIDIER MASSON returned to the United States after the war and worked at various jobs through the years, both in the United States and South America, before settling in Mexico. He lived the last eight years of his life in Chetumel, where he managed a hotel. He died on June 2, 1950, at the age of 64.

ROBERT ROCKWELL joined the 103rd Aero Squadron and eventually became its commanding officer. After the war, he worked in various business endeavors, but retained his commission as a reservist in the Air Service. In 1939, he returned to active duty as a full colonel. He served throughout World War II, before retiring in 1946. He died of a heart attack on January 25, 1958, in San Bernadino, California. He was 65 years old.

WILLIS HAVILAND left the Lafayette Escadrille at Senard on September 18, 1917, and served briefly with Escadrille SPA.102 before enlisting in the US Navy. He served as a Naval Aviator in Italy and ended the war as one of the most highly decorated pilots to have flown for the Lafayette Escadrille. He again served in the Navy during World

War II, until diagnosed with lung cancer. He died at age 54 on November 28, 1944. One of Haviland's biggest contributions to the squadron's legacy was the outstanding photo collection he accumulated during and after the war. His scrapbooks, which are maintained by his grandson, Mr. Willis Haviland Lamm, comprise one of the finest collections of Lafayette Escadrille photographs in existence. Willis Haviland is buried in Arlington National Cemetery.

FREDERICK PRINCE JR. left the Lafayette Escadrille on February 15, 1917, as a result of his powerful father's unwanted political intervention—for which young Fred never forgave him. Their contentious relationship continued, and when the elder Prince finally died in 1953, he willed his estimated $100 million estate to an adopted son and left Fred Jr. with only a yearly stipend of $5,000. Frederick Prince Jr. died on October 5, 1962, on Long Island, New York, at age 77.

A trio of former Lafayette Escadrille pilots share a laugh at an undated reunion dinner, some years after the war. Pictured are Carl Dolan, Robert Soubiran, and Chouteau Johnson. Teetotaler Dolan appeared here to be maintaining his traditional role as the unit's "designated driver," as he nursed his glass of water. He enjoyed a long life to become the final surviving member of the Lafayette Escadrille, dying in his adopted state of Hawaii on the last day of 1981. (Washington and Lee University Archives)

ROBERT SOUBIRAN transferred to the 103rd Aero Squadron and, three weeks before the Armistice, became its commanding officer. In the years that followed, he married and raised a family, while working at various jobs in both France and the United States. He died in Queens, New York, on February 4, 1949, at age 62. Like Willis Haviland, he accumulated a sizable collection of Lafayette Escadrille photographs. The originals can be viewed today in the archives of the National Air and Space Museum's Steven F. Udvar-Hazy Center.

TED PARSONS was the only member of the Lafayette Escadrille to pass up a commission in the US Air Service and remain with the Aéronautique Militaire. When the offer was extended, he was on leave in the States. After returning to France, some of his comrades who were unhappy with the delays and general disorganization in the new American Air Service, advised him against joining. He therefore elected to fly for Escadrille SPA.3, the famed "Storks" squadron of Groupe de Combat 12. Here, he met with further success, knocking down seven additional enemy aircraft, for a total score of eight victories, and receiving a commission as a sous-lieutenant. He ended the war as the senior ranking officer in his squadron and the second-ranking ace to have flown for the Lafayette Escadrille. After the war, Parsons served for three years as an agent in the US Bureau of Investigation (later known as the FBI). Afterward, he transitioned—with the help of an old Lafayette Flying Corps acquaintance-turned-Hollywood director, named William Wellman—into the motion picture industry. Parsons became a writer and technical director for aviation films and also began writing aviation stories. In 1937, he penned his entertaining—though not always completely factual—history of the Lafayette Escadrille, *The Great Adventure*. He later joined the US Navy, where he served with distinction throughout World War II. He retired in 1954 at the rank of rear admiral. He died on May 2, 1968, in Sarasota Florida, at age 75 and is buried in Arlington National Cemetery.

STEPHEN BIGELOW returned home from the war suffering from the residual effects of his facial wound and subsequent infection. Even worse was his mental anguish from the bad memories of lost friends and close calls. The happy-go-lucky piano player never seemed to get past these crippling effects of the war. He married twice, the second union producing a daughter, but, according to *Lafayette Escadrille Pilot Biographies* author, Dennis Gordon, "a listlessness seemed to permeate him...." His health grew steadily worse, and on January 6, 1939—three years after his only daughter's birth—Bigelow died in Boston of tuberculosis, compounded by alcohol abuse. He was 44 years old.

WALTER LOVELL excelled at his administrative position in the US Air Service and, by war's end, was married with a daughter and had attained the rank of major. During the postwar years, he worked at a variety of businesses in both France and the United States. Like so many of his fellow pilots, however, he was not destined to live a long life. He died on Long Island, New York, of a brain abscess on September 9, 1937—his 53rd birthday.

EDWARD HINKLE recovered from the pneumonia that forced him to leave the Lafayette Escadrille, but when he did, no pilot slots were available in SPA.124. Consequently, he served as a ferry pilot and instructor, until returning to the United States to work with the Bureau of Aircraft Production. Like other Lafayette Pilots, he was involved in several different pursuits in the years after the war, but he eventually resumed his career in architecture and engineering design. The resilient Hinkle died on January 20, 1967, in Truth or Consequences, New Mexico, at the age of 90. The oldest man to fly for the Lafayette Escadrille also had the longest life and outlived all but a handful of his fellow members.

HAROLD WILLIS ended up in the POW camp at Villingen, Germany, after his unfortunate August 18, 1917, encounter with Leutnant Schulz. He found the conditions there deplorable—filthy and vermin-infested, with barely enough food to stay alive. He immediately decided he had to get out, so he joined with fellow prisoners to stage a mass escape. On October 5, 1918, Willis and several other men walked out of the camp while the guards were distracted with another escape that was in progress. While on the lam, Willis met up with a fellow prisoner, US Navy Lieutenant Edouard Victor Isaacs. Isaacs, a US Naval Academy graduate from Iowa, had been captured after his ship was torpedoed. The two men waded through swamps and streams and climbed hills and mountains for four days until they reached the Rhine River that formed the border between Germany and Switzerland. They plunged into the swift, icy water and nearly drowned before successfully reaching the opposite bank, free men. Isaacs, who later became a US Congressman, received the Medal of Honor and wrote the book *Prisoner of the U-90* about his experiences. Willis resumed his career as an architect, married, and started a family. At the outset of World War II, he, Paul Rockwell, and Ted Parsons unsuccessfully attempted to organize a new Lafayette Escadrille. Willis later served in the US Army Air Forces, attaining the rank of colonel. After the war, he gained recognition as one of the country's top ecclesiastical architects. He died of cancer on April 17, 1962, in Weston, Massachusetts, at age 73.

KENNETH MARR flew first for the 103rd Aero Squadron, but was soon named the commanding officer of the 94th "Hat in the Ring" Aero Squadron. He ended the war with the rank of major. Afterward, Marr worked for film director John Ford at Paramount Pictures, and while there, met and married actress Alice Ward. Marr later formed a lucrative oil drilling company that enabled him to buy a 5,000-acre sheep ranch in Humbolt County, California. He died at age 78 on December 28, 1963, in Palo Alto, California.

WILLIAM DUGAN served with 103rd Aero Squadron before being assigned to the American Aviation Acceptance Park. After the war, Dugan, now married, returned to Costa Rica and resumed his prewar job as a plantation manager with the United Fruit Company. In January 1921, a son was born to the couple, but a few days later, Mrs. Dugan developed complications and died. The grieving Dugan left his baby son in the care of a nurse and accompanied his wife's body back to New York for burial. He returned to Costa Rica to find that his newborn son had also fallen ill, and on April 29, his three-month-old baby died in his arms. Despondent, he took a job exploring the jungles of Central America for suitable future plantation sites. In 1924, he contracted a fever and returned to New York to recuperate. There, he developed septicemia and died on September 4, 1924. William Dugan, 34 years old, was buried next to his wife and son.

JERRY HEWITT ended the war as an artilleryman in the US Army. He later obtained a law degree but still managed to get into legal trouble. He became involved in a series of shady schemes that resulted in prison terms for embezzlement and larceny. His only defense was, "It is only when I am drinking that I do these things." He died in Washington, DC, on May 24, 1936, an alcoholic vagrant. A group of concerned citizens, upon learning the fate of this former member of the Lafayette Escadrille, rescued his unclaimed body from the morgue and arranged for it to be interred in Arlington National Cemetery. Hewitt was 41 years old.

Hank Jones proudly displays a Sioux Indianhead insignia that was cut from a 103rd Aero Squadron Spad and given to him when he left the squadron. Jones later donated this insignia to the National Museum of the US Air Force, where it is displayed today. It is one of the few surviving examples in existence. (US Air Force)

RAY BRIDGMAN served with the 103rd and 139th Aero Squadrons, before becoming the commanding officer of the 22nd Aero. He ended the war with four confirmed victories. After the war, he completed his studies at Yale, married, and began his career as an educator. He spent most of his life teaching European history at New York University. By 1951, the increasingly reclusive pacifist had become despondent over the state of world affairs, as well as his declining health. On November 9, 1951, he fell or deliberately jumped from the deck of a New York Ferry and drowned. He was 56 years old.

CARL DOLAN served with the 103rd Aero Squadron, and after the war, resigned from the Air Service to become the American Air Advisor to China. Over the years, he continued to serve in a wide variety of government and civilian positions, while remaining in contact with his friends of the Lafayette Escadrille. In November 1981, the 86-year-old Dolan attended a special reunion in France to honor the surviving aces of World War I. This trip affected his health, and Dolan—the last living pilot of the Lafayette Escadrille—died on December 31, 1981, in Honolulu, Hawaii.

JOHN DREXEL was commissioned a major in the US Air Service after his short service with the Lafayette Escadrille. He then occupied high-level military positions until the

Ted Parsons (left) and Hank Jones in their later years, having an animated discussion, possibly about some event that occurred in the skies over France in 1917. (US Air Force)

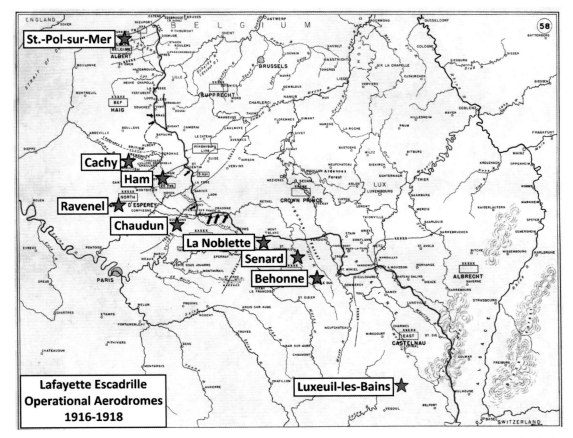

Above: A military map of Northern France, showing the location of all the aerodromes from which the Lafayette Escadrille operated. The irregular red line, extending diagonally from lower right to upper left, represents the front as it existed in 1917. It varied only slightly from this during the 22 months the squadron existed. *(US Military Academy, modified by author)*

Below: An exceptionally clear panorama of a typical Lafayette Escadrille flying field. This photograph, scanned from an original Paul Rockwell negative, was taken on a busy day at Chaudun, early summer, 1917. The view is looking towards the north. Most of the airplanes pictured are Spad VIIs, some of them with their engines running, in preparation for a patrol, while a single Nieuport can be distinguished at the center of the photograph. The official squadron designation had, by this time, changed from N.124 to SPA.124. *(Washington and Lee University Archives)*

"The Valiant 38" Americans who flew for the Lafayette Escadrille. *(Washington and Lee University Archives)*

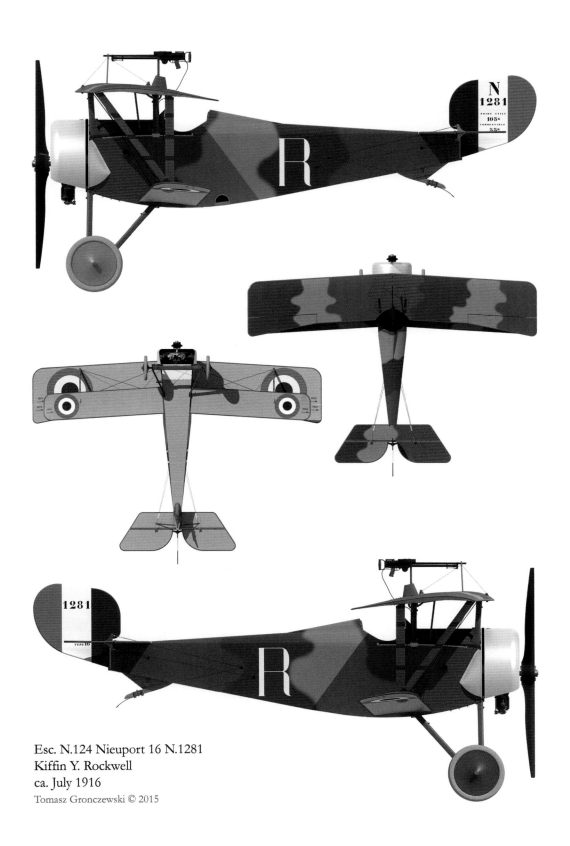

Esc. N.124 Nieuport 16 N.1281
Kiffin Y. Rockwell
ca. July 1916
Tomasz Gronczewski © 2015

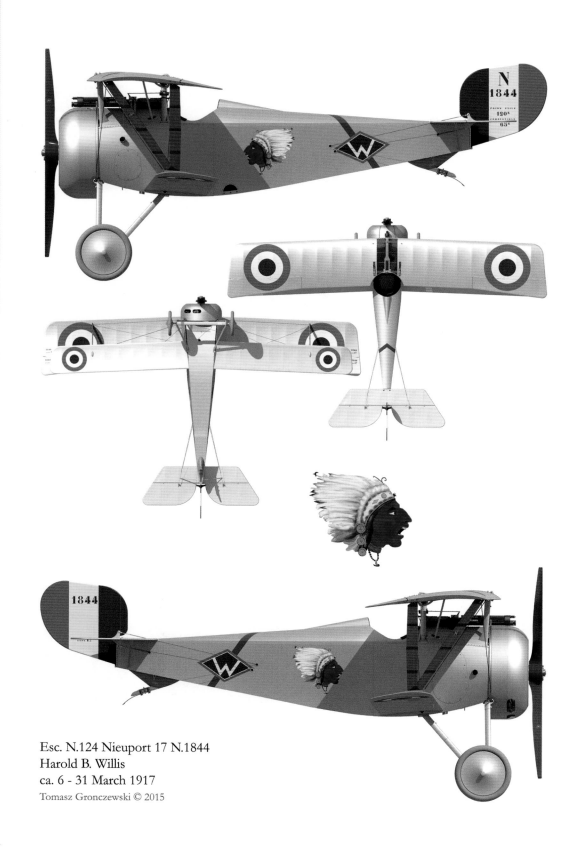

Esc. N.124 Nieuport 17 N.1844
Harold B. Willis
ca. 6 - 31 March 1917
Tomasz Gronczewski © 2015

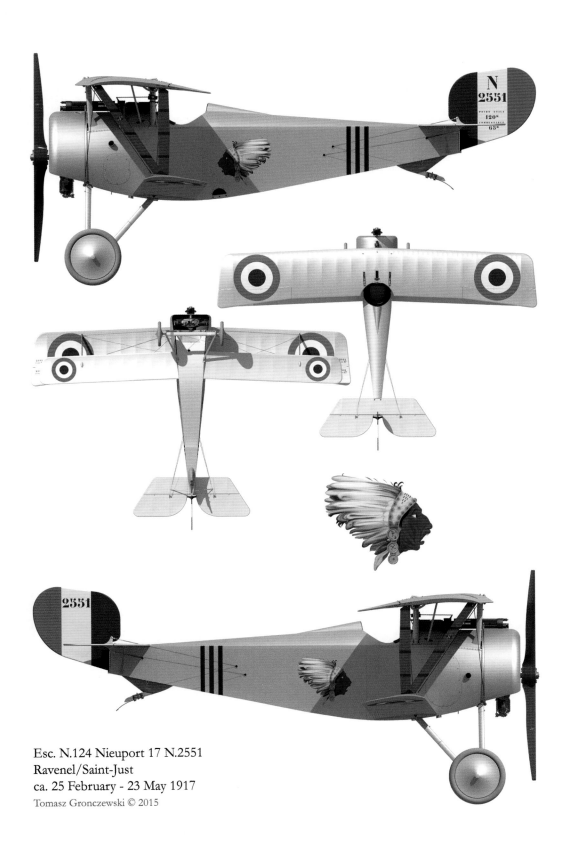

Esc. N.124 Nieuport 17 N.2551
Ravenel/Saint-Just
ca. 25 February - 23 May 1917
Tomasz Gronczewski © 2015

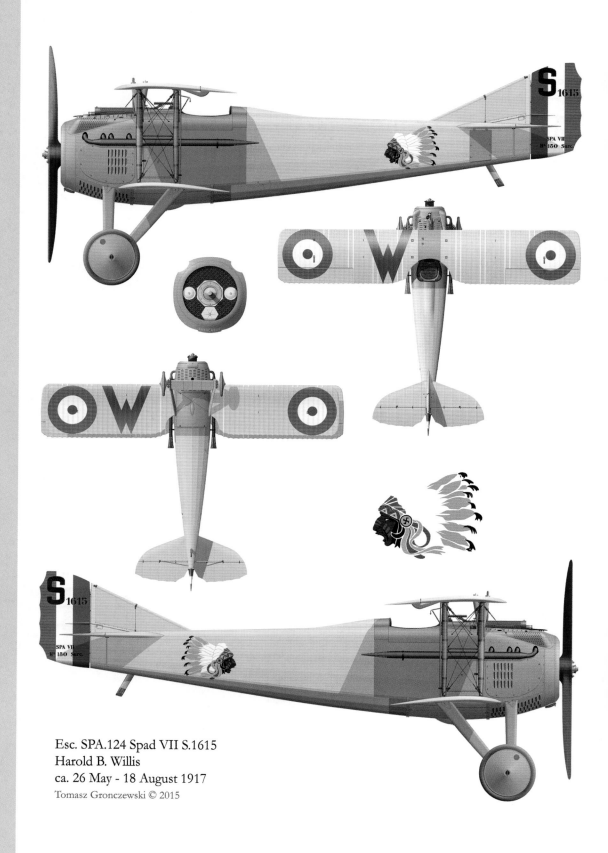

Esc. SPA.124 Spad VII S.1615
Harold B. Willis
ca. 26 May - 18 August 1917
Tomasz Gronczewski © 2015

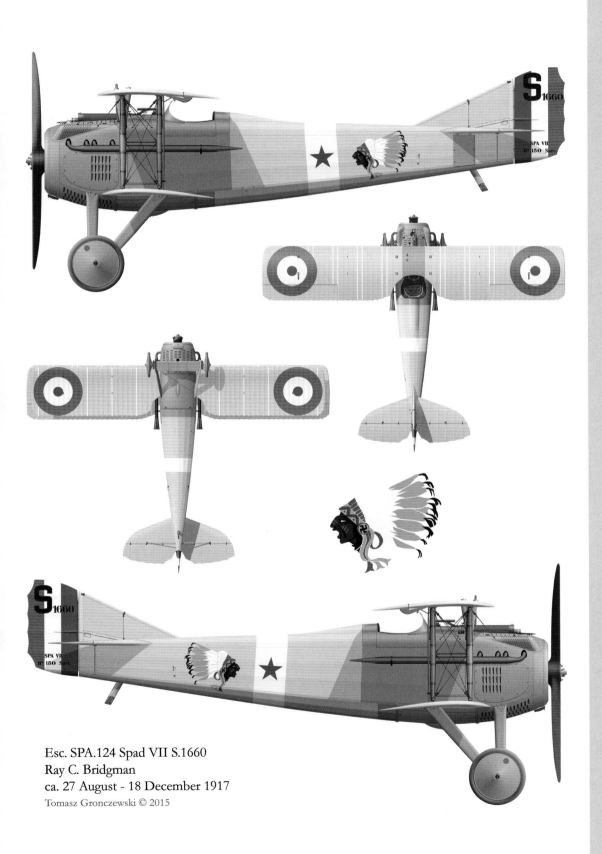

Esc. SPA.124 Spad VII S.1660
Ray C. Bridgman
ca. 27 August - 18 December 1917
Tomasz Gronczewski © 2015

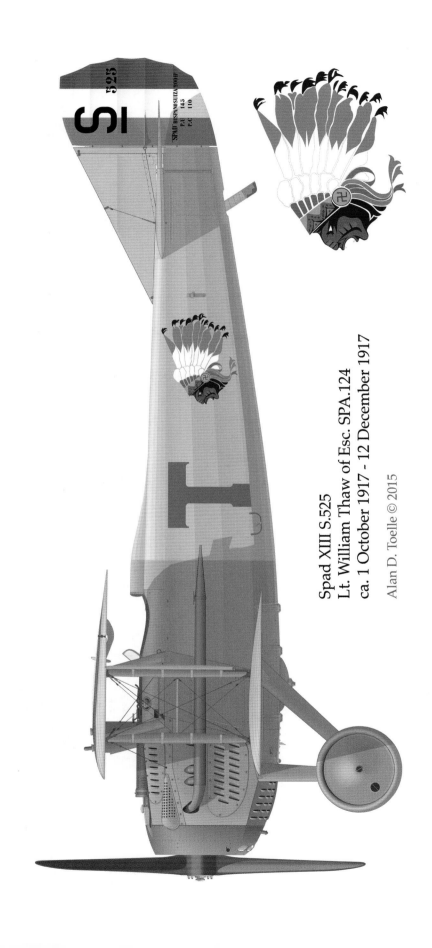

Spad XIII S.525
Lt. William Thaw of Esc. SPA.124
ca. 1 October 1917 - 12 December 1917

Alan D. Toelle © 2015

Armistice, ending the war as a lieutenant colonel. His former squadron mates resented his rank and the key positions to which he was assigned, believing—rightly so—that they were due only to the interventions of his wealthy and influential father. After the war, Drexel moved to England and entered into banking. He lived the rest of his life there and died of a heart attack on March 4, 1958, at the age of 66.

HENRY SWEET JONES flew with the 103rd Aero Squadron until June 1918, when he was reassigned to instructor duties in the United States. After the war, he worked for a railroad and an airline, before signing on with the F.W. Woolworth Company, for which he worked for the rest of his career, managing several different stores. He died, on March 29, 1972, at the age of 79, in Clearwater, Florida.

JAMES NORMAN HALL collected his second and third aerial victories while serving with the 103rd Aero Squadron, and his fourth, as flight commander in the 94th Aero. On May 7, 1918, the fabric covering the upper right wing of his Nieuport 28 fighter ripped loose during a dive over enemy lines. As Hall struggled to maintain control, an antiaircraft shell smashed into his already disabled aircraft. Miraculously, it failed to explode but hit with enough force to bring him down. In the ensuing crash, the injured Hall was taken prisoner. After repatriation at war's end, he was tasked with writing a history of all the American pilots

Captain James Norman Hall's crashed Nieuport 28. Hall had transferred from the Lafayette Escadrille to the US Air Service and eventually became a flight commander in the 94th Aero Squadron. On May 7, 1918, he was hit by an antiaircraft shell as he patrolled over enemy lines. Fortunately for him, the shell failed to explode but it still knocked him out of the sky. He was lucky to survive. (US Air Force)

Here, Hall sits in a German staff car, after his May 7, 1918, crash—with a broken nose, two injured ankles, and a much-needed new canine friend. He later wrote that he "had a homesick quarter of an hour while sitting in their car." A German officer gave Hall this picture while visiting him in the hospital. Hall finished the war as a POW but later enjoyed a highly successful literary career. (US Air Force)

who flew for France in the war. Assisting him was Charles Nordhoff, an American who had flown for Escadrille SPA.99. Their work culminated in the comprehensive two-volume history *The Lafayette Flying Corps*. It was the start of a productive literary collaboration that lasted 28 years, until Nordhoff's death in 1947. Together, they penned such classics as *Falcons of France, Mutiny on the Bounty, Men Against the Sea, and Pitcairn's Island*. James Norman Hall, a soldier, pilot, and author who had served under three different flags, died in his beloved Tahiti of heart disease on July 6, 1951. He was 64 years old.

DAVID PETERSON served in the 103rd, 94th, and 95th Aero Squadrons, the latter as squadron commander. An exceptionally accomplished fighter pilot, he ended the war with six confirmed victories, placing him in the exclusive Lafayette Escadrille "ace club" with Raoul Lufbery, William Thaw, and Ted Parsons. On March 16, 1919, the 24-year-old US Air Service pilot crashed near Daytona Beach, Florida, after his flight controls jammed. He was buried in his hometown of Honesdale, Pennsylvania. When plans were made to move his body to the crypt of the newly built Lafayette Escadrille Memorial, the citizens of Honesdale lobbied against it. As a result, the sarcophagus that bears his name there remains empty.

CHRISTOPHER FORD flew with the 103rd and the 213th Aero Squadrons. He excelled as a fighter pilot, downing three German planes before being brought down by ground fire

After World War I, Paul Rockwell once again served in the French Foreign Legion. Here, he is pictured as a captain. In 1925, he served in Morocco during France's participation in the Rif War. He later served in the US Army Air Forces and retired as a colonel. As the historian of the Lafayette Escadrille, he left behind a treasure trove of precious documents, correspondence, and photographs relating to the squadron and its men that he accumulated throughout his long life. This priceless collection is carefully maintained in the library archives of his alma mater, Washington and Lee University. Rockwell died at the age of 96 and is buried in the Emma Jarnagin Cemetery, Morristown, Tennessee. (Washington and Lee University Archives)

and made a prisoner of war on October 15, 1918. After the Armistice, he remained in the Air Service and served in various capacities until his retirement in 1941. He died of cancer on April 9, 1945, at the age of 52, and was buried at Arlington National Cemetery.

PAUL AYRES ROCKWELL continued his profession as a writer, and in 1925, published *War Letters of Kiffin Yates Rockwell*, in memory of his fallen brother. That same year, he saw action in Morocco as a Foreign Legion aerial observer, during France's participation in the Rif War. In 1930, he published *American Fighters in the Foreign Legion, 1914–1918*, one of the best books ever written on the subject. After he and comrades Willis and Parsons failed in their attempt to establish a new Lafayette Escadrille in France at the beginning of World War II, Rockwell joined the US Army Air Forces, where he served until his retirement in 1946 as a colonel. For the rest of his long and productive life, he remained in close contact with the men of the Lafayette Escadrille, collecting photographs, exchanging correspondence, and hosting reunions. Through his role as historian for the squadron, an unofficial position he took seriously, he became the ultimate authority on all matters having to do with the Lafayette Escadrille. He also became the squadron's harshest critic, often castigating former members—in particular, Bert Hall—who did not measure up to his high standards. Unfortunately his characterization of these men, which was sometimes unfair, painted a false picture of them that still exists today. Later in life, he expressed regret for his unforgiving attitude toward these men, but the damage had been done. Undoubtedly, Paul Rockwell's greatest legacy is his voluminous collection of photographs, letters, and documents that now make up the fabulous Paul Ayres Rockwell collection at the Washington and Lee University Archives. Rockwell died at the age of 96 in Asheville, North Carolina, on August 22, 1985.

WHISKEY AND SODA, like some of their human friends, did not fare well after they left the Lafayette Escadrille. Some of the men visited the beloved mascots at the zoo whenever they were in Paris, and Whiskey in particular, was always glad to see his old comrades. However, the frigid 1916–1917 winter weather, to which the cubs had been subjected in the cold, damp huts at the aerodromes, had ruined their health. Both developed rheumatism and died soon after the war ended.

LEGACY

They shall grow not old, as we that are left grow old:
Age shall not weary them, nor the years condemn.
At the going down of the sun and in the morning
We will remember them. ★

On July 4, 1928, a large crowd gathered in a wooded park on the western outskirts of Paris. Present were former wartime aviators, their families, and numerous dignitaries from both France and the United States. The guests of honor for this solemn occasion included French Minister of War Paul Painlevé and US Ambassador to France Myron T. Herrick. A French honor guard stood at rigid attention and all others in attendance solemnly observed, as biplanes passed low overhead and the bugler sounded taps. The occasion that brought them all together at this time and place was the dedication of an impressive white marble monument that had been several years in the making.

The Memorial

It has now been 100 years since the young American pilots of the Lafayette Escadrille first roared through the skies over war-torn France. Even so, memorials of all shapes and sizes, honoring their deeds and their sacrifices, can still be found in France and the United States. The most important monument, however, is the one that was dedicated on that Independence Day, 1928. The Mémorial de l'Escadrille Lafayette—the Lafayette Escadrille Memorial—lies in the Parisian suburb of Marnes-la-Coquette.

★ Fourth verse of the World War I poem *For the Fallen* by Robert Laurence Binyon, which first appeared in the British newspaper *The Times* on September 21, 1914.

Situated on a 10-acre plot in the beautiful, wooded Parc de Villeneuve-l'Etang, it honors not only the pilots of the Lafayette Escadrille, but all the men of the greater Lafayette Flying Corps who flew for France in World War I. More than just a monument, this imposing creation of French architect Alexandre Marcel, is hallowed ground: it serves as the final resting place for 49 of the approximately 70 American airmen who flew for France and died during or soon after the war. Their remains, along with those of two of their French commanders, Georges Thénault and Antonin Brocard, are entombed in a row of stone sarcophaguses. These coffins, illuminated by 13 ornate stained-glass windows, lie in the semicircular sanctuary, or crypt, that exists below the monument.

The memorial arc—half the size of the famed Arc de Triomphe de l'Étoile—is flanked on either side by a columned wing, and all of this is centered behind a fountained pool. Carved into the monument's stone are an array of symbolic images and inscriptions, both in English and French. The most prominent of these reads, "In Memory of the Heroes of the Escadrille Lafayette Who Died in Defense of Right and Liberty." Also inscribed are the names of the fallen pilots, the battlefields in which they participated, and images of Washington and Lafayette—the latter, to emphasize the friendship that has existed between France and the United States since the American Revolution. The Lafayette Escadrille Memorial remains, today, the most important monument in Europe honoring American airmen of World War I.

The inspiration for the monument came from former Lafayette Flying Corps pilot Edgar Hamilton. After the Armistice, he was one of those assigned to locate the bodies of fallen airmen. He proposed that the remains of those volunteers who had flown for France be brought together in a memorial that would appropriately honor their spirit and sacrifice. His idea was enthusiastically approved, and in March 1923, an association called the "Mémorial de l'Escadrille Lafayette" was formed to begin the process.

The memorial was a true Franco-American joint effort. France donated the land on which it was built, and it was financed with donations from the families of Lafayette Flying Corps pilots and other private donors. It was not, however, without plenty of controversy. Almost from the outset, a fight erupted between William Thaw and Frederick Prince Sr., the father of Norman and Fred Jr. The wealthy father agreed to contribute $20,000 towards the construction of the memorial, but at a price: he stipulated that his dead son, Norman, be recognized as "originator of the idea and inspirer of the purpose of Escadrille Lafayette." Organizers agreed, but Thaw—himself, one of the squadron's originators—challenged the senior Prince's demand, along with his other history-altering claims. The dispute festered for several years, until Thaw's death in 1934. Thaw won the battle, however: on April 19, 1929, Prince gave up and defiantly announced his intention not to have Norman's remains reside in the crypt of the Lafayette Escadrille Memorial. Rather, he decided to move them to a special chapel he funded at the Washington National Cathedral—at a personal cost of more than $200,000.

The second serious controversy erupted, incredibly, on the evening before the July 4, 1928, dedication ceremony. As the attending Lafayette Flying Corps pilots gathered for a dinner at the Hôtel Chatham in Paris, a heated argument arose between some of the men from the Lafayette Escadrille and those of the greater Lafayette Flying Corps, who had served in other French squadrons. The men from the Lafayette Escadrille apparently objected to the names of the fallen Lafayette Flying Corps members appearing along with those from their own squadron. The name on the monument was, after all, "The Lafayette *Escadrille* Memorial." Though seemingly petty, this disagreement nearly derailed the dedication, until calmer voices made themselves heard late into the night and resolved the dispute.

Soon after the 1928 dedication, a prominent American lawyer working in Paris, named William Nelson Cromwell, provided a generous endowment of 600,000 French francs—approximately $24,000—for the formation of the Lafayette Escadrille Memorial Foundation to ensure its future upkeep. Unfortunately, it was not enough to provide the comprehensive maintenance necessary to keep the monument—which was built on damp, low-lying land—in acceptable condition. Consequently, over the decades, it gradually deteriorated into a state of general disrepair: mold covered its surfaces, cracks formed in the stone, and water flooded its subterranean crypt.

Finally, in 2003, the US and French governments joined forces with a sum of $3 million to renovate the structure. Unfortunately, during the course of this work, further structural problems were identified. Subsequent studies indicated the need for a significantly greater amount for a proper restoration. Fortunately, at this writing, another Franco-American partnership—led by military and civilian leaders on both sides of the Atlantic—is well on the way to putting this project into action. However, as might be imagined, in spite of numerous substantial contributions, more funds are needed and will continue to be needed in the future. Those who wish to learn more about this effort and possibly contribute to the worthy cause are urged to go to the Lafayette Escadrille Memorial Restoration Working Group webpage at: *http://www.worldwar1. com/pdf/Lafayette_Project.pdf*

Anyone interested in visiting this historic and still-beautiful memorial can reach it via train from Paris's Saint-Lazare station to the Garches-Marnes-la-Coquette stop. After exiting the train station at Garches, turn left (west) and walk for 1/2 mile to the park's entrance. The memorial is open every day of the week and is well worth the effort.

In spite of its aging problems, the Lafayette Escadrille Memorial continues to serve as a tribute to the heroic young Americans who volunteered to fly and fight for France in the early days of World War I. Equally important, it still functions as an important symbol of the bond of friendship the United States and France have shared for more than 200 years. Periodically, representatives of the air forces of France and the United States gather at the monument to pay homage to the men of the Lafayette Flying Corps.

Other Reminders

There is another important part of the Lafayette Escadrille heritage that reflects France's high esteem for the Americans who served during her hour of need. After the Lafayette Escadrille became the 103rd Aero Squadron of the US Air Service on February 18, 1918, the French Aéronautique Militaire kept the squadron's name alive by retaining the Escadrille de Lafayette in its operational inventory. During World War II, the squadron operated under the auspices of the US Army Air Forces 12th Air Force. Flying American-built Curtiss P-40 Warhawk and Republic P-47 Thunderbolt fighters, it served throughout the Mediterranean theatre of the war. Afterward, this elite unit continued to serve in the French Armée de l'Air, and it remains operational to this day. At this writing, the Escadron de chasse 2/4 Lafayette operates from the French air base at Istres-Le Tubé, flying the Dassault Mirage 2000N jet fighter.

Yet another important part of the legacy of the Lafayette Escadrille is the wealth of literature that the squadron inspired. The sheer number of books and articles—this illustrated history included—that have appeared about this fabled unit over the past century is truly astounding. The list of references found in the bibliography section of this book, though by no means exhaustive, hints at the magnitude of all that has been written about the Lafayette Escadrille. Given this voluminous literary response, it is no exaggeration to assert that this unique squadron is among the most famed and revered in the history of aerial warfare. Its unprecedented renown remains undiminished today.

★ ★ ★

There is nothing glorious about warfare. Decent young people killing other decent young people—whether on the battlefield, the high seas, or in the clear blue sky—is an abomination that defies description. However, if anything good can be said about any war, it is the spirit and courage exhibited by those who accept the responsibility of fighting it. Their willingness to sacrifice life and limb for a cause in which they believe represents courage and nobility of the highest order. The American volunteers who flew for the Lafayette Escadrille exemplified this unyielding dedication to the principle of right over wrong. They had every reason to hate war and what it meant for them, yet they volunteered, fought, and—too often—died for what they considered the cause of freedom and justice.

Soaring in their open-cockpit biplanes through the hazy skies above the Western Front, the men of the Lafayette Escadrille left in their wake a flaming trail of glory and sacrifice. The tale they wrote during that unique slice of time when men fought to the death in the skies over France is one that will never be repeated—and it will never be forgotten.

APPENDIX A
Lafayette Escadrille Operating Locations, 1916–1918

Inclusive Dates*	Location (Department)	Sector
April 20 to May 20, 1916	Luxeuil (Haute-Saone)	Vosges
May 20 to September 14, 1916	Behonne/Bar-le-Duc (Meuse)	Verdun
September 14 to October 18, 1916	Luxeuil (Haute-Saone)	Vosges
October 18, 1916 to January 26, 1917	Cachy (Somme)	Somme
January 26 to April 7, 1917	Ravenel/Saint-Just (Oise)	Oise/Aisne
April 7 to June 3, 1917	Ham (Somme)	Somme
June 3 to July 17, 1917	Chaudun (Aisne)	Aisne
July 17 to August 11, 1917	Saint-Pol-sur-Mer (Nord)	Flanders
August 11, to September 28, 1917	Senard (Meuse)	Verdun
September 28 to December 7, 1917	Chaudun (Aisne)	Aisne
December 7, 1917 to February 18, 1918	La Noblette/La Cheppe (Marne)	Champagne

* Dates vary slightly in different accounts and documents. Moves typically took place over a period of several days, and the date on the relocation order was not necessarily the same as the actual moving date. The dates listed here are from the squadron logbook, the *Journal des Marches et Opérations*.

APPENDIX B
Lafayette Escadrille Roster

Pilot	Arrived*	Departed*	Confirmed Victories w/N/ SPA.124; (w/ Other Units)**	Comments
			French	
Georges Thénault	4/20/16	1/18/18	0	To Pau, School of Aerobatics
Alfred de Laage de Meux	4/20/16	5/23/17	3	Killed in Crash
Charles Nungesser	7/9/16	8/15/16	1 (42)	Temporarily Assigned; Lost during Paris–NY attempt 5/8/1927
Antoine de Maison-Rouge	5/28/17	10/6/17	0	KIA, Esc. SPA.78 1/14/1918
Louis Verdier-Fauvety	10/6/17	2/18/18	0	KIA, Enemy Bombing Raid 8/21/1918
			American	
William Thaw	4/20/16	2/18/18	2*** (3)	To 103rd Aero
Norman Prince	4/20/16	10/15/16	4	Killed in Crash
Elliot Cowdin	4/20/16	6/25/16	0 (1)	US Air Service
Bert Hall	4/20/16	11/1/16	3 (1)	To Esc. N.103
Victor Chapman	4/20/16	6/23/16	0	KIA
Kiffin Rockwell	4/20/16	9/23/16	2	KIA
James McConnell	4/20/16	3/19/17	0	KIA
8. Raoul Lufbery	5/25/16	1/5/18	16	To US Air Service; KIA, 94th Aero 5/19/1918
9. Clyde Balsley	5/27/16	6/18/16	0	Wounded

Pilot	Arrived*	Departed*	Confirmed Victories w/N/ SPA.124; (w/ Other Units)**	Comments
10. Chouteau Johnson	5/27/16	10/31/17	1	To US Air Service, Instructor 2nd AIC
11. Laurence Rumsey	6/4/16	11/25/16	0	Retired from Aviation
12. Dudley Hill	6/9/16	2/18/18	0	To 103rd Aero
13. Didier Masson	6/19/16 6/15/17	2/15/17 10/8/17	1	To Esc. N.471; US Air Service, Instructor, 3rd AIC
14. Paul Pavelka	8/11/16	1/24/17	0	To Esc. N.391, Salonika; Died After Horse-Riding Accident 11/12/1917
15. Robert Rockwell	9/17/16	2/18/18	0	To 103rd Aero
16. Willis Haviland	10/22/16	9/18/17	1***	To Esc. SPA.102; US Navy
17. Frederick Prince	10/22/16	2/15/17	0	To Pau, Instructor
18. Robert Soubiran	10/22/16	2/18/18	0	To 103rd Aero
19. Ronald Hoskier	12/11/16	4/23/17	0	KIA
20. Edmond Genet	1/19/17	4/16/17	0	KIA
21. Edwin Parsons	1/25/17	2/26/18	1 (7)	To Esc. SPA.3
22. Stephen Bigelow	2/8/17	9/11/17	0	Wounded
23. Edward Hinkle	3/1/17	6/12/17	0	Illness
24. Walter Lovell	3/1/17	10/24/17	1	To US G.H.Q., Chaumont
25. Harold Willis	3/1/17	8/18/17	0	POW, Escaped 10/5/1918
26. Kenneth Marr	3/29/17	2/18/18	1***	To 103rd Aero
27. William Dugan	3/30/17	2/18/18	0	To 103rd Aero
28. Thomas Hewitt	3/30/17	9/17/17	0	Retired from Aviation
29. Courtney Campbell	4/15/17	10/1/17	0	KIA
30. Ray Bridgman	5/1/17	2/18/18	0 (4)	To 103rd Aero
31. Charles Dolan	5/12/17	2/18/18	0 (1)	To 103rd Aero
32. John Drexel	5/12/17	6/15/17	0	To US Air Service
33. Henry Jones	5/12/17	2/18/18	0	To 103rd Aero
34. James Hall	6/16/17 10/3/17	6/26/17 2/18/18	1 (3)	Wounded To 103rd, 94th Aero; POW 5/7/1918
35. Douglas MacMonagle	6/16/17	9/24/17	0	KIA

Pilot	Arrived*	Departed*	Confirmed Victories w/N/ SPA.124; (w/ Other Units)**	Comments
36. David Peterson	6/16/17	2/18/18	1*** (5)	To 103rd Aero; Killed in Crash in US 3/16/1919
37. James Doolittle	7/2/17	7/17/17	0	Wounded; Killed in Crash in US 7/26/1918
38. Christopher Ford	11/8/17	2/18/18	0 (3)	To 103rd Aero; POW 10/15/1918

* Arrival and departure dates listed in different sources vary slightly, depending on whether they refer to: (a) the day a pilot arrived/departed, (b) the day he was added/deleted from the roster, or (c) the day he was officially assigned/reassigned. Rarely were these three dates the same.

** The victory credit figures used here are from Dennis Connell and Frank W. Bailey's, "Victory Logs: Lafayette Escadrille and Lafayette Flying Corps," *Cross & Cockade Journal* 21(4), Winter 1980, pp. 351–368. These are probably the best-researched and most accurate figures available.

*** Marr shared his lone victory with Peterson, while Haviland shared his with William Thaw. Thus, the tally of *individual* victories credited to the 38 Americans in the Lafayette Escadrille is 35, but they accounted for only 33 downed enemy aircraft. French pilots Nungesser added 1 and de Laage 3, for a grand total of 37 squadron victories.

SELECTED BIBLIOGRAPHY

Listed here are some of the more useful references dealing directly or indirectly with the Lafayette Escadrille that have appeared over the past century. Included are general histories, which provide good overviews of the topic, as well as first-person accounts and biographies. The latter, although sometimes limited in scope, serve to illuminate the human aspect of the young pilots that a factual overview cannot always provide. All are recommended.

Babbitt, George F. *Norman Prince: A Volunteer Who Died for the Cause He Loved*. Boston: Houghton Mifflin Company, 1917.

Bowe, John and Charles L. MacGregor. *Soldiers of the Legion*. Chicago: Peterson Linotyping Company, 1918.

Brown, Philip C. "Pavelka of the Lafayette," *Cross & Cockade Journal* 19(2), Summer 1978, pp. 97–108.

Cavanaugh, Robert L. "U.S. Army Intelligence Report on l'Escadrille Americaine," *Cross & Cockade Journal* 20(1), Spring 1979, pp. 39–65.

Channing, Grace Ellery (ed). *War Letters of Edmond Genet: The First American Aviator Killed Flying the Stars and Stripes*. New York: Charles Scribner's Sons, 1918.

Chapman, John J. *Victor Chapman's Letters from France, with Memoir by John Jay Chapman*. New York: The Macmillan Company, 1917.

Connell, Dennis and Frank W. Bailey. "Victory Logs: Lafayette Escadrille and Lafayette Flying Corps," *Cross & Cockade Journal* 21(4), Winter 1980, pp. 351–368.

"The Diary of H. Clyde Balsley," *Cross & Cockade Journal* 18(2), Summer 1977, pp. 97–123.

Fisher, Howard G. "Lafayette Escadrille Spad S.VII, S.1777: Whose Aircraft?" *Over the Front*, Fall 2000, pp. 195–205.

Flammer, Philip M. *The Vivid Air: The Lafayette Escadrille*. Athens, GA: The University of Georgia Press 1981.

Flood, Charles Bracelen. *First to Fly: The Story of the Lafayette Escadrille, the American Heroes Who Flew For France in World War I*. New York: Atlantic Monthly Press, 2015.

Franks, Norman L.R. and Frank W. Bailey. *Over the Front: A Complete Record of the Fighter Aces and Units of the United States and French Air Services, 1914–1918*. London: Grub Street, 1992.

Genet, Edmund Charles Clinton. *An American for Lafayette: The Diaries of E.C.C. Genet, Lafayette Escadrille*. Charlottesville, VA: University of Virginia Press, 1982.

Gordon, Dennis. "Dudley Hill of Escadrille Lafayette," *Cross & Cockade Journal* 24(3), Autumn 1983, pp. 253–259.

Gordon, Dennis. *Lafayette Escadrille Pilot Biographies*. Missoula, MT: The Doughboy Historical Society, 1991.

Gordon, Dennis. *The Lafayette Flying Corps: The American Volunteers in the French Air Service in World War One*. Atglen, PA: Shiffer Military History, 2000.

Guttman, Jon. *SPA 124 Lafayette Escadrille: American Volunteer Airmen in World War I*. Oxford, UK: Osprey Publishing Ltd., 2004.

Hall, Bert. *En l'Air*. New York: The New Library, 1918.

Hall, Bert and John J. Niles. *One Man's War: The Story of the Lafayette Escadrille*. New York: Henry Holt and Company, 1928.

Hall, James Norman. *High Adventure: A Narrative of Air Fighting in France*. Boston: Houghton Mifflin Company, 1918.

Hall, James Norman and Charles B. Nordhoff. *The Lafayette Flying Corps in Two Volumes* (Volumes I and II). Boston: Houghton Mifflin Company, 1920.

Hoskier, Ronald Wood. *Ronald Wood Hoskier: Literary Fragments and Remains in Prose and Verse of Ronald Wood Hoskier 1896–1917*. Boston: The McKenzie Engraving Company, 1920.

Hynes, Samuel. *The Unsubstantial Air: American Fliers in the First World War*. New York: Farrar, Straus and Giroux, 2014.

Jablonski, Edward. *Warriors with Wings: The Story of the Lafayette Escadrille*. New York: The Bobbs-Merrill Company, Inc., 1966.

Johnson, Terry L. *Valiant Volunteers, A Novel: Based on the Passion and the Glory of the Lafayette Escadrille*. Bloomington, IN: AuthorHouse, 2007.

McConnell, James R. "Flying for France," *The World's Work 33* (November 1916): 41–53; (March 1917): 479–509.

McConnell, James R. *Flying for France*. Garden City, NY: Doubleday, Page & Company., 1917.

Mason, Herbert Molloy. *The Lafayette Escadrille*. New York: Random House, 1964.

Miller, Roger G. *Like A Thunderbolt: The Lafayette Escadrille and the Advent of American Pursuit in World War I*. Washington, D.C.: Air Force History Museums Program, 2007.

Nordhoff, Charles and James Norman Hall. *Falcons of France*. Boston: Little, Brown, and Company, 1936.

Pardoe, Blaine L. *The Bad Boy: Bert Hall, Aviator and Mercenary of the Skies.* Charleston, SC: Fonthill Media, 2013.

Parks, Dr. James J. "The American Eagle Insignia of the Escadrille Americaine," *Cross & Cockade Journal* 15(4), Winter 1974, pp. 374–375.

Parsons, Edwin C. *The Great Adventure.* Garden City, NY: Doubleday, Doran and Co., 1937. Re-published in 1963 by E.C. Seale & Company, Inc. under the title *I Flew With the Lafayette Escadrille.*

Rockwell, Paul Ayres. *American Fighters in the Foreign Legion 1914–1918.* Boston and New York: Houghton Mifflin Company, 1930.

Rockwell, Paul Ayres. *War Letters of Kiffin Yates Rockwell: Foreign Legionnaire and Aviator France, 1914–1916.* Garden City, NY: Doubleday, Page & Company, 1925.

Rogers, Lt. Colonel Phillippe D., USMC. *L'Escadrille Lafayette : Unité Volontaire de Combat Oubliée de l'Amérique* (English version), http://www.institut-strategie.fr/?p=726, 2012.

Sengupta, Narayan. *The Lafayette Escadrille: America's Most Famous Squadron.* Narayan Sengupta, 2013.

Thénault, Capitaine Georges. *Escadrille N.124, Journal de Marche.*

Thénault, Captain Georges (Walter Duranty, trans). *The Story of the Lafayette Escadrille.* Boston: Small, Maynard & Company, 1921.

Toelle, Alan. "A White-Faced Cow and the Operational History of the Escadrille Americaine N.124 to September 1916," *Over the Front* 24(4) Winter 2009, pp. 292–337.

Vezin, Alain. *Escadron de chasse La Fayette, 1916–2011: Du Nieuport au Mirage 2000N.* Paris, France: Broché, 2012.

Weeks, Alice S. *Greater Love Hath No Man.* Boston: Bruce Humphries, Inc., 1939.

Whitehouse, Arch. *Legion of the Lafayette.* Garden City, NY: Doubleday and Company, 1962.

Winslow, Carroll Dana. *With the French Flying Corps.* London: Constable & Company, Ltd., 1917.

Wynne, H. Hugh. "Escadrille Lafayette," *Cross & Cockade Journal* 2(1), Spring 1961, pp. 1–90.

ARCHIVAL SOURCES

Several archives in the United States and France contain materials relating to the Lafayette Escadrille. The author found the following to be especially useful:

Paul Ayres Rockwell Papers, Washington and Lee University, Leyburn Library, Special Collections and Archives, Lexington, Viginia. This outstanding collection is deserving of special mention. The extensive collection of photographs and documents represents the life's work of the Lafayette Escadrille's self-appointed historian, Paul Rockwell. Paul was the older brother of pilot Kiffin Rockwell and an acquaintance of every member of the squadron. He first served in World War I with the French Foreign Legion, and later as a Paris-based war correspondent for the *Chicago Daily News*. From the first days of the escadrille's existence until his death in 1985 at age 96, Paul collected and saved photographs, letters, and documents from most of the 38 men who flew for the Lafayette Escadrille. No finer collection relating to the famed squadron exists anywhere.

National Museum of the US Air Force Archive, Wright-Patterson AFB, Dayton, Ohio

Carl Dolan Collection, United States Air Force Academy Archives, Colorado Springs, Colorado

The Willis B. Haviland scrapbooks, maintained by his grandson, Mr. Willis Haviland Lamm. This is one of the finest photo collections available relating to the Lafayette Escadrille. Many of the images can be viewed at Mr. Lamm's excellent website, *http://www.wbhaviland.net/index.html*

Henry Lockhart, Jr. Collection, Air Force Historical Research Agency, Maxwell AFB, Montgomery, Alabama

Blerancourt Musée Franco-Américain Archives, Chateau de Blérancourt, Blérancourt, France. This facility contains many documents and a few photographs that might be of interest to researchers. Most of the documents relate to post–World War I activities, especially relating to the establishment of the Lafayette Escadrille Memorial.

Kiffin Y. Rockwell Papers, Virginia Military Institute, Preston Library Archives and Records Management, Lexington, Virginia

James Rogers McConnell Memorial Collections, Accession #2104, University of Virginia, Albert and Shirley Small Special Collections Library, Charlottesville, Virginia

National Air and Space Museum, Archives Division, Washington, DC. Here, researchers can view several collections relating to the Lafayette Escadrille, foremost of which, is the outstanding Robert Soubiran photo collection.

Grinnell College Archives, Special Collections, James Norman Hall Papers

MUSEUMS

The following lists some of the museums having artifacts and/or exhibits relevant to the Lafayette Escadrille, as well as other aspects of World War I aviation:

Blerancourt Musée Franco-Américain, Chateau de Blérancourt, Blérancourt, France

James Rogers McConnell Air Museum, Carthage, North Carolina

Musée de l'air et de l'espace (French Air & Space Museum), Paris-Le Bourget Airport, Le Bourget, France

Musée de la Grande Guerre du Pays de Meaux (Museum of the Great War), Meaux, France

National Air and Space Museum Steven F. Udvar-Hazy Center, Chantilly, Virginia

National Museum of the US Air Force, Wright-Patterson AFB, Dayton, Ohio

New England Air Museum, Windsor Locks, Connecticut

North Carolina Museum of History, Raleigh, North Carolina

Vintage Aero Flying Museum: Home of the Lafayette Foundation, Fort Lupton, Colorado

INDEX

Aero Club of America, 17, 116
aerodrome. *See* listed by name and/or location
Aéronautique Militaire. *See* Air Service, French
Aero Squadron. *See* squadrons, United States
aircraft, French: Blériot, 24, 116, *126*, Penguin
    (Rouleur), 24; Breguet-Michelin BM.2
    bomber, *62*; Caudron, 125, *125*; Maurice
    Farman, 24, 61, 70, 78, 111; Morane
    Saulnier, *93*, 113–14; Nieuport fighter, xvii,
    13, 17, 19, *23*, 26, 35, *35*, 39, 46, 48, 55, 60,
    61, *63*, *64*, 70, 79, 81, 89, 92, 97, 105, 106,
    111, 122, 129, 131, 144, 185; Nieuport 10,
    21; Nieuport 11 (Bébé), 25, *49*, *58*, *68*, 153;
    Nieuport 16, 25, *34*, *63*, *71*, *72*; Nieuport
    17, xxii, 25, *47*, *66*, *69*, *73*, 75, 78, 81, 82,
    82, 85, *86*, *91*, 91, *95*, *101*; Nieuport 21,
    52, *73*; Nieuport 23, 130, *131*; Nieuport
    24, 131; Nieuport 28, 158, 171, *171*; Spad
    fighter, 158, *169*; Spad VII, xii, 91, *100*,
    106, *110*, *118*, 118, 121, 122, *123*, *128*, 128,
    129, 136, *137*, 137, *138*, 141, 143, 145, 156,
    183; Spad XIII, 156, 158
aircraft, German: Albatros, 87, *88*, 109, 114, 136,
    139, 159; Aviatik C, 94; Fokker Eindecker 25,
    26, 27, 87, 88; Roland C.II, 81; Rumpler, 139
air service:
    British Royal Flying Corps, 104, 131; British
        Royal Naval Air Service, 78, 104
    French Aéronautique Militaire, ix, 4–7, 9, 10,
        13, 15, 17, 19, 22, 25, 48, 50, 51, 57, 90,
        98, 99, 100, 104, 117, 126, 139, 144, 145,
        156, 159, 167, 178, 184

German Air Service, 87, 145
US Air Service, ix, xviii, 13, 32, 107, 117, 125,
    126, 131, 144, 145, *146*, 152, 153, *154*,
    157, 158–60, 164, 165, 167, 170–72, 174,
    178, 180–83
alcohol, use and abuse of, 44, 89, 162, 165, 167
American Ambulance Corps. *See* American
    Ambulance Field Service
American Ambulance Field Service, 11, 19, 22,
    48, 50, 100, 117, 127
American Ambulance Hospital, 11
American Cathedral of the Holy Trinity
    (American Cathedral of Paris), McConnell
    service, 106
American Cemetery, 144, 151, 159
American Hospital of Paris at Neuilly-sur-Seine,
    76, 129, 164
Andres, Kurt, German airman and Andrew
    Courtney Campbell Jr., 151
Arlington National Cemetery, members of
    Lafayette Escadrille buried there, 166, 167,
    169, 174
Armée de l'Air, modern-day, 178
Armée de l'Orient, Salonika (Thessaloniki),
    Greece, 96, 181
Avord, France, flying school, 19, 24, 98, 153

Bailey, Frank W., xix, 182n, 183, 184
Balsley, Horace Clyde: 48, *56*, 56, 60, 61, 62, 85,
    164–65, 180, 183; shot down, 60–61; married
    to film star Miriam MacDonald, 165
Bar-le-Duc, France, 39, 45, 55, 75, 179. *See* also

Behonne, France, aerodrome at

Beaurepaire aerodrome. *See* Chaudun

Behonne, France, aerodrome at, Verdun sector,
38, 39, 41, 45, 46, *47*, 48, *49*, 50, *52*, 53, 55,
56, 61, 62, *62*, *63*, *64*, 65, *66*, *67*, 67, *68*, *71*,
72, *73*, 75, 88, 110, 179

von Bernstorff, German Ambassador Johann
Heinrich, encounter with William Thaw, 32

Bessonneau hangar, *56*

Bigelow, Stephen Sohier: 99, 100, 128, *133*, 139,
143, 167, 181; wounded, 139

Binyon, Laurence, fourth verse of *For the Fallen*
quoted, 174

Bley, Louis, mechanic, 61

Boelcke, Oswald, German ace, 26, *59*, 60, 81

"Bottle of Death," 38, 45

Bridgman, Ray Claflin, 116, *133*, *155*, 160,
170, 181

Brocard, Antonin, French commander interred in
crypt of Lafayette Escadrille Memorial, 176

Buc, France, flying school, 24

Bullard, Eugene, member of Lafayette Flying
Corps, first African-American combat
pilot 4, *8*

Cachy, France, aerodrome at, Somme sector,
85–96

Campbell, Andrew Courtney, Jr.: 110, 125; lost
wing, 130–*31*; 132, *133*, 139; collision with
Maison-Rouge, 141; death of, 149, *150*,
151; 181

Cazaux, France, gunnery school, 24

Chanler, William "Uncle Willy" Astor, Victor
Chapman's uncle, 61

Chapman, Victor Emanuel: *8*, 19, 21, *21*, *29*,
31, 35, *35*, 36, *37*, 38, 46, 56, 57, *58*, *59*, 60,
61, 62, *68*, 71, 74, 76, 85, 92, 104, 106, 180,
183; encounter with Boelcke, 57–60; death of,
60–61

Chasseurs Alpins, 14, 132

Chatkoff, Herman "Lincoln:" crash, 124–25, *125*;
World War Veterans Act of 1874, 125

Chaudun, France, aerodrome at, Aisne sector,
119, 121–33, *125*, *127*, *128*, *131–33*, 149–58,
155, 179

Chemin des Dames, 104, 119, 149

Chicago Daily News, 62, 72, 186

"Citizen Genet," Edmond-Charles, 92

Civil War, US, 4, 6, 19, 21

Confederate (States of America), 19, 20, 21

Connell, Dennis, xix, 182n, 183

Corcieux, France, aerodrome where Norman
Prince crashed, 82

Cowdin, Elliot: *18*, 19, *31*, 32, *33*, *34*, 36, *36*, *37*,
56, 62, 85, 100, 164, 180; left squadron, 62

Craonnelle, France, 5, 149

Croix de Guerre, 19, 22, 45, 62, 70, 99, 100, 122,
127, 130, 131

Cromwell, William Nelson, Lafayette Escadrille
Memorial benefactor, 177

Curtiss, Glenn: 97, 116; aircraft factory, 128;
P-40 Warhawk, 178; pusher, as flown by
Ted Parsons, 97, 98; School of Aviation,
Hammondsport, New York, 17; William Thaw
Model E Hydro flying boat, 17

Daniels, Secretary of the Navy Josephus,
posthumous Genet pardon for desertion, 112

Dassault Mirage 2000N jet fighter, 178

Dawn Patrol, The, verse from Bartholomew
Dowling poem, "The Revel," 75n

De Palma, Ralph, racecar driver, as employer of
Robert Soubiran, 87

Dolan, Charles Heave "Carl," Jr.: 116, *117*, 117,
118, *133*, 143, 156, 160, *166*, 170, 181; Dolan
Collection at the US Air Force Academy, 186

Dominguez Field, Los Angeles, California, 97

Doolittle, James Ralph: 129, 130, 131, *133*, 182;
shot down, 130–31, fatal crash, 131

Dowd, Dennis, *5*

Dressy, Jean, 113–114, *115*, 116, 119, 151

Drexel, John Armstrong, 116–117, 118, 125,
170–71, 181

Dugan, William Edward, Jr., *8*, 102, 104, *107*,
127, 128, *133*, 160, 168–69, 181

Dun-sur-Meuse, France, 137, 137, *138*

École des Beaux-Arts, 19, 99

escadrille. *See* squadrons, French

Escadrille Américaine. *See* Lafayette Escadrille

Escadrille des Volontaires. *See* Lafayette Escadrille

Escadrille N.124, SPA.124. *See* Lafayette Escadrille

Escadron de chasse 2/4 Lafayette, modern-day
French squadron, 178

Falkenhayn, General Erich von, German Army
Chief of Staff, 39

The Fatherland, pro-German newspaper, 33

Féquant, Groupe de Combat 13 Commandant Philippe, 85, 105, 141, 145, 155

Ferme de la Noblette (La Cheppe), aerodrome at, Champagne sector, 158, 179

Ferme Ste. Catherine. *See* Behonne, France, aerodrome at

First World War. *See* World War I

Flammer, Philip M., Lafayette Escadrille historian, 161, 183

Fokker, Anthony: 25; Eindecker. *See* Aircraft, German; "Fokker fodder," 25

Fontaine-les-Luxeuil, France, aerodrome at, 79

Ford, Christopher William, 156, *157*, 160, 172, 174, 182

Ford, John, Paramount pictures film director, as employer of Kenneth Marr, 168

Fram, Capitaine Thénault's German shepherd, *31*, 76, *83*, *133*

Franco-American Flying Corps (later, Lafayette Flying Corps Committee), 10, 89, 145

Franz Ferdinand, Archduke, assassination of, 1

French Aero Club, Gold Medal presented to Lufbery, 116

French Foreign Legion (Légion étrangère française), xviii, xxii, 1–10, 15, 17, 19, 22, 31, 48, 52, 53, 57, 60, *62*, 72, 87, 94, 96, 104, 116, 119, 124, *173*, 174, 183, 185, 186

General Guerrero, Federalist gunboat attacked by Didier Masson, 50

Genet, Edmond Charles Clinton: *8*, 92, 94, *95*, 99, 104, 105, 106; death and funeral of, 111–*13*, 114, 115, 119, 139, 151, 153, 181, 183, 184

George, Prime Minister David Lloyd, "Cavalry of the clouds" speech to House of Commons, 30

Gerardmer, France, hospital where Norman Prince died, 83

Germany, German, xvii, xxi, xxii, 2, 4, 7, 21, 24–27, 31–33, 35, 37–39, 45, 46, 48, 55, 57, 58, 59–61, 66, 67, 69–72, 78, 82, 85, 87–90, 92, 98, 104–07, 109, 114, 121, 122, 129, 131, 135, *136*, 136, 137, *138*, 139, 143, 145, *147*, 149, 150, 151, 157–60, 168, *172*, 174

Gordon, Dennis, *Lafayette Escadrille Pilot Biographies* author, 23–24, 167, 184

Gouraud Général Henri, quoted, 160

Graham-White, Claude, aviation pioneer, 116

Great War. *See* World War I

Gros, Edmund, 10, *11*, 89, 104, 127, 144

Groupe de Bombardement 4, 35, *36*, 78, *79*

Groupe de Combat 12, 167

Groupe de Combat 13: formed, 85; at Cachy, 98; at Ravenel, 104; at Ham, 107; at Senard, 135, *136*, 141; 145; at Chaudun, 149, 152, 155; after Lafayette Escadrille disbanded, 160

Groupe des Divisions d'Entraînement (GDE), 24, 92, 97, 129

Grugies, France, Hoskier and Dressy crash site, 114

Habsheim, France, German airfield, 80

Hague Convention (1907), 9

Hall, James Norman: 125, 126, *126*, 127; 151–152, *155*, 159, 160, 171, *171*, *172*, 172, 181, 184, 187; shot down, 128–129, *171–172*; aerial victories, 159, 171; transfer to 103rd Aero Squadron, 160; *Falcons of France* and other works of collaboration with Charles Nordhoff, 172; *High Adventure*, 129; James Norman Hall Papers at Grinnell College, 187; *Kitchener's Mob*, 127

Hall, Weston Birch "Bert:" 19, *20*, 21, *31*, *34*, 35, *35*, 36, *37*, 45, 56, 57, 62, *63*, *64*, 69, 72, 80, *83*, 87, 89, 104, 164, 174, 180, 184, 185; animosity with squadron mates, 57, 89; feud with Paul Rockwell, 89; aerial victories, 45, 69, 164; *One Man's War*, 69, 184

Ham, France, aerodrome at, Somme sector, 107, *109*–19

Hamilton, Edgar, Lafayette Flying Corps pilot who inspired Lafayette Escadrille Memorial, 176

Happe, Capitaine Felix, "Le Corsaire Rouge," 35, *36*, 39, 78, *79*, 82

Harvard College, 17, 18, 19, 21, 48, 87, 92, 93, 99, 100

Haviland, Willis Bradley: 86, 87, *91*, *94*, 96, 99, 102, 111, 114, 116, *127*, *128*, 130, *133*, 141, *142*, 165, 166, 167, 181, 182n; aerial victory, 116; left Lafayette Escadrille, 141–*42*; photo collection maintained by Willis Haviland Lamm, 166, 186

Herrick, US Ambassador Myron T., 4, 175

Hewitt, Thomas Moses "Jerry," Jr., 103, *104*, *107*, 111, 121, 133, 141, 169, 181

Hill, Dudley Lawrence: 50, *51*, 56, *64*, *83*, *94*,

114, *133*, *155*, 160, 165, 181, 184; transfer to
103rd Aero Squadron, 160
Hindenburg Line, 104
Hinkle, Edward Foote, 99; Lafayette Escadrille
Sioux insignia, 100; 101, *107*, 124, 168, 181
Hispano-Suiza, engine, 91, 118; company, 124
Hoskier, Herman and Harriet, 92, 114, *115*
Hoskier, Ronald Wood: 92, *93*, 99; death of,
113–*15*; 116, 119, 151, 181, 184
Hôtel de la Pomme d'Or, Luxeuil-les-Bains,
France, 78
Hôtel du Lion Vert, Luxeuil-les-Bains, France, 29
Hôtel Chatham, Paris, France, 177

Immelmann, Max, 26
Isaacs, US Navy Lieutenant Edouard Victor, escape
from POW camp with Harold Willis, 168
Issoudun (3rd Aviation Instruction Center), 152,
153, 181

Jadgstaffel, Jasta. *See* squadrons, German
Jay, John (US Chief Justice and Victor Chapman
ancestor), 19
Johnson, Charles Chouteau: 22, 48, 56, 62, *63*,
64, *71*, *83*, 116, *127*, 128, *133*, 153, 154, *154*,
165, *166*, 181; aerial victory, 116; transfer to
US Air Service, 153–54
Jones, Henry Sweet "Hank," 117, *118*, *133*, 149,
160, *169*, *170*, 171, 181
Journal des Marches et Opérations, flight log for N/
SPA.124, 104, 179

Kämmerer, Leutnant Heinrich, Jasta 20 pilot, 105
Kenilworth Field, Buffalo, New York, James
Doolittle fatal crash, 131

Laage de Meux, Lieutenant Alfred de: 14, 15, 16,
31, 35, 37, 46, 64, 67, 81, 83, 94, 105, 107,
109, 113, *113*, 115, *133*, 152, 180, 182n; aerial
victories, 67, 109; death of, 117–19
Lafayette Escadrille (Escadrille N.124, SPA.124):
Escadrille Américaine: vii, xii, xvii, 8, 12,
13, 16, 18, 19, 20, 22, 27, 29, 30, 31, 36,
38, 39, 41, 44, 45, 48, 53, 64, *64*, 65, 72,
76, 81, 83, 85, 87, 90, 185; publicity of,
30; diplomatic problems prompting name
change, xii, xvii, 90
Escadrille des Volontaires, xii, xvii, 90
Lafayette Escadrille (l'Escadrille Lafayette):

ix, xi; name changes, xii–xiii, xvii; facts
about, xviii–xx; xxii; origins of, 4, 6–14;
at Luxeuil, 29–39; at Behonne, 41–74;
at Luxeuil (return), 75–84; at Cachy, 86,
89–93, 95, 96; at Ravenel/Saint-Just,
97–100, 101, 102, 103, 104, 106, 107;
at Ham, 109, 110, *110*, 111, 112, 114,
115, 116, 117, 118, 119; at Chaudun,
121, 122, 124, 125, *125*, 126, 127, *127*,
128, 129, 130, 131, *131*, 132, *133*, 134;
at Saint-Pol-sur-Mer, 130–34; at Senard,
135, 136, 138, 139, 141, 142, 143–45,
146; at Chaudun (return), 149, 150,
151, 152, 153, *153*, 155, *155*, 156, 157,
158, 159, 160; at Ferme de la Nolette,
158–60; transfer to 103rd Aero Squadron,
ix, xviii, 117, 160; aftermath, 161–62,
164–65, 166, 167–71, *170*, 172, 173,
174; Indianhead insignia, xx, 86, 90, 91,
97, 100, 101, 137, 169; legacy of, 175–78;
list of operating locations, 179; roster,
180–83; research resources, 183, 184,
185, 186, 187
Lafayette Escadrille Memorial (Mémorial de
l'Escadrille Lafayette), Parc de Villeneuve-
l'Etang, Marnes-le-Coquette, France, 96, 114,
144, 150, 151, 159, 163, 172, 175, 176, 177,
186; directions to, 177
Lafayette Escadrille Memorial Restoration
Working Group, webpage, 177
Lafayette Flying Corps, xii, xiii, 167, 172, 176,
177, 182, 183, 184
Lafayette Flying Corps Committee. *See* Franco-
American Flying Corps
Lafayette, Marquis de, ix, 1, 4
Legion of Honor (Légion d'honneur), 62, 68,
83, 109
Le Prieur rockets, *71*
Le Rhône engine, 25, *52*, 78
Lewis machine gun, 25, *26*, 37, *52*, 60, *68*, 78,
82, *91*
Lovell, Walter: 99, *100*, 100, 101, 102, 111, 112,
127, 128, *133*, 136, 139, 152, 156, 167, 181;
aerial victory, 136
Lufbery, Gervais Raoul Victor: xix, 46, *47*, 48,
56, 56, 61, *64*, 69, 70, 73, 74, 76, 78, 79–83,
85, 87, *94*, 94, 105, *107*, 109, *110*, 111, 116,
122, *123*, 124, 125, 128, *133*, 133, *137*, 139,
140, 143, 144, 145, 146, 153, *155*, 156; with

Marc Pourpe, 48; crashes, 69–70, 81; in jail, 76; French Aero Club Gold Medal, 116; his success, 122–23, 124; death of, 158, *159*; 172, 180

Luxeuil-les-Bains, France, aerodrome at, Voges sector, ix, xvii, 13, 15, 17, 19, *21*, 21, 22, 25, 29, *29*, *31*, 31, 32, 34, 35, *35*, 36, *36*, 37, *37*, 38, 41, 45, 56, 75, 76, 78, *79*, 80, 81, 83, 85, 88, 179

MacMonagle, Douglas: 127, 128, *133*; death of, 143–*44*; 144, 151, 181

Maison-Neuve aerodrome. *See* Chaudun

de Maison-Rouge, Lieutenant Antoine Arnoux: 119, 133, 141, 143, 152, 180; aerial collision with Campbell, 141; death of, 143

Maistre, Général Paul, 149

Malmaison offensive, 149

Marcel, Alexandre, architect for Lafayette Escadrille Memorial, 176

Marne, Second Battle of the, 104

Maron, France, Lufbery's death, 158

Marr, Kenneth "Siwash:" 102, 104, *107*, *128*, *133*, 139, 141, 144, *150*, *155*, 160, 168, 181, 182n; aerial victory, 139; marriage to film actress Alice Ward, 168

Marshall, Emil, *83*, 89

Martin biplane, 50

Masson, Pierre Didier: 50, *64*, *67*, 81, 82, *83*, 85, 87, 88, 98, 106, 125, *127*, *133*, 152, *153*, 165, 181; with Louis Paulhan, 50; in Mexican Revolution, 50; aerial victory with dead engine, 81–82

Mata Hari, 66

McAdoo, Mrs. William Gibbs, 130

McConnell, James Rogers: xv, xix, *6*, *21*, 22, *23*, *29*, *31*, 31, 32, 34, 35, *35*, 36, *37*, 45, 48, 55, 56, 57, 60, 61, 62, *64*, 69, 70, 71, 77, 78, 80, 86, 88, 89, *94*, 98, 102, 104–06, 109, 111, 112, 119, 129, 151, 180, 184, 187, 187; ambulance driver, 6, 22; *Flying for France*, 22, 31, 70, 184; back injury in crash, 70; superstitious comment at Cachy Christmas party, 94, 106; death of, 104–06; McConnell Collection at University of Virginia, 187

Médaille Militaire, 19, 38, 45, 55, 62, 70, 72, 129

Mémorial de l'Escadrille Lafayette. *See* Lafayette Escadrille Memorial

Mexican Revolution, 50

Monday "hex," 104, 111, 112, 121, 143, 149, *150*, 151

National Museum of the US Air Force, 169, 186, 187

Nivelle, Général Robert, 98, 104

Nordhoff, Charles, 172

North Carolina, xvi, xxi, 1, 4, *6*, 21–*23*, 187

Norton-Harjes Ambulance Corps, 6, 92, 104, 129

Nungesser, Charles: 65, *66*, 66, *67*; silent movie *Sky Raider*, 163; transatlantic attempt with François Coli in *l'Oiseau Blanc*, 163–64; 180, 182n

Oberndorf, Germany, bombing raid on Mauser arms works, 80–83

Obregón, General Álvaro, Mexican Revolution, 50, 98

Painlevé, French Minister of War Paul, at dedication of Lafayette Escadrille Memorial, 175

Pardoe, Blaine, author of Bert Hall biography *The Bad Boy*, 89, 185

Paris, France: xvi, xxi, 1, *3*, 4, *8*, 10, 11, 19, 24, 36, 44, 46, 48, 56, 61, 62, 65, 66, 75, 76, 77, 85–89, 93, 96, 99, 100, 106, 116, 117, 124, 128–30, 143, 152, 155, 162, 163, 164, 174, 175, 177, 180, 186, 187; "City of Light," 75, 128, 162

Parsons, Edwin Charles "Ted:" 4, 17, 24, 44, 92, 97–100, 103, 105, *107*, 110–14, 119, 125, *127*, 128–30, 132, *133*, 133, 139, *140*, 141, 143, 155, 159, 162, 167, 168, 172, 174, 181, 185; aerial victory, 139; *The Great Adventure* 4, 167, 185

Pau, France, 17, 24, 180, 181

Paulhan, Louis, 50

Pavelka, Paul "Skipper:" 50, *52*, 53, 70, 71, *72*, 77, 80, *83*, 92, *94*, 96, 104, 106, 181, 183; death of, 96

Pershing, General John J., 164, 165

Pétain, Général Philippe, 41, 135, 141

Peterson, David McKelvey, 128, *128*, 130, *133*, 139, 141, *155*, 160, 172, 182, 182n; aerial victories, 139, 172; transferred to 103rd Aero Squadron, 160; death of, 172

Petit-Détroit (Flavy-le-Martel), France, site of McConnell crash, 105–06

Plaa-Porte, Michel, mechanic, *35*, *68*

Place des États-Unis, Paris, France, Washington and Lafayette statue, 130

Plattsburg, New York, military training camp, 99

Plessis-Belleville (GDE), 24, 92, 129

Posttraumatic Stress Disorder (PTSD), shell shock, rigors of WWI combat flying, 41–45

Pourpe, Marc, 48, 158

Prince, Frederick Henry, Jr., 86, 87, 98, 99, 106, 166, 181

Prince, Frederick Sr., 17, 166, 176

Prince, Norman: 9, 10, 17, *18*, 19, *21*, 21, *31*, 32, *33*, *35*, 36, *37*, 49, 55, 56, 60, 61, *64*, *67*, 68, 69, 70, 71, 72, 74, 80, 81, 82, *82*, 83, 85, 86, 90, 106, 176, 180, 183; attempts to establish an all-American squadron, 9–10; Christmas trip home, 32, *33*; aerial victories, 71, 72, 81–82; death of, 81, *82*, 83

Princip, Gavrilo, assassin, 1

Ravenel, France (Saint-Just-en-Chaussée), aerodrome at, Oise/Aisne Sector, 96, 97–107, 179

Republic P-47 Thunderbolt fighter, 178

Revolutionary War, US, ix, 4

Rickenbacker, Eddie, 43

"ringers," false members of the Lafayette Escadrille, 161

Ritscherle, Karl, German airman and Andrew Courtney Campbell Jr., 151

RMS *Carpathia*, and Ted Parsons, 98

Rochambeau, Compte de, 1, 4

Rockwell Brothers, Paul and Kiffin, 4, 19, 87

Rockwell, Kiffin Yates: crash site today, xxi–xxii; in Foreign Legion, 2, *3*, 4, *5*, 6, 8; at Luxeuil, *21*, 21, 22, *29*, 30, *31*, 32, 35, *35*, 36, 37; aerial victories, *37*, 38, 39, 72; at Behonne, 46; 53, 55, *56*, 56, 57, 60, 61, 62, *63*, *64*, 67, *68*, 69, 71, 72, 74; wounded, 46; reaction to Chapman death, 61; dissatisfaction with Thénault, 55, 56, 67, 68; return to Luxeuil, 76, 77, 78, 79, 80, 81, 85, 89, 90, 104, 106, 112, 139, 174, 180, 185, 187; death of, 78–80

Rockwell, Paul Ayres: xvi, 2, *3*, 22, 60, *62*, 64, 76, 80, 89, 105, 106, 127, 133, 136, 144, 152, 154, 156, 168, *173*, 174, 185, 186; vendetta against Bert Hall, 89, 174; book *War Letters of Kiffin Yates Rockwell*, 22, 174, 185; book *American Fighters in the Foreign Legion, 1864–1868*, 174, 185; participation in Rif War, *173*,

collection at Washington and Lee University, 174, 186

Rockwell, Robert Lockerbie "Doc," 76, *83*, *94*, 114, *133*, 143, 144, *155*, 160, 165, 181

Roderen, France, Kiffin Rockwell crash site, xxi, 79

Rose, Commandant Charles de Tricornot de, 4

Rumsey, Laurence Dana, Jr.: 48, *49*, 56, *64*, *83*, 89, 90, 165, 181; left squadron, 90

Saint-Just-en-Chaussée aerodrome. *See* Ravenel

Saint-Pol-sur-Mer (Dunkirk), France, aerodrome at, Flanders sector, 130–34

Savage Arms Company, logo that inspired Lafayette Escadrille Seminole insignia, 90

Schulz, Leutnant Wilhelm, Jasta 16b pilot who shot down Harold Willis, *138*, 139, 168

Schunke, Leutnant der Reserve Wilhelm, Jasta 20 pilot who shot down Hoskier and Dressy, 114

Seeger, Alan: citation for verse from *Ode in Memory of the American Volunteers Fallen for France,* xxii (note); reference to *I Have a Rendezvous with Death*, 119

Seminole and Sioux Indianhead insignia for Lafayette Escadrille, xx, *86*, 90, *91*, 97, *100*, *101*, *137*, *169*

Senard, France, aerodrome at, Verdun sector, 135–47, *136*, *137*, *144*, *147*

Sillac, Jarousse de, French Ministry of Foreign Affairs, 10

Société Pour L'Aviation et ses Dérivés. *See* aircraft, French, SPAD

Soda, lion cub mascot, 102, *133*, 155, *155*, 174

Somme Offensive and sector, 75, 85–96, 119, 179

Soubiran, Robert: *86*, 87, 99, 104, *128*, *133*, 160, *166*, 167, 181; photo collection, 86, 167, 187

Sperry Gyroscope Company, 116

squadrons, French, escadrille: C.11, 124; C.18, 50; C.42, 13, 17; F.44, 139; MS.38, 19; N.49, 116; N.57, 70; N.65, 66, 85, 152; N.67, 85; N.68, 50; N.103, 89; N.112, 85; N.124 (*also* SPA.124, Escadrille Américaine, Escadrille des Volontaires, Lafayette Escadrille). *See* Lafayette Escadrille; N.391, 181; N.471, 181; SOP. 66, 136; SOP.111, 136; SPA.3 "Storks," 181; SPA.78, 180; SPA.99, 172; SPA.102, 181; V.B.106, 48; V.B.108, 17, 19; V.B.113, 17

squadrons, German: Jadgstaffel (Jasta), 87; Jasta 5,

88; Jasta 20, 105, 114; Jasta 16b, 138
squadrons, United States: 22nd Aero, 170; 94th
  Aero, "Hat in the Ring," 158, 168, 171, *171*,
  172, 180, 182; 95th Aero, 172; 103rd Aero,
  ix, xviii, 117, 158, 160, 164, 165, 167, 168,
  169, 170, 171, 172, 174, 178, 180, 181, 182;
  138th Aero, 165; 139th Aero, 165, 170; 213th
  Aero, 174; 3rd Pursuit Group, 164; 5th Pursuit
  Group, 165
SS *Dunedin*, and Clyde Balsley, 48
SS *St. Paul*, and the Rockwell brothers, 1
Stinson Flying School, San Antonio, Texas, 156
stresses of flying in World War I. *See* Posttraumatic
  Stress Disorder (PTSD), shell shock
Suchet, Caporal, Lafayette Escadrille Seminole
  insignia artist, 90

Thaw, Benjamin, at Genet's funeral, 113
Thaw, William: 9, 13, 15, *16*, 17, 18, 19, *31*, 32,
  33, *35*, 36, *37*, 45, 46, 56, 57, 62, *64*, 71, *73*,
  77, *83*, 85, 87, 88, 90, 100, 102, 104, 106,
  107, *113*, 114, 116, 122, *128*, *132*, *133*, 145,
  153, *155*, 160, 164, 172, 176, 180, 182n; flight
  under East River bridges and around Statue of
  Liberty, 17; Christmas trip home, 32, *33*; aerial
  victories, 45–46, 116; wounded, 46; awarded
  Legion of Honor, 62; transfer to 103rd Aero
  Squadron, 160
Thénault, Capitaine Georges: 13, *14*, 15, 16, *21*,
  21, *31*, 35, *35*, 36, *36*, *37*, 46, 55, *56*, 60, 61,
  63, 64, 68, *69*, 70, 72, 75, 76, 78, 79, 80, 81,
  83, 85, 89, 103, 104, *107*, 111, *115*, 121, 122,
  130, *133*, 143, 152, 160, 162, *163*, 176, 180,
  185; after the war, 162–63; *The Story of the
  Lafayette Escadrille*, 163
Toelle, Alan, 72, 185
Toul, France: aerodrome, 158; Sebastopol
  cemetery, *159*
Trinkard, Charles, *5*

University of Virginia, 22, 23, 48, 110, 151, 187
US declaration of war on Germany, *107*, 107
US military: Army, 48, *73*, *146*, 152, 165, 169;
  Army Air Forces, 168, 173, 174, 178; Army
  Air Service. *See* air service, US Air Service;
  Naval Academy, 21; Naval Aviator, 141;

Navy, 50, 86, 94, 106, 111, 112, 165, 167,
  168, 181
Vadelaincourt, France, evacuation hospital, 60
"Valiant 38," nickname for the men of the
  Lafayette Escadrille, xviii
Vanderbilt, William K., Lafayette Escadrille
  benefactor, 10
Verdier-Fauvety, Lieutenant Louis: 152, 160, 180;
  death of, 160
Verdun, Battle of and sector, 39, 41, 45, 46, 53,
  57, 64, 68, 72, 75, 78, 85, 98, 110, 127, 134,
  135, 149, 179
Vickers machine gun, *69*, 78, 91
victory credits, aerial: 46, 65, 66, 67, 69, 70, 80,
  81, 94, 109, 114, 116, 139, 141, 152, 154,
  156, 158, 159, 164; difficulty in achieving, xix;
  Lufbery's expertise, 122–*23*, 124; squadron
  listing, 180–83, 182n
Villa, Francisco "Pancho," 98
Villingen, Germany, POW camp, 168
Virginia Military Institute (VMI), 2, 21, 187
Voge, Madame, billiard parlor matron, *29*
Vosges Mountains, xvii, xxi, 13, 32, 35, 75, 102

Washington and Lee University, xvi, 21, 174, 186
Washington National Cathedral, Norman Prince
  chapel, 176
Weeks, Alice, "Legion Mom" and friend of Kiffin
  Rockwell, 42, 185
Wellman, William, former Lafayette Flying Corps
  pilot and Hollywood director, 167
Whiskey, lion cub mascot, 76, 77, 90, 100, 102,
  133, *140*, 154–55, *155*, 174
Willis, Harold Buckley: 99, *107*, 113, 116, *127*, 128,
  130, *133*, 143, 168, 174, 181; Lafayette Escadrille
  Sioux insignia, 100–*01*; shot down, 135–39, *138*
Wilson, President Woodrow, 2, 130, *133*
Woodworth, Benjamin, ambulance driver killed in
  Chatkoff crash 124–25, *125*
World War I, ix, xi, xii, xv, xvii, xviii, xix, xxi,
  1, 2, 6, 11, 17, 25, 41, 42–45, 50, 62, 72, 121,
  122, 124, 126, 137, 161–63, 170, 173, 175–77,
  184, 186, 187
World War II, 129, 163, 165, 167, 168, 174, 178
World War Veterans Act of 1874, relating to
  Herman Chatkoff injuries, 125